WAR

Before

Civilization

WAR

Before

Civilization

Lawrence H. Keeley

Oxford University Press
New York   Oxford

Oxford University Press

Oxford   New York
Athens   Auckland   Bangkok   Bogotá   Bombay
Buenos Aires   Calcutta   Cape Town   Dar es Salaam
Delhi   Florence   Hong Kong   Istanbul   Karachi
Kuala Lumpur   Madras   Madrid   Melbourne
Mexico City   Nairobi   Paris   Singapore
Taipei   Tokyo   Toronto   Warsaw

and associated companies in
Berlin   Ibadan

Library of Congress Cataloging-in-Publication Data
Keeley, Lawrence H.
War before civilization / Lawrence H. Keeley.
p.   cm.   Includes bibliographical references and index.
ISBN 0-19-509112-4
ISBN-13 978-0-19-511912-1 (Pbk.)
ISBN 0-19-511912-6 (Pbk.)
1. Warfare, Prehistoric.   2. Fortification, Prehistoric.
3. Weapons, Prehistoric.   I. Title.
GN799.W26K44   1996
355'.009'01—dc20   94-8998

10 9 8 7

Printed in the United States of America

To my mother, Ruth; my son, Pete;

and the memory of my father, Lawrence

PREFACE

This book had its genesis in two personal failures—one of a practical academic sort, the other intellectual. As a result of these, I realized that archaeologists of the postwar period had artificially "pacified the past" and shared a pervasive bias against the possibility of prehistoric warfare.

My practical failure involved two unsuccessful research proposals requesting funds to investigate the functions of recently discovered fortification surrounding some Early Neolithic (ca. 5000 B.C.) villages in northeastern Belgium. Such sites represented the settlements of the first farmers to colonize central and northwestern Europe. These two proposals to the U.S. National Science Foundation (which had supported my previous research) requested funds to excavate several Early Neolithic village sites near to the already excavated "frontier" site of Darion. My Belgian colleague, Daniel Cahen, had found that Darion had been surrounded by an obvious fortification consisting of a 9-foot-deep ditch backed by a palisade. My research proposal claimed that Darion's defenses indicated that this Neolithic frontier was a hostile one and predicted that excavations at nearby sites would reveal similar fortifications. The archaeologists who reviewed these proposals could not accept the defensive nature of the Darion "enclosure" and therefore could not recommend funding a project predicated on what they regarded as an erroneous interpretation. A third proposal was successful only after I rewrote it to be neutral about the function of the Darion ditch-palisade, which was referred to as an "enclosure" rather than as a fortification. In other words, only when the proposal was cleansed of references to that archaeological anathema, warfare, was it acceptable to my colleagues.

With our new funding, our excavations at four other Early Neolithic sites soon documented that two of them had also been fortified. We had been right after all: on the Early Neolithic frontier, at least when it reached Belguim, fortified villages were rather common; one just had to know how to look for them. Despite having normally inflated academic egos, Daniel and I were shocked by this vindication. I recall that as we drove home on the day our excavations at the site of Waremme-Longchamps had revealed a deep ditch and palisade, our conversation was very limited. It consisted of a stunned silence periodically punctuated by one or the other of us stating in an amazed tone, "We have a ditch and palisade!" Our mutal amazement was based on the prejudices we shared with the very colleagues who had given my early, unsuccessful proposals a skeptical review. Subconsciously, we had not really believed our own arguments: we, too, had assumed that Darion's fortifications were an aberration and had used them only as an excuse to satisfy our curiosity about the other sites in its vicinity. This realization about our own expections later led to a series of conversations among Daniel, Anne Cahen-Delhaye (a specialist in later Bronze and Iron Age archaeology), and me about the difficulty archaeologists of our generation had in accepting evidence of prehistoric warfare. Later, reflecting on my own education and career, I realized that I was as guilty as anyone of pacifying the past by ignoring or dismissing evidence of prehistoric warfare—even evidence I had seen with my own eyes.

My first excavations, as a college freshman, were on a prehistoric "shell-mound" village site on San Francisco Bay, where we uncovered many burials of unequivocal homicide victims. It never occurred to me or my fellow students that the skeletons with embedded projectile points we excavated evidenced a homicide rate that was extraordinarily high. This brutal physical evidence we were uncovering never challenged our acceptance of the traditional view that the native peoples of California had been exceptionally peaceable.

Even more tellingly, in my senior thesis, I used all the rhetorical tricks I accuse my colleagues of here to deny the obvious importance of warfare in early Mesoamerican civilizations. Since grammar school, I had been fascinated by military history and avidly read every book on the subject I could get my hands on. For my B.A. thesis at the end of the 1960s, I chose a topic—the role of militarism in the rise of Mesoamerican civilizations—that seemed to unite my personal interest in military history with my developing academic interest in prehistory. In fact, it was a final decree of divorce, since I concluded (dutifully following the current consensus of archaeological opinion) that the first civilization in Mesoamerica had developed in especially peaceful circumstances. In other words, I argued that militarism and warfare had no role in the evolution of the Olmec, Teotihuacan, and Classic Maya civilizations and that warfare and soldiers had become important only when these more or less "theocratic" civilizations collapsed.

A quarter-centry later, it is abundantly clear that this prevailing view was quite wrong. The percentage of violent deaths at the prehistoric California Indian village I had helped excavate has recently been tabulated by my college classmate, Bob Jurmain, and it is at least four times the percentage of violent deaths suffered by inhibitants of the United States and Europe in this bloody century. The Classic Maya city-states, one of the subjects of my senior thesis, clearly were at war very frequently and were ruled by particularly militant kings. Ironically, the *archaeological* evidence that all was not peaceful in the Mayan realm was readily available when I wrote my senior thesis (gruesome murals at Bonampak, fortifications at Becan and Tikal, countless Mayan depictions of war captives and their armed captors, and so on). But like the archaeologists whose work I relied on, I dismissed this data as either unrepresentative, ambiguous, or insignificant. Only as more and more Mayan hieroglyphic writing has been deciphered during the last decade has archaeological opinion shifted from its erroneous conception of the peaceful Maya.

Like most archaeologists trained in the postwar period, I emerged from the first stage of my education so inculcated with the assumption that warfare and prehistory did not mix that I was willing to dismiss unambigous *physical* evidence to the contrary. If my initial lack of success in obtaining funding for my own research made me aware of the predjudices of most of my colleagues, my own reactions and memories stimulatred by my subsequent success drove home the fact that I had worn the same blinders.

A few years later, I learned another important lesson. Archaeological opinion quickly became much more open-minded about the probability of armed conflicts in the Early Neolithic of western Europe. In 1989, when Cahen and I published a report in an international journal on our first full field seasons, the prepublication reviewers (some of whom were almost certainly the same referees who had skeptically reviewed my unsuccessful NSF proposals) were uniformly favorable. This is not to say that these colleagues were completely convinced that the enclosures we had found were fortifications, but, by then, they were more than willing to entertain the possibility. Other information published in the late 1980s was also challenging archaeologists' bias on this issue. Some German publications during this period documented that Early Neolithic enclosures were actually common—more than fifty enclosed sites had already been discovered during the past fifty years—but these findings had been published in such obscure local journals that they were not widely known. In addition, a very thorough report was published in 1987 (again, in a local journal) on an Early Neolithic mass grave found near Stuttgart that contained the remains of thirty-four men, women, and children killed by blows to the head inflicted by characteristicly Early Neolithic axes. By the beginning of this decade, few Early Neolithic specialists would deny that war existed in what had previously been regarded as a peaceful golden age. The resistance that we archaeologists showed to the notion of prehistoric war, and the ease with which it was overcome when the relevant evidence was recognized, impressed me and convinced me that a book on this subject would be worthwhile. Physical circumstantial evidence has an extraordinary ability to overcome even the most ingrained ideas.

Indeed, archaeology is a peculiarly robust social science. Like all fields, it has unacknowledged blind spots, unconscious prejudices, and declared theoretical biases; but the extremely physical and material nature of the things it studies provides a constant basis for correcting erroneous intellectual notions. Unlike scholars whose evidence consists of the spoken or written word, archaeologists lack the license to dismiss any facts uncongenial to their prejudices by selective ad hominem skepticism, clever sophistry, or the currently fashionable denial that there is any "real past" (that is, that the past is merely an ideological construction and as many pasts exist as there are conceptions of it). For archaeologists, the human past is unequivocally real: it has mass, solid form, color, and even occasionally odor and flavor. Millions of pieces of it—bones, seeds, stones, metal, and pottery—sit on lab tables and in museum drawers all over the world. The phrase "the weight of evidence" has a literal meaning for archaeologists because their basic evidence is material; and because it is circumstantial, only repeated occurrences of it can be interpreted convincingly. Archaeology is the study of patterns of *effects*, repetitions of human behaviors that leave enduring marks on the physical world. Warfare—the armed conflict between societies— whether its scale is large or small, is such a pattern and leaves very enduring effects. In this work, I have tried to muster a mass of evidence to convince not just archaeologists and historians but also the educated public that the notion of prehistoric and primitive warfare is not an oxymoron.

Chicago   L. H. K.
May 1994

Acknowledgments

This project began when the chairman of my department, Jack Prost, encouraged me in the strongest possible terms to apply for a fellowship at the University of Illinois at Chicago's Institute for the Humanities to write a book on this subject. I was granted the fellowship and enjoyed a year free of teaching and departmental duties in the company of a superb group of scholars: Bruce Calder, Jody Enders, Peter Hale, Mae Henderson, and Jim Schultz from UIC's departments of history, French, art history, English/African-American studies, and German, respectively. They helped me enlarge my view of my subject, suggested changes in my presentation of material, and raised issues I had not considered. Their good-humored tolerance in debate, devotion to scholarship, and mutual encouragement refuted all of the popular hand-wringing about the state of the humanities in our nation's universities. I also owe much to the director of the Institute, Gene Ruoff, a distinguished scholar of English Romanticism, for extraordinary encouragement, assistance (yes, even financial!), and astute advice. I am most grateful—both to him for sustaining the Institute administratively and to him and his executive board for accepting a "naive realist" natural scientist into their midst. I hope that this book somehow repays the trouble taken on my behalf by everyone concerned with the UIC's Institute for the Humanities.

No one is his or her own best critic. Some friends and colleagues have read partial drafts of this book, offering advice and criticism: Jack Prost, Gene Ruoff, Jim Phillips, Bob Hall, Quentin Calkins, Brian Hayden, and my wife, Lesley. A number of colleagues have also provided information, references, and reprints used in this book: April Sievert, Anne Cahen-Delhaye, Paul-Louis Van Berg, Marcel Otte, Larry Kuznar, David Frayer, Waud Kracke, Nancy Fagin, Ron Weber, Brian Hayden, Polly Wiesner, Doug Bamforth, Bob Jurmain, John Beaton, Tom Hester, Ellen Steinberg, Pat Lyons, Jonathan Haas, Bob Hall, and Jim Phillips. None of these helpful people is responsible for any errors of commission or omission perpetrated by me in this work.

I would also like to acknowledge the inspiration of several eminent anthropologists, whom I know only from their work but upon whose data and ideas I have especially relied: Andrew Vayda, Robert Carneiro, Mervyn Meggitt, Paula Brown, William Divale, Thomas Gregor, and Robert Edgerton. Their unblinking realism, comparative approaches, and unapologetic rationality are balm indeed in this era of vacuous "notions" and completely subjective "deep readings." Any future dissertations on this subject must be founded, as was mine, on the work of these extraordinary anthropologists.

I am most grateful to my editor, David Roll, for finding merit in this work and assisting in its completion. I also appreciate the efforts of Gioia Stevens in seeing it into print.

The research that provided the germ of this book was conducted in conjunction with my friend and colleague, Daniel Cahen. We are grateful to various ministries of the Belgian government and to the National Science Foundation of the United States for funding our research on the Early Neolithic. Many after-dinner discussions with Daniel and with Anne Cahen-Delhaye helped me define the problem addressed here and understand how pervasive it was. I would treasure our long friendship and their unstinting hospitality even if these had not been so academically productive.

Last but not least, I thank my wife, Lesley, for her unfailing support of my efforts by reading, exhorting, comforting, and permitting me to neglect my responsibilities as a homeowner, father, and husband. Even more humbling was the the generous and proud response of my son, Pete, who told his friends that the reason I was "always busy" was that I was writing a "big book." While I was immersed in the most depressing aspects of human behavior, my family served as a constant reminder that the more hopeful and cheerful facets of human existence far outnumber its darker ones.

CONTENTS

WAR
Before
Civilization

ONE

The Pacified Past

The Anthropology of War

War has long been a sensational topic. Warfare concentrates and intensifies some of our strongest emotions: courage and fear, resignation and panic, selfishness and self-sacrifice, greed and generosity, patriotism and xenophobia. The stimulus of war has incited human beings to prodigies of ingenuity, improvisation, cooperation, vandalism, and cruelty. It is the riskiest field on which to match wits and luck: no peaceful endeavor can equal its penalties for failure, and few can exceed its rewards for success. It remains the most theatrical of human activities, combining tragedy, high drama, melodrama, spectacle, action, farce, and even low comedy. War displays the human condition in extremes.

It is thus not surprising that the first recorded histories, the first written accounts of the exploits of mortals, are military histories. The earliest Egyptian hieroglyphs record the victories of Egypt's first pharoahs, the Scorpion King and Narmer. The first secular literature or history recorded in cuneiform recounts the adventures of the Sumerian warrior-king Gilgamesh. The earliest written parts of the Books of Moses, the "J-strand" (called so because in its passages the name given God is Yahweh or, corruptly, Jehovah), culminate in the brutal Hebrew conquest of Canaan. The earliest annals of the Chinese, Greeks, and Romans are concerned with wars and warrior kings. Most Mayan hieroglyphic texts are devoted to the geneologies, biographies, and military exploits of Mayan kings. The folklore and legends of preliterate cultures, the epic oral traditions that are the precursors to history, are equally bellicose. Indeed, until this century, historiography was dominated by accounts of wars and the political intrigues that led up to them. Because history, strictly speaking, consists of written accounts and because writing is confined to civilized societies, civilized warfare is the subject of a long-standing and voluminous literature. For example, more than 50,000 complete books have been devoted to the American Civil War alone, and scores more are published each year. What the literate world knows as warfare is therefore civilized warfare.

But recorded history represents less than half of 1 percent of the more than 2 million years that humans have existed. In fact, prehistory ended in some areas of the world a mere thirty years ago. At the dawn of the European expansion (A.D. 1500), only a third of the inhabited world was civilized; all of Australasia and Oceania, most of the Americas, and much of Africa and north Asia remained preliterate and tribal. These long chapters in humanity's story and all the recent "peoples without history" are the special focus of anthropology—of the archaeologists who study the former and of the ethnographers who have observed the latter.

What, then, has anthropology said about the warfare conducted by prehistoric and "primitive" societies? The simple answer is: very little. By recent count, only three complete books (and a handful of anthologies and ethnographies) devoted exclusively to primitive warfare have been published in this century, far fewer than are published on the American Civil War each year.[1] Information on the topic is not lacking, but it is tucked away in technical journals or scattered as brief passages in ethnographic and archaeological reports. Compared with the tens of thousands of volumes and countless articles on civilized military history, however, this imbalance is striking, considering how much of humanity prehistoric and primitive peoples represent. The subject of war among ancient and modern tribal peoples remains prone to glib speculation, the caprices of intellectual fashion, and the deeper currents of secular mythology.

Even today, most views concerning prehistoric (and tribal) war and peace reflect two ancient and enduring myths: progress and the golden age. The myth of progress depicts the original state of mankind as ignorant, miserable, brutal, and violent. Any artificial complexities introduced by human invention or helpful gods have only served to increase human bliss, comfort, and peace, lifting humans out of their ugly and hurtful state of nature. The contradictory myth avers that civilized humans have fallen from grace—from a simple and primeval happiness, a peaceful golden age. All the accretions of progress merely multiply violence and suffering; civilization is the sorry condition that our sinfulness, greed, and technological hubris have earned us. In the modern period, these ancient mythic themes were elaborated by Hobbes and Rousseau into enduring philosophical attitudes toward primitive and prehistoric peoples.

HOBBES AND ROUSSEAU

The English philosopher Thomas Hobbes (1588–1679) reached his conclusions about warfare and society via a series of logical arguments. In his great work, *Leviathan,* he first established that, in practical terms, all men were equals because no one was so superior in strength or intelligence that he could not be overcome by stealth or the conspiracy of others. He found humans equally endowed with *will* (desires) and *prudence* (the capacity to learn from experience). But when two such equals desired what only one could enjoy, one eventually subdued or destroyed the other in pursuit of it. Once this happened, all hell broke loose. The similar desires of others tempted them to emulate the winner, and their intelligence required them to guard themselves against the fate of the loser. When no power existed to "overawe" these equals, prudent self-preservation forced every individual to attempt to preserve his *liberty* (the absence of impediments to his will) by trying to subdue others and by resisting their attempts to subdue him. Hobbes thus envisioned the original or natural condition of humanity as being "the war of every man against every man." In this primeval state of "warre,"[2] men lived in "continual fear and danger of violent death"; and, in Hobbes's most famous phrase, their lives were therefore "solitary, poor, nasty, brutish and short." He claimed vaguely that "savage people in many places in America" still lived in this violent primitive condition but gave no particulars and never pursued the point further.

Humans escaped this state of war only by agreeing to *covenants* in which they surrendered much of their liberty and accepted rule by a central authority (which, for Hobbes, meant a king). And since "Covenants, without the sword, are but words," the king (or state) had to be granted a monopoly over the use of force to punish criminals and defend against external enemies. Without the state to overawe humans' intelligence by force, mediate their selfish passions, and deprive them of some of their natural liberty, anarchy reigned. Civilized countries returned to this condition when central authority was widely defied or deprived of its power, as during rebellions. All civilized "industry" and the humane enjoyment of its fruits depended on a peace maintained by central government; the "humanity" of humans was thus a product of civilization.

Hobbes acknowledged that nation-states between themselves remained in a "posture of war." But because they thereby protected the industry of their subjects, "there does not follow from it that misery which accompanies the liberty of particular men." In other words, a world of states necessarily tolerated some wars and much preparation for war, but these preserved havens of peace within each state. In the primitive condition, there was no peace anywhere.

Hobbes never claimed that humans were innately cruel or violent or bio-logically driven to dominate others. The condition of war was a purely social condition—the logical consequence of human equality in needs, desires, and intelligence. It could be eliminated by social innovations: a covenant and coercive institutions of enforcement. War would recur only if these covenants were broken or if the police powers of the central state waned. His argument was certainly intended as an apology for absolute monarchy; but later, yielding to circumstance, he admitted that it applied equally well to other forms of strong central government, even republics. Whatever his views on the ideal form of the state, the point of central relevance here is that Hobbes considered the inertial "natural" state of humanity to be war, not peace.

For the past two centuries, the most influential critic of Hobbes's view of primitive society and "man in a state of nature" has been Jean-Jacques Rousseau (1712–1778). Rousseau disdained the logical rigor of the philosopher, the plodding empiricism of the historian and the scientist, and the unbridled invention of the romancer, but he combined a semblance of all three with an assertive style to become an intellectual sensation. Like Hobbes, he constructed an origin myth to explain the human condition, but his denied civilization its humanity while proclaiming the divinity of the primitive.

Rousseau, like Hobbes, asserted the natural equality of mankind but saw humans in their natural state as being (justly) ruled by their passions, not their intellects. He argued that these passions could be easily and peaceably satisfied in a world without the "unnatural" institutions of monogamy and private property. Any tendency toward violence in the natural condition would be suppressed by humans' innate pity or compassion. This natural compassion was overwhelmed only when envy was created by the origins of marriage, property, education, social inequality, and "civil" society. He claimed that the savage, *except when hungry*, was the friend of all creation and the enemy of none. He directly attacked Hobbes for having "hastily concluded that man is naturally cruel" when in fact "nothing could be more gentle" than man in his natural state.[3] Rousseau's Noble Savage lived in that peaceful golden age "that mankind was formed ever to remain in." War only became general and terrible when people organized themselves into separate societies with artificial rather than natural laws. Compassion, an emotion peculiar to individuals, gradually lost its influence over societies as they grew in size and proliferated. When artificial, passionless states fought, they committed more murders and "horrible disorders" in a single engagement than were ever perpetrated in all the ages that men had lived in a state of nature.

Unlike Hobbes, Rousseau seemed genuinely interested in whether his contentions were confirmed in the observations of real "savages" then being encountered by European explorers. His disciples accompanied French explorations and brought back mixed reports.[4] The explorer Louis de Bougainville reported that Tahitians exactly fulfilled Rousseau's predictions, although to reach this conclusion Bougainville had to ignore their rigid class stratification, their arrogant chiefs, and some of the most horrific warfare on record (Chapters 4–7). But another explorer told Rousseau of a sudden unprovoked attack on French explorers by the very simple and previously uncontacted aboriginal Tasmanians, despite the most peaceful gestures by the completely naked French emissaries. Rousseau was shocked: "Is it possible that the good Children of Nature can really be so wicked?" Of course, Noble Savage apologists then and since have remarked that such fracases were only the result of the natives' misunderstanding of the emissaries' intentions or anxiety that the explorers meant to stay. Even so, what had happened to the savages' natural compassion and lack of jealousy? Similar cases of tribesmen at first contact "shooting first and asking questions later" (which with hindsight seems prescient on their part) did not trouble Rousseau or his disciples to the point of reconsidering their assumptions. They were too thoroughly convinced that the natural state of human society was a peaceful combination of free love and primitive communism to see these violent first encounters as anything but rare aberrations.

Despite Rousseau's influence, Hobbes's view of primitive life held the upper hand during the nineteenth century, which not coincidentally was the heyday of European imperialism and colonization. One of the principal apologies for Western imperialism was the pacification of ever-warring savages by European conquest, missionary activity, and administration. The natives, living in Hobbesian turbulence, could enjoy the comforts of Christianity and the benefits of civilization only after they were pacified and controlled by Europeans. Europeans also awarded their own the highest ranking among the few civilizations they recognized (such as those of Asia and the Near East) because they reckoned that theirs had progressed further than any other from the violent and impoverished state of nature. Not surprisingly, the soldiers, missionaries, and colonial functionaries sent out to establish Western dominion brought back accounts that emphasized the Hobbesian features of societies they sought to conquer and transform. These portraits were the only information available to the first anthropologists as the discipline emerged during the 1860s. Only a handful of anti-imperialists, reformers, and self-consciously iconoclastic artists—few of whom had ever directly observed real primitives—clung to Rousseau's pacific view of uncivilized life.

THE CONCEPT OF PRIMITIVE WAR

In the early part of the twentieth century, the mass of unsystematic observations of prestate societies that had accumulated during European expansion was superseded by the new data of ethnography. Trained in the new technique of participant observation, anthropologists went out to live with the subjects of their studies for months and even years, learned their language, and made observations of their customs and behavior with their own eyes. The young science of anthropology had left its armchair.

All of this data, old and new, indicated that with only rare exceptions primitive life was not particularly peaceful. It was no longer possible to declare, as the eminent sociologist William Sumner did at the turn of the century, that primitive man "might be described as a peaceful animal" who "dreads" war.[5] In 1941, the great ethnographer Bronislaw Malinowski could argue that "anthropology has done more harm than good in confusing the issue by . . . depicting human ancestry as living in the golden age of perpetual peace." Yet it was also clear that, contrary to Hobbes, life in small-scale societies was *not* "solitary, poor, nasty, brutish and short." Anthropologists who actually lived among such people, got to know them as individuals and as friends, and participated in their daily affairs found it very difficult to maintain a Hobbesian disdain for their way of life. Ethnography exposed primitive cultures as perfectly valid and satisfying ways of being human and found that they often possessed features that were preferable to comparable aspects of Western civilized life.

Few of these ethnographers were explorers, however, and they usually lived with people who had already been pacified by Western administration.[6] Thus they had to rely on their informants' memories of precontact warfare and had little opportunity to observe it directly. But such accounts tended to idealize or bowdlerize behavior. While informants' descriptions of many aspects of social life could be enhanced or corrected by the anthropologists' direct observations, independent checks on their descriptions of warfare were usually impossible. For example, an ethnographer studying the Sambia of New Guinea found that Sambia warriors "unconsciously repress the gory parts of war tales, tranforming the once traumatic into drama" when recounting their war experiences.[7] When such idealized native accounts were filtered, by the questions asked, through the intense interest of anthropologists in customary rules and rituals, the images of primitive combat that emerged had a very stylized, ritualistic allure.

In *The Face of Battle*, historian John Keegan notes an exactly corresponding tendency in military historians' accounts of civilized battles.[8] Some of these make bloody combat between groups of frightened, overexcited men seem no more hurtful than a barroom brawl or a prosy Romantic thunderstorm. In these accounts, individuals and groups are motivated by a hunger for glory or avenge for previous defeats, by a desire to maintain the reputation of the regiment, retain the good opinion of their comrades, or gain the notice of superiors. The soldiers are very rarely depicted as driven by hatred of the enemy and never as fighting for the base motives of material gain or fear of punishment. Were such accounts our only source of information, we could easily conclude that modern Western warfare has been highly ritualized, psychologically motivated, and not particularly deadly. Only actual casualty statistics and rare unedited eyewitness memoirs by front-line soldiers challenge such impressions. But anthropologists, with very few exceptions, have had information of only the historiographic type to guide them in generalizing about uncivilized warfare.

In some rare instances, ethnographers were able to observe actual primitive combat. But even these observations showed a marked bias toward pitched or formal battles.[9] Because such battles are the primary goal and most dramatic events of *modern* warfare, the eyes of ethnographers were drawn to comparable clashes in the tribal societies they studied. They noticed that these primitive battles were often suspended after only a few deaths, and—even if they were renewed after a brief interval—the total number killed in a series of battles was usually small. The ethnographers seldom analysed casualties in relation to the small numbers who fought and thus could not compare them on this basis to larger-scale civilized battles. The raids, ambushes, and surprise attacks on villages that constitute a major component of tribal warfare were seldom observed and paid little notice. The general impression drawn from rare glimpses of formal battles was that primitive warfare was not very risky.

By midcentury, it became possible to save the Rousseauian notion of the Noble Savage, not by making him peaceful (as this was clearly contrary to fact), but by arguing that tribesmen conducted a more stylized, less horrible form of warfare than their civilized counterparts waged. This view was systematized and elaborated into the theory that there existed a special type of "primitive war" very different from "real," "true," or "civilized" war.

The architects of this concept of *primitive war*, Quincy Wright and Harry Turney-High, were academics of vastly different character and experience. Despite the essential similarity of their views, neither of them ever acknowledged in print the existence of the other's work.

Quincy Wright (1890–1970) was professor of international law at the University of Chicago. He directed that university's long-term study of the causes of war, which began in 1926. This project eventually involved a large number of faculty members and graduate students from a variety of disciplines, including anthropology. The study of war by primitive societies was but a small part of this great enterprise but had a considerable effect on much subsequent thinking by anthropologists.[10] Wright's two-volume summary of this project, *A Study of War*, was published in 1942. An abridged edition of this work remains in print today. Not surprisingly, Wright took a rather lawyerly view of war and was especially concerned with identifying the laws and customs that might moderate or even eliminate it. Indeed, he defined *war* as a temporary legal condition permitting hostile groups "to carry on a conflict by armed force."[11] His attitude toward war seems one of judicial disapproval for such a wasteful and brutal way of settling disputes.

Harry Holbert Turney-High (1899–1982) was, for most of his career, a professor of anthropology at the University of South Carolina. But unlike most academics, he maintained a lifelong involvement with the modern military, rising from a private in the cavalry to a colonel of military police in the U.S. Army Reserves. He served in Europe during World War II as a military police-men but apparently never saw actual combat.[12] As an ethnographer, he collected "memory culture" data on the Flathead and Kutenai Indians of Montana and wrote the standard ethnography on these groups. The character of tribal warfare remembered by these fringe Plains tribes and his own admiration for the princi-ples of warfare he learned in training as a cavalryman obviously strongly influ-enced his views of primitive warfare. His seminal book, *Primitive War* (1949), remains the only anthropological synthesis on warfare; it is still in print.

Rather than viewing war as a temporary legal condition, Turney-High saw it as a social institution that served a variety of functions. Not only could war be useful, especially in a civilized context, but it was also an exciting diversion. Turney-High reserved his disapproval for what he saw as substandard, half-hearted, or cowardly warfare, not war itself. Writing in a rollicking, opinionated style, he radiated contempt for anyone ignorant or heedless of the civilized soldier's craft and trade, whether the uninformed were social scientists, tribal warriors, or modern guerrillas. Indeed, one has the uneasy sense that Turney-High thought a little whiff of cordite smoke, some military discipline, and a touch of wholesome field punishment would do everyone a world of good.

Despite the difference in their basic definitions of war and their studied silence about each other's work, both Wright and Turney-High agreed that primitive warfare differed drastically from warfare conducted by civilized states. Militarily, Wright thought primitives "resemble more the apes and the ants" than they did civilized men. Turney-High drew a very sharp line, literally a "military horizon," above which real warfare was conducted by states and below which occurred only the submilitary combat of primitives. He spoke of primitive warfare as being childish, "reflecting the ways of human infancy." Both men agreed that this distinction between primitive and civilized warfare was rooted in a fundamental difference in aims and motivation.

In civilized or real warfare, the motives or goals were economic and political—for example, plunder, more territory, or hegemony. Turney-High characterized these as "rational and practical." By contrast, primitives were said to fight for personal, psychological, and social motives. Wright argued that the military goals of primitive societies primarily involved maintaining "the solidarity of the political group" and secondarily satisfying "certain psychic needs of human personality." Their lists of primitive motives included tension release for violent impulses that could be conveniently redirected toward outsiders; pursuit of personal prestige and status, including initiation to manhood; and revenge. Both Turney-High and Wright asserted the widely repeated claim that primitive people commonly went to war for adventure or sport—literally, to escape boredom.[13] Given Turney-High's characterization of the motives of states, he clearly implied that the motives of primitive societies were irrational and impractical. Comparable purely psychological motives only occasionally appeared in civilized warfare in the motivations of individual soldiers or small units.

Wright and Turney-High dismissed the possibility that warfare might function to produce material advantages for primitive groups because the conscious pursuit of such advantages was characteristic only of states. They saw all features of primitive war making as flowing directly from impractical, personal goals, which could be achieved without "victory" and, indeed, could be served only if warriors had a very good chance of surviving combat.

Both Wright and Turney-High judged primitive warfare to be technically defective compared with civilized warfare.[14] They independently listed the various deficiencies of primitive war:

1. Poor mobilization of manpower because of reliance on completely voluntary participation
2. Inadequate supply and logistics
3. Due to deficiencies 1 and 2, an inability to conduct protracted campaigns
4. No organized training of units
5. Poor command and control
6. Due to deficiencies 4 and 5, undisciplined units and flighty morale
7. Few weapons specialized for war and neglect of fortification
8. No professional warriors or military specializations (such as swordsmen, bowmen, and cavalrymen)
9. Ineffective tactics and neglect of certain principles of warfare

In short, they found primitive warfare desultory, ineffective, "unprofessional," and unserious.

The highly voluntary nature of recruitment for war parties in tribal societies, Turney-High claimed, led to ineffective or defective mobilization. The ability of warriors in some tribes to desert a war party because of ill omens or dreams was even more disastrous. He suggested that "a good stiff jolt of punishment" would have quickly remedied such malingering. Although he conceded that social pressure alone was sufficient to raise large war parties in some tribes, he also believed the system of physical compulsion used by the Zulu, Dahomean, Celtic, and modern states was superior.[15] Typically, Wright, and especially Turney-High, gauged the military efficacy of a practice by how closely it resembled that of the modern military, rather than by its effects. In the case of mobilization, the key effect involved the proportion of a society's potential manpower that was actually mobilized for combat, an issue neither scholar ever addressed.

Turney-High noted that the inadequate supplies provided to warriors by their subsistence economies limited the possibilities for perpetuating campaigns or sieges beyond the first encounter. He linked the issues of adequate supplies and logistics to "a social organization capable of producing an economic surplus by a high agriculture" (presumably he means a state supported by short-fallow agriculture) and "a means of transporting such food." Thus the absence of extended military campaigns was the direct consequence of poor logistics that, in turn, reflected a primitive economy and social organization. By implication, the only way a gardening tribe or hunting band could conduct an extended campaign would be by first becoming an agricultural state.

Both scholars noted that primitive warriors were ill-disciplined and rather selective about obeying their leaders' commands. The military virtues of discipline and ready obedience were the product of training, practice, and exercise. Turney-High remarked that only states could afford such training and that only state leaders had the power to compel obedience.[16] At the same time, he repeatedly implied that such discipline was essential for victory and that only states were capable of winning victories. He had nothing but disdain for the capriciousness and heedlessness of primitive warriors:

> His is an undisciplined rabble which really does not stand and die when ordered by some alleged chief. A stand-up battle with quality troops against odds was no more his idea of fun than it is of his cultural descendent, the guerrilla. The primitive warrior . . . loves a sure thing. Turning an apparently hopeless cause into a winning one by valor and skill is not his way.[17]

Wright's characterization of primitive warriors as "flighty" was not so openly contemptuous, but it carried the same message.

One feature that permeated Turney-High's discussion of primitive war—and distinguishes it from Wright's—was his profound belief that the tactical principles or laws of war taught to modern officers in training represented timeless requirements for effective warfare. He compared them to scientific laws and claimed that they could be used to predict or guarantee military success and failure. For him, to the degree that primitive warriors ignored or violated these commandments, their warfare was necessarily frivolous and ineffective.

According to Turney-High, primitive warriors did adhere to some of these principles or "laws" but characteristically ignored or disobeyed several others.[18] Indeed, their application of some might even be superior to that of civilized soldiers. He found that tribal warriors generally obeyed the principles that prescribed Offensive Action, Surprise, Intelligence, Utilization of Terrain, and Mobility. They were quite variable in their use of the rules for Fire and Movement, with many groups merely exchanging missiles at a distance and never closing with their foes. They were surprisingly poor at the law of Security, often being surprised or ambushed and neglecting the use of fortifications. They rarely adhered to the commandments of Concentration at the Critical Point and Exploitation of Victory in that they failed to focus on key objectives or enemy weak points and to pursue defeated foes. Of course, Cooperation of Specialized Forces—another rule—was impossible for groups lacking specialized units such as cavalry and artillery. He insisted that primitives did not use the Correct Formations, but he was vague on this point. Given that his other accusations implied a lack of sophistication or complexity, it is surprising that he also found primitive warriors failing to observe the principle of Simplicity of Plans, either by having none at all or by having plans that were too standardized.

These principles, for which Turney-High claimed the status of social science laws, are contradictory and rather vague, especially in practice. For example, achieving "security" usually requires locating forces at other than the "critical point" and often necessitates restraint in the "exploitation of victory." Many civilized units or armies have paid a high price by adhering to the injunction to exploit victories by racing headlong into piecemeal defeat by their rallied or reenforced foes. Fortifications exemplify "security" but are inimical to "mobility" and "offensive action." Actually, few of these principles can be taken at face value or unequivocally. With examples like the disastrous trench offensives of World War I and Napoleon's Russian campaign, it might be more honest to restate one principle as "offensive action except when inadvisable." Others of these laws suffer from a debilitating vagueness. How simple should plans be? How does one recognize the critical point except in hindsight? Because of their proverbial vagueness and contradictoriness, these tactical laws are much more readily employed, like proverbs, in rationalizing outcomes than as scientific prescriptions for generating victories. Ironically, Turney-High's "immutable Laws of War" are no longer taught to aspiring war leaders at the great Western military academies.[19]

For all of his disparagement of primitive warfare, Turney-High repeatedly recognized that the concentrated economic surplus, power of coercion, and centralized decision making of states were the basic determinants of his "true war." The absence of these features in primitive societies explained most or all of their military "deficiencies." In other words, Turney-High's military horizon was not so much a tactical Rubicon as a political and economic one.

One tactical principle missing from Turney-High's list is the importance of superior numbers (usually codified as the principle of Mass). This important feature of warfare he airily dismisses with the assertion that "good small armies have time and again humiliated large masses."[20] In fact, any number of good small armies have been ground into dust by less artful large masses. For example, the nimble Finns in 1939 and 1940 and the formidable Germans in 1941 and 1942 certainly humiliated the more massive Soviet Army initially, but they were soon overwhelmed as thoroughly as any armies in history. Like so many historians enamored of tactics, leadership, and discipline, Turney-High's focus was on victory in battle, not wars. As the Romans fighting Hannibal showed, one can lose every battle but the last one and still win the war. That crucial last battle has almost always gone to the side with the larger manpower reserves and stronger economy.

Both Wright and Turney-High agreed that because of its frivolous motivations and technical deficiencies, primitive warfare had few important effects, nor was it particularly dangerous.[21] Wright concluded that casualties and destructiveness only increased with social evolution. Both scholars simply *assumed* that fighting for practical goals with civilized techniques automatically made war more terrible and, conversely, that irrational goals with simple techniques made war ineffective. Neither author supported these assumptions with any facts or figures. Although Wright did have casualty figures from a few tribal groups (presumably because they contradicted his conclusions) they appeared only in an appendix.[22] He even experienced difficulty supporting his trend of increasing death and destruction with historical data from Europe.[23] Turney-High never bothered with figures at all. He believed that since primitive warriors were always defeated by civilized soldiers, the point was self-evident.[24] He did, however, concede that primitive societies "made some very credible stands against the white man, in spite of their small populations and simple weapons," implying that primitive warfare was not always entirely ineffective or safe. Essentially, Wright and Turney-High's conclusions concerning the efficacy of primitive war amounted to aesthetic judgments of form and style, rather than practical or scientific evaluations of effects.

Subsequent students of precivilized life seem to have paid little heed to Wright and Turney-High's technical points about the social contexts and techniques of primitive war. But no one seems to have forgotten their dismissal of primitive war as a relatively harmless sport, directed toward impractical goals and incapable of affecting any essential aspects of social existence. From this filtration, the postwar concept of a relatively benign primitive war was born.

THE CONTROVERSY OVER CAUSES

As the concept of ineffective and unimportant primitive war became embedded in textbooks and teaching, anthropologists devoted little attention to warfare during the 1950s.[25] The situation changed dramatically in the 1960s, however, for a host of anthropological and nonanthropological reasons. During the late 1950s and early 1960s, ethnographers were able to observe the final stages of tribal warfare in highland New Guinea and in Amazonia. Anthropologists were again directly confronted with the realities of warfare among small-scale societies. Explanations of these new observations became entangled in the theoretical and political debates of the times. These arguments also reopened the Hobbes versus Rousseau question and revived the mythologizing impulses that have invariably attached themselves to this debate.

The anthropological debates about war are part of a wider theoretical battle in anthropology between cultural ecology and cultural materialism on one side and a variety of opposing "-isms" on the other. Cultural materialism proposes that most cultural practices are explainable by reference to the material conditions of life—ecology, technology, demography, and basic economy.[26] Various anthropological opponents to cultural materialism deny this proposition, preferring explanations that refer to the independent realms of social dynamics, differing ideologies, or other nonmaterial factors.

The materialist perspective focuses on the adaptive consequences of war. One early materialist view was that warfare redistributes or controls human populations to bring them into a better balance with available scarce resources, especially productive land.[27] There was also the implication that warfare should intensify with increasing population pressure on critical resources. The combatants may or may not be aware of these material causes, and they often use a fairly standard set of pretexts or justifications for fighting. Nevertheless, a common result of tribal warfare is that one side obtains from the other various means of production in the form of land, livestock, and additional labor. Some materialists argued that societies undertake warfare only when forced to do so by competition over food or other essential resources. Peace is the inertial or natural state to which societies revert when essential material needs can be cheaply supplied by nonviolent means.[28]

This type of theory simply elaborates Rousseau's contention that primitive man is an enemy to others only when he is hungry. Yet the materialists were by no means completely Rousseauian; many of them (for instance, Andrew Vayda, Robert Carneiro, Marvin Harris, and William Divale) asserted that tribal warfare could be exceptionally vicious and inflict high casualty rates. Indeed, Robert Carneiro argued that warfare played a key role in social evolution, especially the development of states.

In the late 1960s, a substantial shock to the materialist interpretation of war was administered by Napoleon Chagnon's influential and popular ethnography on the Yanomamo of Venezuela and Brazil.[29] Chagnon described the Yanomamo as being embroiled in almost constant warfare. The men displayed a considerable propensity for violence against everyone. Yet Yanomamo villages were surrounded by abundant unoccupied territory; the fighting between them was apparently motivated only by desires to exact revenge and to capture women; and they experienced difficulty in obtaining sufficient food only as a *result* of warfare. Chagnon literally declared that the Yanomamo exemplified the Hobbesian state of "warre."

Many antimaterialists have concentrated on the social features that escalate disputes between individuals into warfare between groups or make peace difficult to establish and maintain—in other words, on formal causes rather than material or final ones.[30] This conception is neo-Hobbesian in that it derives primitive warfare especially from the absence of statelike institutions of external justice and mediation. The neo-Hobbesians deny that one gains anything from war except a bleak social survival. For example, C. R. Hallpike claims that nonstate societies "engage in warfare because among other reasons they cannot stop, not because they derive any benefit from fighting. In the absence of any central authority they are condemned to fight forever . . . since for any one group to cease defending itself would be suicidal."[31]

Neo-Hobbesians argue that the booty obtained by warriors and the larger territories often acquired by victors are merely occasional effects and have no bearing on the causes of warfare. Indeed, the neo-Hobbesians seem quite unconcerned with the content or nature of the disputes that lead to fighting, apparently believing that a dispute over almost any matter can lead to war, if no powerful third-party authority exists to adjudicate or suppress it. To judge from the various social and ideological factors they repeatedly discuss, neo-Hobbesians see war as a permanent social condition in which the potential for combat is always present, even if it actually breaks out only intermittently. The actual episodes of fighting receive—and by these scholars' principles require— no general explanation.

Neo-Hobbesians also view prestate warfare as being very frequent and consider a state of war a latent condition of prestate existence. Yet like Wright and Turney-High, they deny that it has any important practical causes or consequences except bare survival of the social group. By contrast, some materialists see primitive wars as having important demographic and economic causes and effects; but, like the proponents of benign primitive war, they do not see war as "normal" to (and therefore necessarily common among) prestate societies. Indeed, materialists echo Wright and Turney-High in accepting that warfare becomes more frequent and terrible as the size, density, and complexity of economic and political organizations increase (that is, with social evolution). Thus recent anthropological theory has tended toward two extreme and opposed conceptions: primitive warfare is uncommon but rewarding, or it is very common but unrewarding. In either case, important aspects of Wright and Turney-High's concept of primitive war survive.

The essential focus of almost all these arguments has been the perennial question: What causes war? The intense interest in this question, to the neglect of the actual conduct or immediate effects of warfare, is undoubtedly attributable to its assumed practical utility. Just as we cure or eradicate disease by eliminating its causes, so anthropologists frequently premise their examinations of warfare on the hope that it may be extinguished by rooting out its (single) cause. These arguments between the materialist and antimaterialist schools concerning warfare represent only a flank of a larger theoretical battle among anthropologists. Because of the pervasive polarization, both sides have claimed that their own favored theories suffice to explain warfare and assert that any resort to the other side's hypotheses is logically unnecessary.

Though many partisans in these debates imply that the warfare of a particular region—or even all warfare—has a single cause, no complex phenomenon can have a single cause. There are efficient, formal, material, and final causes, as well as necessary and sufficient conditions. Even something as straightforward as catching an infectious disease usually entails more than just exposure to a viral or bacterial agent because the illness will not develop if the host possesses an inborn or acquired immunity. Since infectious diseases actually have multiple causes, they can be defeated by various means: eliminating exposure to the disease by quarantine or by destruction of animal vectors, killing the active agent with antiseptics or antibiotics, mitigating adverse symptoms with antitoxins, inducing immunity with vaccination, and so on. In this example, quarantine and antibiotics eliminate an efficient cause; vaccination removes a formal cause; and antitoxins ignore causes but palliate the effects. The complexity of the concept of cause means that seemingly contradictory views are often actually complementary because they focus on different categories. The anthropological debates about the causes of warfare may represent a classic case of unacknowledged complementarity.

PREHISTORIC PEACE

If social anthropologists of various persuasions have retained theoretical elements derived from the concept of a stylized, ineffective, and insignificant primitive war, archaeologists during the past twenty-five years have been even more accepting. Less by sustained argument than by studied silence or fashionable reinterpretation, prehistorians have increasingly pacified the human past. The most widely used archaeological textbooks contain no references to warfare until the subject of urban civilizations is taken up.[32] The implication is clear: war was unknown or insignificant before the rise of civilization. In several recent collections of papers dealing with more specialized topics—such as prehistoric frontiers, migrations, trade, and "farmer–forager interactions"—the only mentions of warfare relate to historic civilized frontiers and civilized economies.[33] The possibility that warfare might have been involved with these matters before the rise of urban states is not dismissed; it is simply never mentioned.

A few specific examples from my area of expertise, European prehistory, should clarify the character of this interpretative "pacification." The earliest farmers to appear in Britain during the period known as the Early Neolithic, beginning about 4000 B.C., constructed ditched and palisaded enclosures called causewayed camps by archaeologists. In Brian Fagan's very popular textbook on prehistory, the function of these enclosures is discussed in entirely peaceful terms. Noting that several such camps were "littered with human bone," Fagan concludes that "perhaps these camps were places where the dead were exposed for months before their bones were deposited in nearby communal burials." In an excellent survey of the early farming cultures of prehistoric Europe, Alasdair Whittle suggests that the "interrupted ditches backed by solid barriers" (log palisades banked or daubed with earth from the ditches) typical of these camps merely expresses the "symbolism of exclusion." According to these syntheses or summaries, either causewayed camps were the Neolithic equivalent of the famous Parsi Towers of Silence of India or their deep ditches and palisaded ramparts stood as elaborate symbols bearing the message Keep Out![34]

A far different impression is conveyed by the reports of the archaeologists who have conducted extensive excavations of some of these enclosures.[35] At several camps, the distribution of thousands of flint arrowheads, concentrated along the palisade and especially at the gates (Figure 1.1), provides clear evidence that they "had quite obviously been defended against archery attack," making it extremely probable that the enclosures were "built with this intention." Moreover, the total destruction by fire of some of these camps seems to have been contemporaneous with the archery attacks. At one such site, intact skeletons of two young adult males were found at the bottom of the ditches, buried beneath the burned rubble of the collapsed palisade-rampart. In one poignant instance, the young man had been shot in the back by a flint-tipped arrow and was carrying an infant in his arms who had been "crushed beneath him when he fell." Whatever ritual or symbolic functions of the enclosures might have had, they were obviously fortifications, some of which were attacked and stormed.

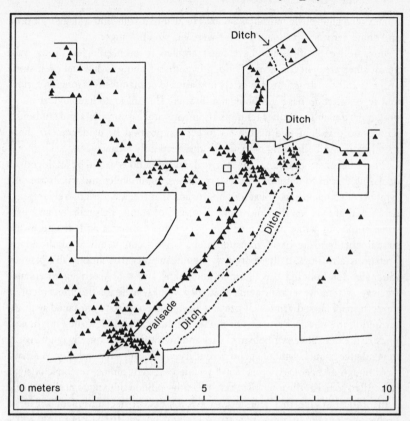

Figure 1.1 Distribution of arrowheads at a Neolithic causewayed camp in England. Concentrations were found along the line of the palisade and fanning inward from the gates. (Redrawn after Dixon 1988: 83 by Ray Brod, Department of Geography, University of Illinois at Chicago)

A Belgian archaeologist who has excavated many Iron Age burials was criticized by several colleagues at a recent conference for referring to burials from this period as "warrior" graves, even though they contained spears, swords, shields, a male corpse clothed in armor, and in some instances the remains of a chariot. The critics asserted that these weapons and armor were merely status symbols and had only a symbolic function rather than a practical military one. Similarly, copper and bronze axes from the Late Neolithic and Bronze Ages, formerly referred to as battle axes, are no longer classified as weapons but are considered a form of money. The 5,000-year-old Austrian glacier mummy recently reported in the news was found with one of these moneys mischievously hafted as an ax. He also had with him a dagger, a bow, and some arrows; presumably these were his small change.

Interpretive pacifications have been applied to archaeological finds from many other areas of the world.[36] Such hypotheses about individual prehistoric artifacts and constructions are rarely implausible or manifestly wrong. Weapons and forts often *do* have symbolic significance. But these archaeological interpretations depend on rather tenuous arguments and assumptions and studiously ignore more violent interpretations directly supported by evidence. In short, they ignore the bellicosely obvious for the peaceably arcane.

These deconstructionist archaeological interpretations would be analogous to declaring that in contemporary Western culture automobiles and trucks are only symbols of status, masculinity, and liberty and that freeways are merely impractical ritual arenas for the enactment of rituals of status, masculinity, and personal autonomy while never mentioning that these artifacts and structures are fundamentally a means of transportation.[37] Such completely symbolic interpretations also neglect the extremely significant fact that among the primary rationales for building the German autobahns and the American interstate-freeway system were arguments that they would facilitate the movement of modern mechanized armies. If present-day archaeologists were faced with interpreting the physical remains of modern industrial societies, they might emphasize the derivative symbolism of cars and highways while quietly ignoring the dependence of such symbolism on practical economic or even military concerns.

Although archaeologists may have pacified the past almost unconsciously, a handful of social anthropologists have recently codified this vague prejudice into a theoretical stance that amounts to a Rousseauian declaration of universal prehistoric peace. In some recent papers and books, Brian Ferguson and a number of other scholars have argued that the instances of tribal warfare described by Westerners, including ethnographers, were the product of disequalibrium induced by Western contact and did not represent the primitive condition.[38] Specifically, such warfare was a product of decimation by introduced diseases, native population movements induced by civilized colonization, social disruption associated with slave raiding, and hostilities engendered by conflicts over civilized trade goods. These Western derangements created a "tribal zone" of Hobbesian war of an unspecified radius around any civilized outpost or observer. Whenever civilized observers moved out to previously uncontacted groups, they would either still be within this zone of war or, if they moved beyond the disrupted region, merely transmit the virus of war themselves by bringing Western goods for trade and gifts or by introducing new diseases. Thus no civilized observer could ever view anything but the Hobbesian warfare created by European contact. Ferguson concludes that the "wild violence noted by Hobbes was not an expression of 'man in a state of nature' but a reflection of contact with Hobbes' Leviathan—the states of Western Europe. To take the carnage as revealing the fundamental nature of human existence is to pass through the looking glass."[39] This argument is based on the well-documented observation that contact with Westerners altered a wide variety of native behaviors and attitudes, including those involved in warfare. Undoubtedly, native warfare changed with increasing external contact, but important questions remain with regard to the character and speed of the changes and (especially) the nature of the situation prior to contact.

Since these neo-Rousseauian scholars characterize any evidence of Hobbesian social or demographic features, tribal traditions, and mythologies among prestate societies as being consequences of contact, they appear to believe that the resulting transformations, which touched almost every facet of social life and culture, occurred almost instaneously. Thus the proponents of prehistoric peace not only reject the validity of certain ethnographic observations uncongenial to their view of the primitive condition, but also deny the legitimacy of ethnography altogether. That is the substance of arguing that ethnographic descriptions merely mirror civilized behavior and do not provide a window on the precivilized way of life. But if ethnographers' observations can tell us nothing useful about the conditions of life peculiar to prestate nonindustrial societies, why bother with ethnography or ethnographers at all? An undistorted image of civilization is much more immediately discernible in the work of economists, sociologists, and historians. One suspects that because the uncivilized villagers described by ethnography often appear to have lived in a Hobbesian state, certain scholars have metaphorically "destroyed the village in order to save it."

This hypothesis attributes an exceptional potency—indeed, a peculiar radioactivity—to civilized people and their products. Were there never epidemic diseases before Western contact? Were there never uncivilized items of trade that excited the practical appetites of primitive consumers and were worth fighting over? Did new weapons never diffuse to modify prehistoric warfare? Were there never population movements or expansions before civilization? If any of these conditions existed before civilized expansion, then, by these arguments, the causes of war should also have existed. As we shall see in the following chapters, there is evidence that such things happened before civilized observers soiled the preliterate world. In this case, the tribal-zone hypothesis would be reduced to the claim that civilized contact merely brought some new weapons to fight with and new items to fight over to prestate regions, not the more general reasons for fighting or the institution of war itself.

Most neo-Rousseauians are vague about what they suppose the precontact situation to have been. Their assertions that "wild violence" and carnage were caused by civilized contact imply they imagine that precontact conditions approached Rousseau's primitive peace. This hypothesis of prehistoric peace is analogous to my father's facetious claim that the flesh of a watermelon is really white until the skin is broken and it turns instantly red. As with my father's story, it is impossible to disprove by direct observation. It requires no great diligence to show that any primitive group, at the moment of its ethnographic description, has been subjected to an epidemic, possessed civilized trade goods, or sustained some form of disruption from the presence of a European observer in their midst. Ferguson does acknowledge that archaeology has the capacity to look inside the watermelon before it is cut, but neither he nor his colleagues ever mention any archaeological support for their declaration of prehistoric peace.

In the past few decades, the hypothesis of unserious, ritualized primitive war has thus been transformed—through the consistent deemphasis of prehistoric violence by archaeologists and later through the explicit arguments of some social anthropologists—into an neo-Rousseauian concept of *prehistoric peace*.

RESONANCE OF THE PACIFIED PAST

The neo-Rousseauian tenor of these postwar anthropological views on war and civilization has penetrated and resonated with other aspects of Western intellectual and popular culture. Let me cite a few recent expressions of such concurrences ranging from academic discourses by nonanthropologists to expressions in popular culture.

Directly reflecting the idea of primitive war, two military historians discussing the Iron Age of early Western civilization see it as the germinal period of real war:

> In less than 2000 years, man went from a condition in which warfare was relatively rare and mostly ritualistic to one in which death and destruction were achieved on a modern scale. . . . The Iron Age also saw the practice of war firmly rooted in man's societies and experience and, perhaps more importantly, in his psychology. War, warriors and weapons were now a normal part of human existence.[40]

Thus, before civilization, war was rare, ritualized, abnormal, and foreign to human psychology.

Recently, in a letter to an academic newsletter, a professor of sociology contrasted "the emotional richness and cultural diversity of traditional African tribal life" to "the enhanced capacity for destructiveness that the emergence of all civilizational structures brought forth, such as organized mass warfare."[41] Rousseau's view of civilization as emotionally impoverished, culturally confining, and destructively warlike compared with traditional tribal life could not be more baldly restated.

In William Manchester's quasi-memoirs of his service in the marines during World War II, he asserts that although the natives of Papua–New Guinea lived in a Stone Age culture, "it is equally true that their simple humanity would prevent them from even contemplating a Pearl Harbor, an Auschwitz or a Hiroshima."[42] Surprise attacks, slaughters of noncombatants, and general massacres are therefore unknown in a world of New Guinea tribesmen. As we shall see in later chapters, Manchester could not have been more wrong.

Reflecting several of the ideas of prehistoric peace, the plot of Jamie Uys's film comedy *The Gods Must Be Crazy* centers on a Coke bottle that is tossed from a passing airplane and lands in an African San (Bushmen) encampment. The Bushmen's encounter with this civilized artifact soon leads to conflict and fighting in the previously harmonious camp. The angry headman then undertakes a quest to return this evil item to the unhelpful gods who dropped it. Reaching a civilized outpost, he is eventually arrested and gets embroiled in a guerrilla war. The film is a broad farce, but the little San's good sense and peacefulness are always favorably contrasted with the foolishness, cold hearts, and violence of the civilized people he meets. The underlying message is that the selfish strife and heartless wars characteristic of civilization emanate from even its most prosaic artifacts.

In intellectual and popular culture, war has come to be regarded by many as a peculiar psychosis of Western civilization. This atmosphere of Western self-reproach and neo-Rousseauian nostalgia is prevalent in the views espoused by many postwar anthropologists.

The pacification of the past now epidemic in anthropology is just the latest turn in the long struggle between the myths of progress and the golden age, between Hobbesian and Rousseauian conceptions of the nature of primitive societies and of the prehistoric past. Relying perhaps on the time-honored archaeological method of ethnographic analogy, archaeologists have increasingly ignored the phenomenon of prehistoric warfare (inasmuch as it had been declared by ethnologists to be weightless and unimportant). They have written warfare out of prehistory by omitting any mention of evidence of prehistoric violence when they synthesize or summarize the raw data produced by excavation. Some social anthropologists have recently become more aggressively pacifist, dismissing all ethnographic descriptions of primitive warfare as being the product of civilized interference with more peaceful precontact (that is, truly prehistoric) primitive life. If these ideas are correct, anthropology has little to say about war.

But the proponents of primitive war and prehistoric peace have tended to neglect the very evidence that is crucial to their propositions. With regard to the intensity, dangerousness, and effectiveness of primitive war, it is vital to study the direct effects of precivilized conflict: the casualty rates, the destruction, and the gains or losses of territory and other vital possessions. If uncivilized societies were very peaceful before literate observers could record them, archaeology should be able to provide the documentation. The evaluation of these ideas (and, of course, any ideas contrary to them) requires careful surveillance of both ethnographic and archaeological data, with special attention to questions of how recent tribal and ancient prehistoric warfare was actually conducted and what the direct results of such conflicts were. Since implicit in any discussion of primitive warfare is a contrast with the corresponding forms of civilized conflict, it is also vital to make direct comparisons between the two in equivalent terms. Only then is it possible to achieve a realistic view of all warfare and to determine whether anthropology has anything to offer us in our attempts to understand and eventually eliminate the awful scourge of war. The purpose of this book is to provide just such a survey and evaluation.

TWO

The Dogs of War

The Prevalence and Importance of War

A s we have seen, many recent popular and academic views of precivilized warfare agree that it was a trivial and insubstantial activity. Proponents of primitive war and the pacified past claim or imply that peaceful societies were common, fighting was infrequent, and active participation in combat was limited among nonstate peoples until they either evolved into or made contact with states and civilizations.

If these views are correct, they should be supported by broad surveys of ethnographic and archaeological evidence. Ethnographic data should indicate that nonstate societies were commonly pacifistic, resorted to combat much less frequently than did ancient or modern states, and mobilized little of their potential manpower for the warfare they did conduct. In the more thoroughly studied regions, archaeology should recover very little evidence of violent conflicts before the development of indigenous states or the intrusion of foreign states. As we shall see, on the contrary, the available evidence shows that peaceful societies have been very rare, that warfare was extremely frequent in nonstate societies, and that tribal societies often mobilized for combat very high percentages of their total man-power.

LEVELS OF SOCIAL COMPLEXITY

Before proceeding with any ethnographic survey, we must review some terms that are used by anthropologists in roughly classifying the size and complexity of societies. These terms include *bands, tribes, chiefdoms, states,* and *civilized* or *urban states.* They loosely describe the population size and the economic and political complexity of various societies.

Bands are small, politically autonomous groups of twenty to fifty people with an informal headman. They usually consist of a few related extended families who reside or move together. Typically, bands are hunter-gatherers or foragers. Several such *micro-bands* usually congregate for a few weeks each year into a *macro-band* of several hundred people for ceremonies, festivities, courting and marriage arrangements, and the exchange of goods. Such macro-bands usually speak a distinct dialect and are sometimes referred to as *dialect tribes.* The classic examples of societies with band organization are the Eskimo of the central Arctic, the Paiutes of the American Great Basin, and the Aborigines of central Australia.

The term *tribe* covers a multitude of social and political organizations. Tribes generally incorporate a few thousand people into a single social organization via pan-tribal associations. These associations are usually kin groups that trace descent to a common hypothetical or mythological ancestor. But nonkin associa-tions, such as *age-grades* (groups of young men who were initiated together) and *sodalities* (voluntary nonkin associations such as dance societies, clubs, etc.), can also integrate a tribe. Tribes are collections of such associations or kin groups that unite for war. While tribal leaders may be called big men or chiefs, they are not formal full-time political officials, and they usually exercise influence rather than what we would call power. In most cases, there is no central political organization except informal councils of "elders" or local chiefs. Foraging, pastoral, and agricultural economies are all found among tribes. Tribes are so various in their features that it is difficult to list classic cases, but the Indian tribes of the Plains, the southwestern Pueblos, and the Masai of East Africa are familiar examples.

Chiefdoms are organizations that unite many thousands or tens of thousands of people under formal, full-time political leadership. The populace of a chief-dom is usually divided into hereditary *ranks* or incipient social classes, often consisting of no more than a small chiefly or noble class and a large body of commoners. Both the means of production and economic surpluses are concentrated under the control of the chief, who redistributes them. A central political structure integrates many local communities. This central body may consist of a council of chiefs, but in most cases a single head chief controls a hierarchy of lesser chiefs. Accession to chiefship is hereditary, permanent, and justified on religious or magical grounds. But a chief, unlike a king, does not have the power to coerce people into obedience physically; instead, he must rely on magical and economic powers to enforce his dictates. Some typical examples, ranging from weak to strong chiefdoms, include some Pacific Northwest Coast tribes, many Polynesian societies, early medieval Scottish clans, and some traditional petty kingdoms in central Africa.

States are also political organizations that incorporate many tens or hundreds of thousands of people from numerous communities into a single territorial unit. They have a central government empowered to collect taxes, draft labor for public works or war, decree laws, and physically enforce those laws. Essentially, states are class-stratified political units that maintain a "monopoly of deadly force"—a monopoly institutionalized as permanent police and military forces. *Civilized* states are simply those with cities and some form of record keeping (usually writing). Since few people in the world today are not citizens of some state, examples are unnecessary.

The term *primitive*, when used in its usual sense in anthropology, merely refers to a technological condition—that of using preindustrial or preliterate technology. In social terms, primitive refers to societies that are not urban or literate. Precisely such societies are the traditional subject matter of anthropology. But because the word has negative connotations in everyday speech, *primitive* has fallen out of favor. It has been erratically replaced by a number of inelegant neologisms such as *preliterate* or *nonliterate*, *prestate* or *nonstate*, *preindustrial* and *small-scale*. The term *tribal societies* usually encompasses bands, tribes, and weak chiefdoms but excludes strong chiefdoms and states. In the broadest sense, all these terms refer to societies that are simpler in technology and some aspects of social organization—and usually smaller in size—than societies that have produced historical records. Primarily for stylistic variety, all these terms are used interchangeably here.

IS WARFARE UNIVERSAL?

According to the most extreme views, war is an inherent feature of human existence, a constant curse of all social life, or (in the guise of real war) a perversion of human sociability created by the centralized political structures of states and civilizations. In fact, cross-cultural research on warfare has established that although some societies that did not engage in war or did so extremely rarely, the overwhelming majority of known societies (90 to 95 percent) have been involved in this activity.

Three independent cross-cultural surveys of representative samples of recent tribal and state societies from around the world have tabulated data on armed conflict, all giving very consistent results. In one sample of fifty societies, only five were found to have engaged "infrequently or never" in any type of offensive or defensive warfare.[1] Four of these groups had recently been driven by warfare into isolated refuges, and this isolation protected them from further conflict. Such groups might more accurately be classified as defeated refugees than as pacifists. One California Indian tribe, the Monachi of the Sierra Nevada, apparently did occasionally go to war, but only very rarely. The results of this particular survey indicate that 90 percent of the cultures in the sample unequivocally engaged in warfare and that the remaining 10 percent were not total strangers to violent conflict.

In another larger cross-cultural study of politics and conflict, twelve of a sample of ninety societies (13 percent) were found to engage in warfare "rarely or never."[2] Six of these twelve were tribal or ethnic minorities that had long been subject to the peaceful administration of modern nation-states—for example, the Gonds of India and the Lapps of Scandinavia. Three were agricultural tribes living in geographically isolated circumstances, such as the Tikopia islanders of Polynesia (who were defeated refugees) and the Cayapa tribe of Ecuador.[3] The final three were nomadic hunter-gatherers of the equatorial jungles and arctic tundra: the Mbuti Pygmies of Zaire, the Semang of Malaysia, and the Copper Eskimo of arctic Canada. Most of these peaceful societies were recently defeated refugees living in isolation, lived under a "king's peace" enforced by a modern state, or both. The real exceptions, representing only 5 percent of the sample, were some small bands of nomadic hunter-gatherers and a few isolated horticultural tribes.

In a study of western North American Indian tribes and bands, again only 13 percent of the 157 groups surveyed were recorded as "never or rarely" raiding or having been raided—meaning, in this case, *more than once a year.*[4] Of these 21 relatively peaceable groups, 14 gave other evidence of having conducted or resisted occasional raids, presumably only once every few years. This leaves only 7 truly peaceful societies (4.5 percent of the sample) that apparently did not participate in any type of warfare or raiding. All these were very small nomadic bands residing in the driest, most isolated regions of the Columbia Plateau and the Great Basin.[5] Again, we find the most peaceful groups living in areas with extremely low population densities, isolated by distance and hard country from other groups.

Even highly nomadic, geographically isolated hunter-gatherers with low population densities are not universally peaceable. For example, many Australian Aboriginal foragers, including those living in deserts, were inveterate raiders.[6] The seeming peacefulness of such small hunter-gatherer groups may therefore be more a consequence of the tiny size of their social units and the large scale implied by our normal definition of warfare than of any real pacifism on their part. Under circumstances where the sovereign social and political unit is a nuclear or slightly extended family band of from four to twenty-five people, even with a sex ratio unbalanced in favor of males, no more than a handful of adult males (the only potential "warriors") are available. When such a small group of men commits violence against another band or family, even if faced in open combat by all the men of the other group, this activity is not called war but is usually referred to as feuding, vendetta, or just murder.

Thus many small-band societies that are regarded by ethnologists as not engaging in warfare instead evidence very high homicide rates.[7] For example, the Kung San (or Bushmen) of the Kalahari Desert are viewed as a very peaceful society; indeed, one popular ethnography on them was titled *The Harmless People.* However, their homicide rate from 1920 to 1955 was four times that of the United States and twenty to eighty times that of major industrial nations during the 1950s and 1960s. Before local establishment of the Bechuanaland/Botswana police, the Kung also conducted small-scale raids and prolonged feuds between bands and against Tswana herders intruding from the east. The Copper Eskimo, who appear as a peaceful society in the cross-cultural surveys just discussed, also experienced a high level of feuding and homicide before the Royal Canadian Mounted Police suppressed it. Moreover, in one Copper Eskimo camp of fifteen families first contacted early in this century, *every* adult male had been involved in a homicide. Other Eskimo of the high arctic who were organized into small bands also fit this pattern. Based on figures from different sources, the murder rate for the Netsilik Eskimo, *even after the Mounties had suppressed interband feuding,* exceeds that of the United States by four times and that of modern European states by some fifteen to forty times. At the other end of the New World, the isolated Yaghan "canoe nomads" of Tierra del Fuego, whose only sovereign political unit was the "biological family," had a murder rate in the late nineteenth century "10 times as high as that of the United States."[8] Thus armed conflict between social units does not necessarily disappear at the lowest levels of social integration; often it is just terminologically disguised as feuding or homicide.

Both Richard Lee and Marvin Harris, defending the pacifistic nature of Kung and other simple societies compared with our own, decry the "semantic deception" that disguises the "true" homicide rates of modern states by ignoring the murders inflicted during wars.[9] Let us undertake such a comparison for one simple society, the Gebusi of New Guinea. Calculations show that the

United States military would have had to kill nearly the *whole* population of South Vietnam during its nine-year involvement there, in addition to its internal homicide rate, to equal the homicide rate of the Gebusi.[10] As their ethnographer Bruce Knauft notes, "Only the most extreme instances of modern mass slaughter would equal or surpass the Gebusi homicide rate over a period of several decades."[11] There is, then, an equal semantic deception involved in manufacturing peaceful societies out of violent ones by refusing to characterize as war their only possible form of intergroup violence, merely because of the small size of the contending social units.

If many of the "peaceful" hunter-gatherer bands did in reality engage in armed conflict, were any of them genuine pacifists? Perhaps the most striking case of peaceful hunters involves the Polar Eskimo of northwestern Greenland.[12] In the early nineteenth century, they consisted of a small band of some 200 people whose circumstances seemed ideally suited to a postapocalyptic science-fiction plot or perhaps a heartless social science experiment. Their icy isolation had been so complete for so long that they were unaware that any other people existed in the world until they were contacted in 1819 by a European explorer. This tiny society, whose members eked a precarious livelihood from a frozen desert, not surprisingly avoided all feuds and armed conflicts, although murder was not unknown.[13] When other Eskimo from Canada and southwestern Greenland reached them after hearing of their existence from Europeans, relations with these strangers and with the Europeans they encountered were always quite amicable. The Polar Eskimo thus provide a counterexample to the recent theory that contact with Western civilization and its material goods inevitably turns peaceful tribesmen into Hobbesian berserkers.

There are a few other examples of peaceful hunter-gatherers.[14] The Mbuti Pygmies and Semang of the tropical forests of central Africa and Malaysia seem to have completely eschewed any form of violent conflict and can legitimately be regarded as pacifistic. However, the Pygmy foragers were in fact politically subordinate to and economically dependent on the farmers who surrounded them (Chapter 9). Although they frequently engaged in nonlethal violence involving weapons, the last small "wild" band of Aborigines in the western Australian desert, the Mardudjara, never (at least while ethnographers were present) permitted such fighting to escalate into killing. Although they possessed shields and specialized fighting weapons, the Mardudjara had no words in their language for feuds or warfare. The Great Basin Shoshone and Paiute bands mentioned earlier apparently never attacked others and were themselves attacked only very rarely; most just fled rather than trying to defend themselves. But these few peaceful groups are exceptional. The cross-cultural samples indicate that the vast majority of other hunter-gatherer groups did engage in warfare and that there is nothing inherently peaceful about hunting-gathering or band society.[15]

Pacifistic societies also occur (if uncommonly) at every level of social and economic complexity. Truly peaceful agriculturalists appear to be somewhat less common than pacifistic hunter-gatherers. In the cross-cultural samples discussed earlier, almost all the peaceful agricultural groups could be characterized as defeated refugees, ethnic minorities long administered by states, or tribes previously pacified by the police or by paramilitary organs of colonial or national states.[16] Low-density, nomadic hunter-gatherers, with their few (and portable) possessions, large territories, and few fixed resources or constructed facilities, had the option of fleeing conflict and raiding parties. At best, the only thing they would lose by such flight was their composure. But with their small territories, relatively numerous possessions, immobile and labor-expensive houses, food stores, and fields, sedentary farmers or hunter-gatherers who attempted to flee trouble could lose everything and thereupon risk starvation. Farmers and sedentary hunter-gatherers had little alternative but to meet force with force or, after injury, to discourage further depredations by taking revenge. Groups that depended on very localized, essential resources—such as desert springs, patches of fertile soil, good pastures, or fishing stations—had to defend these or face severe privation. Even nomadic pastoralists in extensive grasslands had to defend their herds, wherever they might be. For obvious reasons, then, agriculturalists, pastoralists, and less nomadic foragers have seldom been entirely peaceful. But such pacifistic farmers have occasionally appeared.

The best-known peaceful agriculturalists are the Semai of Malaysia, who strictly tabooed any form of violence (although their homicide rate was numerically significant).[17] Their reaction to any use of force involved "passivity or flight." Interestingly, they were recruited as counterinsurgency scout troops by the British during the Communist insurgency in Malaya in the 1950s. The Semai recruits were profoundly shocked to discover that as soldiers they were expected to kill other men. But after the guerrillas killed some of their kinsmen, they became very enthusiastic warriors. One Semai veteran recalled, "We killed, killed, killed. The Malays would stop and go through people's pockets and take their watches and money. We did not think of watches or money. We thought only of killing. Wah, truly we were drunk with blood." However, when the Semai scouts were demobilized and returned to their villages, they quietly resumed their nonviolent life-style. The low density of population, shifting settlement, and abundances of unused land probably allowed the Semai, unlike many other farmers, the option of flight from violent threats.[18] But their strong moral distaste for violence was undoubtedly important in maintaining their peacefulness.

Peaceful societies even exist among industrial states. For example, neither Sweden nor Switzerland has engaged in warfare for nearly two centuries; their homicide rates are among the lowest in the world. Like many peaceful tribal societies, Switzerland is to some degree geographically isolated behind its mountains. Sweden was once home to the legendarily belligerent Vikings and remained one of the most warlike societies in Europe until the eighteenth century. Nevertheless, Sweden has fought no wars since 1815. Both nations traditionally maintain modern military forces; indeed, every Swiss male between the ages of twenty and fifty is a military reservist, while Sweden is one of the world's leading arms exporters. But they and a few other nations in Asia and South America offer testimony that there is nothing inherently warlike about states.

Thus pacifistic societies seem to have existed at every level of social organization, but they are extremely rare and seem to require special circumstances. The examples of Sweden and the Semai demonstrate that societies can change from pacifistic to warlike, or vice versa, within a few generations or, (as with the Semai) within the lifetime of an individual. As these examples and the case of the Polar Eskimo establish, the idea that violent conflicts between groups is an inevitable consequence of being human or of social life itself is simply wrong. Still, the overwhelming majority of known societies have made war. Therefore, while it is not inevitable, war is universally common and usual.

THE FREQUENCY OF WARFARE IN STATE AND NONSTATE SOCIETIES

How frequent are primitive wars, and do nonstate societies engage in warfare less frequently than states or civilized societies? These questions are related to the question of how intense primitive warfare is. Again turning to cross-cultural research, we find that many of the myths about primitive war are untrue.

The three cross-cultural surveys mentioned earlier also include data on the frequency of warfare. All these studies show that warfare has been extremely frequent among primitive societies.[19] In the sample of fifty societies, 66 percent of the nonstates were continuously (meaning every year) at war, whereas only 40 percent of the states were at war this frequently. In this survey, warfare was therefore found to be less frequent in state societies. The larger sample of ninety societies, however, indicated that the frequency of war increased somewhat with greater political complexity; 77 percent of the states were at war once a year, whereas 62 percent of tribes and chiefdoms were this war prone. Nevertheless, 70 to 90 percent of bands, tribes, and chiefdoms went to war at least once every five years, as did 86 percent of the states. All these figures support yet another survey, which found that about 75 percent of all prestate societies went to war "at least once every two years before they were pacified or incorporated by more dominant societies" and that warfare was no more frequent "in complex societies than in simple band or tribal societies." In the sample of U.S. western Indian tribes, which consisted wholly of nonstate societies, 86 percent were raiding or resisting raids undertaken more than once each year. And such high frequencies of fighting were not peculiar to North America.[20] For example, during a five-and-a-half-month period, the Dugum Dani tribesmen of New Guinea were observed to participate in seven full battles and nine raids. One Yanomamo village in South America was raided twenty-five times over a fifteen-month period. These independent surveys show that the great majority of nonstate societies were at war at least once every few years and many times each generation. Obviously, frequent, even continuous, warfare is as characteristic of tribal societies as of states.

The high frequencies of prestate warfare contrast with those of even the most aggressive ancient and modern civilized states. The early Roman Republic (510–121 B.C.) initiated a war or was attacked only about once every twenty years. During the late Republic and early Empire (118 B.C.–A.D. 211), wars started about once every six or seven years, most being civil wars and provincial revolts.[21] Only a few of these later Roman wars involved any general mobilization of resources, and all were fought by the state's small (relative to the size of the population), long-service, professional forces supported by normal taxation, localized food levies, and plunder. In other words, most inhabitants of the Roman Empire were rarely directly involved in warfare and most experienced the Pax Romana unmolested over many generations.

Historic data on the period from 1800 to 1945 suggest that the average modern nation-state goes to war approximately once in a generation.[22] Taking into account the duration of these wars, the average modern nation-state was at war only about one year in every five during the nineteenth and early twentieth centuries. Even the most bellicose, such as Great Britain, Spain, and Russia, were never at war every year or continuously (although nineteenth-century Britain comes close). Compare these with the figures from the ethnographic samples of nonstate societies discussed earlier: 65 percent at war continuously; 77 percent at war once every five years and 55 percent at war every year; 87 percent fighting more than once a year; 75 percent at war once every two years. The primitive world was certainly not more peaceful than the modern one. The only reasonable conclusion is that wars are actually more frequent in nonstate societies than they are in state societies—especially modern nations.

MOBILIZATION

The informal and voluntary mobilization for war supposedly characteristic of tribal societies is often cited as evidence of the lack of importance and effectiveness of primitive versus civilized war. The idea is that if war really represented an important activity, instead of just a sport or dangerous pastime, these primitive societies would muster all of their strength.

Figure 2.1 shows some selected information on the size of war parties or armies in relation to the male populations of the social units from which they were drawn. While in most nonstate societies every male over the age of thirteen or fourteen is a potential warrior, not all of them participate in any particular war, battle, or raid. In general, tribal military formations are "all-volunteer" and usually muster proportions of their potential manpower similar to those achieved in the volunteer armed forces of states. Although modern conscript armies during active warfare generally represent a high percentage of the male population, on many occasions nonstate societies mobilize a higher proportion of their manpower. In World War II, neither the Soviet Union nor the United States, despite the tremendous power of coercion enjoyed by modern states, managed *during the whole war* to mobilize any greater proportion of its manpower than have some tribes and chiefdoms.

The reasons why mobilization cannot be complete are essentially the same for any society. Many males are too young, too old, too ill, or temperamentally unsuited to endure the stresses of combat. Because the sexual division of labor in most societies trains men and women to be proficient in different tasks, a

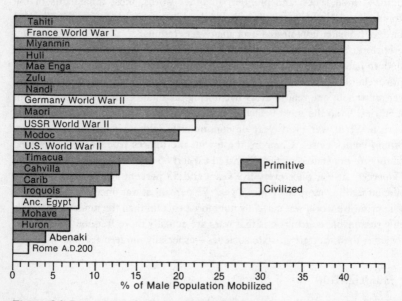

Figure 2.1 Percentages of male populations mobilized for combat by various tribes, ancient states, and modern nations (see Appendix, Table 2.1).

society's economy may not be sustained if it is denuded of men to hunt, tend stock, clear gardens, or do whatever other essential work lies on the male side of the division. Although women may be able to take over some of these tasks, training and developing skill at them take time. It may be very unwise to focus all of a group's manpower at one point on a border or beyond it, leaving women, children, and property vulnerable to attack from another quarter.

Women have very rarely engaged in combat, but have often played auxiliary roles in mobilization and logistics.[23] Before hostilities commenced, they might shame cowards, taunt the hesitant, and participate in dances of incitement. Among some groups, women have accompanied war parties to carry weapons and food. During combat, they might serve as a cheering section, supply first aid, or collect spent enemy missiles to resupply their own warriors. In some cases, either by choice or by necessity (such as when the enemy breached their fortifications), some women might actually fight. For example, female warriors were apparently not unusual in northern South America. In general, though, women's role has been to maintain the home front, tend gardens and stock, and nurse the wounded. While war may be everyone's business, it has usually been men's work.

In civilized war, ancient and modern, tremendous manpower (and woman-power) is required just to equip and supply military formations. The higher "warrior" proportions of modern wartime states in Figure 2.1 disguise the fact that only a fraction of the men mobilized actually engaged in combat.[24] In Napoleon's armies, at any given time, only about 58 to 77 percent of his soldiers were "effectives." The rest were convalescing, in training, garrison troops, or members of support units. During World War II, only about 40 percent of American servicemen served in combat units. The others were involved in administration, logistical support, and training; and an even smaller percentage carried a rifle, sailed on a warship, or flew in a warplane. The "tooth to tail" ratio between combat and support troops was 1:14 for the U.S. Army in Vietnam and is now about 1:11. This diminution in the proportion of actual combatants in armies means that no modern state army can or does engage all of its mobilized manpower. These proportions reflect the huge geographic scale of modern military operations and the heavy, complex technology involved. Of course, every person mobilized is lost to the home economy and peaceful pursuits, but the fact remains that very few of them actually engage in combat. By contrast, in ancient armies and primitive war parties, almost every participant was an effective. If mobilization figures are modified to reflect the higher proportion of noncombatants in modern armed forces, the mobilization *for combat* of tribal societies would compare even more favorably with those of modern states. This finding also implies that males in nonstate societies are far more likely to face combat than is the average male citizen of a modern nation. By the measure of manpower mobilization, then, war is no less important to tribes than to nations.

PREHISTORIC WARFARE

With regard to prehistory, nothing comparable to the surveys of historical and ethnographic societies cited earlier exists as yet. Any attempts to survey 2 million years of human prehistory for evidence of violence and armed conflict face several daunting difficulties. The first is that most regions of the world are poorly known archaeologically—the rare exceptions being Europe (especially the west), the Near East, and parts of the United States. The most unequivocal evidence of armed conflict consists of human skeletons with weapon traumas (especially, embedded bone or stone projectile points) and fortifications. However, humans have buried their dead for only the past 150,000 years or so; before this, the human remains that have been found were often disturbed and fragmented by scavengers and natural forces. Even during the past 150,000 years, many prehistoric peoples disposed of their dead in ways—for example, cremation and exposure—that left no remains for anthropologists to study. Only among some peoples—those for whom the use of stone- and bone-tipped weapons (which can survive embedded in or closely associated with human skeletons) was commonplace—is it easy to distinguish accidental traumas from those inflicted by humans. The use of these weapons occurred only during the past 40,000 years, and in many regions perishable wooden and bamboo spears and projectiles continued to be used until modern times. Until humans began living in permanent villages, fortifications would have not repaid the labor required to construct them (Chapter 3). But humans seem to have become sufficiently sedentary only during the past 14,000 years, and permanent villages are common in most regions only after the adoption of farming (8000 B.C. at the earliest). Thus it is possible to document prehistoric warfare reliably only within the past 20,000 to 30,000 years and in a only a few areas of the world. Granting these limitations, what does the archaeological evidence say about the peacefulness of prehistoric peoples?

Some authors have claimed that the evidence of homicide is as old as humanity—or at least as old as the genus *Homo* (that is, over 1 million years).[25] But many of the traumas found on early hominid skeletons have been proved by subsequent investigation to have had nonhomicidal causes or cannot be distinguished from accidental traumas of a similar character.[26] For instance, the paired "spear wounds" found on some South African Australopithicine skulls are now recognized as punctures created by leopard canines as the predator carried these luckless ancestors of ours, gripping their heads in its teeth. As another example, Neanderthals seem to have been especially accident prone, compared with the modern humans who followed them. Neanderthals' bones evidence many injuries and breakages (one study determined that 40 percent of them had suffered head injuries). Which, if any, of these injuries were caused by human violence cannot be determined. Since the heavy musculature and robust bones of Neanderthals imply that their way of life was much more strenuous and physically demanding than that of more recent humans, it seems probable that most of the traumas in question were accidental. Why they so often "forgot to duck" remains a mystery, however.

Whenever modern humans appear on the scene, definitive evidence of homicidal violence becomes more common, given a sufficient sample of burials.[27] Several of the rare burials of earliest modern humans in central and western Europe, dating from 34,000 to 24,000 years ago, show evidence of violent death. At Grimaldi in Italy, a projectile point was embedded in the spinal column of a child's skeleton dating to the Aurignacian (the culture of the earliest modern humans in Europe, ca. 36,000 to 27,000 years ago). One Aurignacian skull from southern France may have been scalped; it has cut-marks on its frontal (forehead). Evidence from the celebrated Upper Palaeolithic cemeteries of Czechoslovakia, dating between 35,000 and 24,000 years ago, implies—either by direct evidence of weapons traumas, especially cranial fractures on adult males, or by the improbability of alternative explanations for mass burials of men, women, and children—that violent conflicts and deaths were common. In the Nile Valley of Egypt, the earliest evidence of death by homicide is a male burial, dated to about 20,000 years ago, with stone projectile points in the skeleton's abdominal region and another point embedded in its upper arm (a wound that had partially healed before his death). The one earlier human skeleton found in Egypt bears no evidence of violence, but the next more recent human remains there are rife with evidence of homicide.

The human skeletons found in a Late Palaeolithic cemetery at Gebel Sahaba in Egyptian Nubia, dating about 12,000 to 14,000 years ago, show that warfare there was very common and particularly brutal.[28] Over 40 percent of the fifty-nine men, women, and children buried in this cemetery had stone projectile points intimately associated with or embedded in their skeletons. Several adults had multiple wounds (as many as twenty), and the wounds found on children were all in the head or neck—that is, execution shots. The excavator, Fred Wendorf, estimates that more than half the people buried there had died violently. He also notes that homicidal violence at Gebel Sahaba was not a once-in-a-lifetime event, since many of the adults showed healed parry fractures of their forearm bones—a common trauma on victims of violence—and because the cemetery had obviously been used over several generations. The Gebel Sahaba burials offer graphic testimony that prehistoric hunter-gatherers could be as ruthlessly violent as any of their more recent counterparts and that prehistoric warfare continued for long periods of time.

In western Europe (and more poorly known North Africa), ample evidence of violent death has been found among the remains of the final hunter-gatherers of the Mesolithic period (ca. 10,000 to 5,000 years ago).[29] One of the most gruesome instances is provided by Ofnet Cave in Germany, where two caches of "trophy" skulls were found, arranged "like eggs in a basket," comprising the disembodied heads of thirty-four men, women, and children, most with multiple holes knocked through their skulls by stone axes. Indeed, some archaeologists, impressed by the abundant evidence of homicide in the European Mesolithic, date the beginnings of "real" war to this period.

Indications of conflict, as reflected by violent death and the earliest fortifications, become especially pervasive in western Europe during the ensuing Neolithic period (the era of the first farmers, ca. 7,000 to 4,000 years ago, depending on the region).[30] Some archaeologists have argued that real warfare begins only when hunters become farmers. This mistaken point of view does have some especially grim support in the remains of Neolithic mass killings at Talheim in Germany (ca. 5000 B.C.) and Roaix in southeastern France (ca. 2000 B.C.). At Talheim, the bodies of eighteen adults and sixteen children had been thrown into a large pit; the intact skulls show that the victims had been killed by blows from at least six different axes.[31] More than 100 persons of all ages and both sexes, often with arrowpoints embedded in their bones, received a hasty and simultaneous burial at Roaix. The villages of the first farmers in many regions of western Europe were fortified with ditches and palisades. Several of these early enclosures in Britain, after being extensively excavated, yielded clear evidence of having been attacked, stormed, and burned by bow-wielding enemies. The early agricultural tribes and petty chiefdoms of Neolithic Europe were anything but peaceful.

Interestingly, the historically blood-soaked Near East has yielded little evidence of violent conflict during the Early Neolithic.[32] Although extensive and elaborate fortifications were erected during this period at Jericho, they became common in the Near East only in the later Neolithic and in the Bronze Age.

When we turn to the United States—specifically to those areas that have been subject to intensive archaeological scrutiny and where large samples of human burials have been excavated, such as the Southwest, California, the Pacific Northwest Coast, and the Mississippi drainage—violent deaths are at least in evidence and, in some periods, were extremely common.[33] Fortifications were constructed at various times and in various regions by prehistoric farmers in the Mississippi drainage and in the Southwest, as well as by the prehistoric sedentary hunter-gatherers of the Northwest Coast.[34] As with the best-studied regions of the prehistoric Old World, the prehistoric New World was also a place where the dogs of war were seldom on a leash.

In each of these regions, the indications are that warfare was relatively rare during some periods; nothing suggests, however, that prehistoric nonstate societies were significantly and universally more peaceful than those described ethnographically. The archaeological evidence indicates instead that homicide has been practiced since the appearance of modern humankind and that warfare is documented in the archaeological record of the past 10,000 years in every well-studied region. In the chapters that follow, it will become clear that archaeological evidence strongly supports ethnographic accounts concerning the conduct, consequences, and causes of prestate warfare.

There is simply no proof that warfare in small-scale societies was a rarer or less serious undertaking than among civilized societies. In general, warfare in prestate societies was both frequent and important. If anything, peace was a scarcer commodity for members of bands, tribes, and chiefdoms than for the average citizen of a civilized state.

THREE

Policy by Other Means

Tactics and Weapons

From Chapter 2, it is clear that primitive war, like its civilized counterpart, engages the efforts of a considerable proportion of the populations concerned and is even more frequently resorted to than among modern states. But if this warfare is conducted in an unserious fashion and has little effect on the societies involved, archaeologists and historians are justified as regarding it as a minor and peripheral activity.

Perhaps no aspect of prestate societies has been treated with more condescension by civilized observers than the way such groups have conducted their wars. The methods of primitive war have been characterized as undangerous, unserious, stylized, gamelike, and ineffective. These methods are seen as mere customs rather than tested techniques for obtaining positive results. They supposedly bear only a puerile resemblance to the complex, deadly military science of civilized warfare. In such analyses, primitives are described as taking special pains in tactics and weaponry to minimize casualties and destruction. Primitive warriors are accused of neglecting precisely the means and methods that have proven so brutally effective in civilized warfare. Certainly, a smaller, equalitarian society with a simple technology and subsistence economy has to conduct warfare differently from a modern, highly organized state with a complex technology and surplus economy. But as we shall see, such a difference does not necessary mean that tribal warfare has been safe and ineffective.

TACTICS AND LEADERSHIP

As noted in Chapter 1, Harry Turney-High made important distinctions between the tactics used in civilized warfare and those employed in primitive warfare. He judged the latter to be equal or superior to its civilized counterpart in its devotion to the offensive, its use of surprise, its scouting and intelligence, its utilization of terrain, and its tactical mobility. At the same time, he found four main deficiencies: inadequate training, poor unit discipline, and weak battlefield leadership; poor logistics, leading to an inability to sustain campaigns; no strategic planning beyond the first battle; and tactical defects, including poor coordination of fire and movement, no specialized warriors or units, poor concentration of force, overreliance on a single formation, and weak security and defense. He related most of the superior features of civilized warfare to the centralized coercive power, surplus-concentrating economies, and large organized populations of urban states.

As Brian Ferguson points out, recent cross-cultural research indicates that there is no Rubicon dividing the tactics of states from those of nonstates; instead, one finds an evolutionary continuum.[1] Turney-High himself acknowledged countless exceptions to his dichotomy. Indeed, one cross-cultural survey indicates that the greatest tactical "deficiencies" are observed in the simplest societies, whereas some chiefdoms may display none. While Turney-High's military horizon may have proved illusory, the fact remains that the warfare of nonstates differs by various degrees from that conducted by states, especially urban ones. These differences may affect the degree of military success or failure enjoyed or suffered by a society, and they are closely correlated with sociopolitical and economic organization. These essential variable features can be roughly categorized as matters of command and control or of logistics, which correspond (not coincidentally) to the anthropological headings of social organization and economy.

The war parties of most nonstates, compared with civilized armies, have lacked unit discipline. The discipline of state military formations is the consequence of unit (as opposed to just individual) training, hierarchical subordination, and physical compulsion. In some respects, of course, tribal warriors were much better trained for war than are their civilized counterparts. Their preparation usually spanned their whole childhood instead of the few weeks or months that civilized warriors train before facing combat. From an early age, warriors constantly practiced wielding real weapons and dodging missiles, receiving criticism and advice from experienced warriors, and being inured to deprivation and pain by means of various ordeals and rites of passage. Yet such training zfocuses entirely on the individual, not on the group or on teamwork. It also establishes no sense of subordination to leaders or plans, which require group or unit training. The drilling in unit tactics and the group training practiced by a few chiefdoms on the Pacific Northwest Coast and in Polynesia were a rare feature even at this level of social organization.[2] To maintain a close formation in combat and maneuver effectively requires just the trained discipline that primitive warriors have rarely possessed.

Many commentators have also noted the weakness in command of primitive war parties. While many groups had battlefield leaders who were men of renown and redoubtable fighters, these individuals usually led from the front by example and exhortation. They seldom exercised any central control over the behavior of the individuals they led in active combat. "Fight-leaders" among the New Guinean Mae Enga ran back and forth between the front line and an observation point to the rear—exhorting, encouraging and fighting in the former and assessing the situation in the latter.[3] Although cowards were often shamed, they, like those who failed to heed the suggestions of their leaders, were not physically punished. Any punishment for flight or heedlessness was administered, if at all, solely by the enemy. Attempts to punish physically a warrior in an egalitarian society would be foolhardy and disruptive, since the culprit would have the support of kinsmen in resisting or retaliating for such abuse.

But even though maintenance of lines, adherence to plans, and obeisance to leaders seem not to have been habits ingrained by upbringing or special training in prestate warriors, this does not mean these behaviors were absent. The reputation for courage (and, more important, for success) in combat that primitive war leaders possessed inspired confidence in the efficacy of their advice and plans. As a result, these plans were usually followed—but only while they continued to succeed. In circumstances where chiefs or state rulers wielded the power of physical coercion, adherence to plans and commands was compulsory, not voluntary. Conversely, where physical coercion and subordination were decentralized in the nonmilitary sphere, warriors' obedience and subordination were voluntary—but not necessarily absent. As Turney-High noted, only states can devote time and resources to training officers and drilling soldiers to obey their orders, and "only men with the patience of civilization will submit to it."[4] It is not a mystical patience that makes civilized men easier to reduce to strict subordination and military discipline; it is their habituation to hierarchy and obedience as a result of being raised in a *state*, which by definition is a polity with class stratification and monopolized coercive powers. These social features also appear, but to a lesser degree, in chiefdoms; hence trained units and practiced maneuvers occasionally occur among such societies. The weak command systems common in primitive warfare merely reflect the prevailing level of social organization.

Few primitive societies could sustain active combat or continuous maneuvering of their war parties beyond a few days, simply because ammunition and food were soon exhausted. In New Guinea, certain groups fought battles lasting for several days or even weeks, but only because the fighting was so local that troops could retire each evening to their own homes and return replenished the next dawn. In instances where fighting became protracted and the crops suffered from neglect, truces might be arranged so that these could be tended. Thus in one instance of warfare between Jalemo villages in New Guinea, an informal truce developed after several weeks of fighting so that men could take care of their gardens; otherwise, famine would have resulted on both sides. When the new crops were ready to harvest, the fighting was resumed.[5] Most nonstate societies did not produce the surplus food or population necessary for prolonged episodes of combat. But they nevertheless could and did maintain a state of war with frequent battles and raids over very long periods, lasting in some cases for generations. Although their episodes of combat were briefer, they might be much more frequent than in civilized war. The weak logistics of primitive societies affected only their ability to sustain *combat* and continuous maneuvering, not necessarily their capacity to conduct *war*.

Without logistic support sufficient to continue combat or maneuver beyond the first encounter, what need did prestate societies have for strategic (as opposed to tactical) planning? Without centralized leadership empowered to enforce compliance with strategic designs and without units trained to execute them, such planning would have been pointless. Most tribal groups had the logistic and leadership capacity to conceive and execute plans for battles and raids. Furthermore, ruses, maneuvers to the flank or rear, and coordinated movements by separate parties were commonly planned and executed by war leaders and warriors of even the simplest societies.[6] One Murngin Aborigine group in Australia defeated another by faking a rout by a small party, which led their disordered pursuers onto the group's main body concealed in some woods. The same tactic, employed by the Oglala Sioux and planned by Chief Red Cloud, was catastrophically successful against the U.S. Army's Fetterman command in 1866 and was the keystone of one of the few Indian campaigns (a successful one) against the United States.[7] A common tactic in New Guinea was to infiltrate a party, before or during a formal battle, and to attack from the flank or rear when the enemy was fully engaged to the front. Indeed, one of the

earliest representations of warfare—between two small parties of Spanish Neolithic archers (Figure 3.1)—depicts a simultaneous center advance and flank
attack. During the first Indian-colonist war in New England, some allied Indians suggested a plan to the colonists for a surprise attack on a hostile village,
with a blocking force set in ambush; one historian, who served in Vietnam as a
marine, judged that "in all the years since 1637 no one has really improved on
this plan."[8] That such plans sometimes went awry can no more be held against
the planning abilities of primitive leaders than can be those of civilized leaders
when these were thwarted by weather, incompetence, "the fog of war," or (most
often) an uncooperative enemy. And just like the soldiers of Grant in 1864 or of
the German general staff in 1914, when their plans were thwarted, tribesmen
had to resort to opportunism and a strategy of attrition. Tribal warriors or their
recognized leaders conceived and executed plans to exactly the degree of

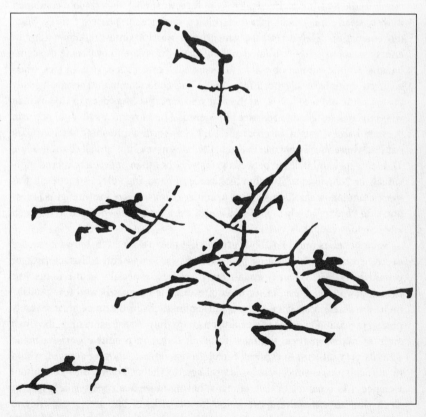

Figure 3.1 Neolithic cave painting of battle between two groups of archers, Morella
la Villa, Spain. (Traced from photo in Watkins 1989: 15)

elaborateness and sophistication that their social organization, cultural proscription of leadership, and economic surplus permitted. In this regard, they were no different from civilized soldiers and commanders.

Other tactical strengths and deficiencies of primitive warfare were determined by social and economic organization. Concentrating force at a weak point in an enemy's or one's own defenses requires coherent subunits to move and central leadership (with the power to order movements) to observe such spots. As we have seen, many nonstate societies were too few in numbers to subdivide war parties and too egalitarian in social organization to accept powerful leaders. Moreover, societies without specialization in the economic realm were unlikely to develop specialized warriors or units. Again, the point of comparison is social and economic, not directly military.

While most primitive warriors were enthusiastic deliverers of "fire" (commonly at the maximum effective range of their weapons), they seldom combined it with steady movement in a determined advance or phased retreat. Such movements or delayed retreats, which bring warriors into the killing zone of enemy weapons, require trained and enforced discipline to overcome the combatants' wholly rational objection to facing such extremes of risk. In fact, when civilized units have advanced into this killing zone, commanders have usually posted a line of "file closers" at the rear whose purpose has been to kill any man who ran back or failed to advance as ordered. The movements that did occur in prestate battles usually involved the back-and-forth skirmishing seen in Dani battles, where the distance between battle lines never substantially closed (Plate 1). Hand-to-hand fighting between groups, rather than between scattered individuals or "champions," seldom took place in band and village societies; it was more common in chiefdoms. Many primitive combats were just firefights unless one side "broke." Only then would clubs, axes, and lances be used to dispatch any enemies caught.

Some scholars (most notably Turney-High) have claimed that prestate tactics overrelied on surprise because poor security was supposedly a characteristic of primitive warfare. Security entails alert watches, especially in the hours just before dawn; and these, in turn, require disciplined guards who fear punishment for dereliction. Even the most disciplined civilized armies must severely punish the common crime of sleeping on guard duty. At the same time, the small scale of raiding parties, the most frequent threat in primitive warfare, made security very difficult to achieve. Small groups of men, moving at night, would be difficult for anyone, warrior or soldier, to detect before they committed violence. (As a matter of fact, animals, having more acute senses, less love of sleep, and an instinctive appreciation for the risks of life, are far superior to civilized or primitive humans at security—hence watchdogs and the famous

Capitoline geese.) The Dani of New Guinea erected watchtowers that they kept manned with small groups of ready warriors; but even this system could not prevent small raids from succeeding. At best, a group could hope to deter such raids by ensuring that, once the raiders had exposed themselves, they did not escape. Since scholars usually give prestate warriors high marks for scouting and intelligence, it seems contradictory to suggest that they were easy to surprise. Conversely, if poor security was a frequent feature of tribal warfare, then surprise attacks should be very effective; and if they were so effective, then in what sense could tribesmen be criticized for overrelying on them?

Turney-High's accusation that primitive warriors used "improper" formations or only the simple line, sometimes bent into the "surround," is rather mysterious to anyone familiar with the battle maps of military history, which almost invariably consist of two lines of rectangular unit symbols facing each other. For example, the Mae Enga used a very reasonable formation that put shield-bearing spearman forward, with unshielded archers firing between and over them.[9] Nevertheless, Turney-High asserts that use of correct formations is the key feature, the acid test, that distinguishes real civilized war from primitive war.[10] However, when he has an opportunity to elaborate on tribal warriors' failure to observe this principle, he gives no examples, claiming instead that it is hard to generalize and that the "correct formation must be determined for each engagement."[11] Consequently, it remains impossible to understand what formations uncivilized warriors should have been using or what is so improper about the ones they did use.

All the supposed tactical deficiencies of prestate warfare have been a direct consequence of the weaker authority of leaders, more egalitarian social structure and values, lower level of surplus production, and smaller populations of nonstate societies. Hence the gradualistic differences one finds in the conduct of warfare as preserved in ethnographic and historical records are not traits reflecting the sophistication of military knowledge or technique but features almost exactly mirroring social organization, economic efficiency, population size, and the cultural values correlated with them. To argue that the warriors or war making of a village society is ill-disciplined, weakly led, constrained by inadequate logistics, "unprofessional," disorganized, and so on is to state a tautology: these terms describe not how they make war but how they live. There is as much simple truth as hyperbole in Turney-High's declaration: "Warfare *is* social organization."

Many students of warfare share a delusion that war is an independent realm of selection. Their idea is that the raw competition involved in warfare selects for weapons and techniques that increase the probability of military success. These more efficient arms and methods then spread by diffusion and trade or by the propagation of the societies that master them at the expense of those that do not. But one cross-cultural survey found a higher correlation between military sophistication (a compound of features judged more efficient) and political system than between military sophistication and military success.[12] If competitive selection is the moving force behind military sophistication, then societies that are successful (that is, are expanding their territory) and that go to war most frequently (that is, are experiencing the most intense competition) should be the most militarily sophisticated, independent of their political and economic systems. But this is not the case. A reanalysis of the same data indicates that political and economic organization, in combination, are excellent predictors of military sophistication, whereas the frequency of war and military success are very poor predictors of it.[13] Statistically, these data imply that socioeconomy is three times more important than competitive selection in determining military techniques. The poor correlation of military success and war frequency with military sophistication also implies that perhaps the most sophisticated (read "civilized") tactics and techniques are not necessarily advantageous in every setting. These results alone hardly provide sufficient grounds on which to decide such a large and complex question so it will be considered further later on (especially Chapters 5 and 6).

In any case, in the widest view of warfare, competitive selection seems to play a relatively minor role in creating the differences observed between various societies' methods of making war. Instead, a society's demography, economy, and social system provide the means for and impose limits on military technique. For example, the Plains tribes did not develop armies equal in size, training, and discipline to those of their nation-state foes; did not centralize leadership; and did not conduct prolonged campaigns or ruthlessly press their advantages after victories. These failures were not the result of their being dim-witted or heedless of the stakes involved, but of their having neither the economic nor the social means to do otherwise.

STRATEGIES

If nonstates could be said to have implemented strategies in war, they were of the attritional and total-war varieties. Attrition was achieved by frequent low-casualty battles and raids, occasionally by surprise massacres. Total-war strategies were manifested in the plunder of wealth and food; destruction of houses, fields, and other means of production; and killing or capture of women and children. All these were common features of primitive warfare. Since in most cases such strategies were customary and unspoken, they must be inferred from the conduct and effects of warfare. Therefore, evidence for them is discussed in later chapters.

WEAPONRY

Students of military weapons usually divide them into two classes: fire (or missile) and shock. Fire weapons injure with projectiles—such as arrows, javelins, darts, stones, or pellets—and they are effective at some distance. Shock weapons—for example, lances, clubs, axes, and swords—require contact between warriors and injure by blows or cuts. A very rare third category of weapons might loosely be called chemical. These involve noxious or heated substances that injure by direct poisoning or burning. The potency of weapons is usually evaluated in terms of their range, accuracy, rate of fire, and striking power; but psychological and social considerations may be much more important in determining their military effectiveness.

No primitive or ancient fire weapon can surpass the accuracy and striking power of shock weapons.[14] The accuracy of shock weapons is the result of trigonometry and guidance. Most of us experience little difficulty in squarely striking the head of a finishing nail even with a tack hammer, but replicating this feat with a rifle bullet fired from just a few yards away is extraordinarily difficult. Tiny differences in the firing angles of missiles rapidly compound with distance into large variations in the impact point. The heavier weight of shock weapons means greater inertia, which contributes to accuracy since they are not subject to diversion by wind; and they impart a greater force at impact than that generated by necessarily lighter missiles. Once a missile is released, it is unguided, whereas a shock weapon's path can be adjusted to track the target. A single blow from such weapons can severely wound or kill outright an unarmored opponent. It is no surprise, then, to read of skulls being crushed, brains dashed out, limbs fractured or severed, and torsos pierced through by such weapons. For example, an Aztec warrior could decapitate a Spanish horse with a single blow of his obsidian-edged sword-club.[15] Although primitive projectiles may be "improved" with poison or other features that increase the likelihood of wound infection and severity (see discussion following), shock weapons are usually sufficiently lethal that any improvement is superfluous. The potential "rate of fire" of shock weapons is also very rapid, limited only by the weight of the weapon, the reflex speed, and muscular endurance of their wielder.

On the negative side, the maximum range of shock arms is seldom greater than a couple of meters. Long lances or pikes can double this reach, but only at the expense of accuracy, mobility, and impact. Moreover, these very short ranges create severe psychological and social difficulties that render shock weapons the weapon of choice among only the more severely disciplined armies of high chiefdoms and states. These weapons are very dangerous to an opponent, but they put their wielder at great risk. To employ them against a comparably armed opponent, a warrior must close to a distance where both parties are in maximum danger of being killed or terribly wounded. And more important, to reach this closure the warrior must pass through the killing zone of the enemy's fire weapons, with each step forward increasing their accuracy and their impact force. It is no accident that the use of body armor is highly correlated with the use of shock weapons, since the former can dramatically decrease the risks of injury from missiles and can ameliorate those from close combat.[16] Many groups equipped themselves with shock weapons but employed them only to dispatch fleeing or captured foes after these had been routed. Only units disciplined by training and fear of punishment could be expected to traverse the missile zone and close for shock action with an unbroken enemy.

Shock weapons are more likely than missile weapons to be specialized for war. For example, maces and clubs find little or no use in everyday life. Similarly, employing a thrusting spear or lance in hunting requires too close an approach to wary prey to be useful, except against large aggressive animals (such as jaguars, lions, boars, bears, and men) inclined to attack rather than flee. Daggers, unlike knives, seldom have any function but violence against other humans. Thus tomahawks, maces, lances, daggers, and swords are excellent weapons of war but often have no other purpose.

Of course, axes have prosaic nonviolent as well as military functions. But just because axes are used for woodworking does not mean that this is always their primary or most important function. Until local laws prohibited the practice, Mae Enga men in highland New Guinea always carried an ax tucked in their belts and felt "naked" without them.[17] This habit was not the result of their being subject to sudden impulses to clear forest or work wood, but of their never knowing when they might need to fight. The groundstone axes of the Early Neolithic (ca. 5000 B.C.) in northwestern Europe are an archaeological parallel. Because these pioneer farmers cleared forests to establish their fields and felled many trees to make their longhouses, many scholars have assumed that their axes were exclusively woodworking tools. Yet it seems strange that a mere carpenters' tool would be the only grave good buried with men—and only a few of the oldest men at that—since this practice implies that male status was based on woodworking. Moreover, some of the axes found were made of rather course, friable types of stone that would not have held an edge sharp enough for woodcutting. The find at Talheim (Chapter 2) of a mass of victims with holes in their skulls exactly the shape of Early Neolithic axes and adzes solves these mysteries. These implements were male status symbols because, whatever other purposes they may have had, they were weapons. Some of them did not need a durable sharp edge because they worked perfectly well for busting heads. It is likely that these prehistoric axes—like those of the New Guinea tribesmen— were often employed for woodworking and for felling trees, but the only *documented* use for them is homicide.[18]

Missile or fire weapons, the second weapons category, far outrange hand-held shock arms, but their accuracy, rate of fire, and striking power are significantly poorer.[19] Among fire weapons, arrows can kill at maximum distances of from 50 to 200 meters depending on their weight, their point type, and the power of the bow. The rate of fire of bows is potentially high, approximately five to ten aimed shots per minute. In addition, compared with smooth-bore muskets, bows are much more accurate. Indeed, experiments and calculations from historical data have led two historians to conclude that ancient composite-bow archery was twenty times more effective at causing casualties than eighteenth-century musketry. However, the low impact force of arrows (the result of their small mass) meant that body armor and shields provided sufficient defense except at very close distances.

The *atl-atl,* or spear-thrower, can deliver a javelin or dart (a fletched javelin) with a higher impact force but over a shorter range than an arrow. The Australian spear-thrower was deadly within a range of 40 meters and permitted a maximum cast of 80 to 100 meters.[20] The fletched darts thrown by Aztec *atl-atls* may have had a slightly longer effective range and greater accuracy, but the lighter missile would have lessened their impact. In fact, both the central Mexicans and the conquistadors found that quilted cotton body armor was usually effective at stopping them. There is no established information on the rate of fire of a spear-thrower, but it must be lower than that of a bow.

The hand-thrown javelin was commonly used as an auxiliary weapon by many nonstate groups and was important in that role even in ancient civilized armies. Although its force on impact is superior to that of the arrow (because of its greater mass), its range is very short.[21] Mae Enga warriors could cast them to a maximum distance of only 50 meters and were accurate to only 30 meters; the range at which javelins are deadly must thus be less than 30 meters. The Roman legions launched their iron-tipped javelins (*pilae*) at just that distance when charging, but their purpose was more to distract foes and to immobilize their shields in the few seconds before the Roman charge arrived than to inflict substantial injury.

The sling was also used as an auxiliary fire weapon by some tribes—especially in South America—as well as by ancient civilized armies.[22] Although some modern experiments have cast doubt on the efficacy of this weapon, both biblical and classical accounts testify to its effectiveness. For example, plummet-shaped shots could penetrate flesh, and Roman slingers were recruited into service only if they could hit a man-sized target at 185 meters. The sling's status as an auxiliary weapon was probably due to its low lethality; only a direct hit on an unprotected head would be likely to kill the person struck, and it was inaccurate except in the hands of the most skilled users. But an enemy stunned or knocked down by a shot could be dispatched with a war club or lance, as was done in Polynesia.

Missile weapons were all clearly derived from those used in hunting. Those employed in war were often exactly the same as those used in the chase, although some models for warfare were deadlier than the corresponding hunting versions.[23] Points of war projectiles were commonly weakened or hafted in such a way that when the shaft was extracted, the point or some part of it would remain in the wound. For example, the Wintu and several other tribes in California used tightly hafted side-notched arrowheads on hunting arrows but loosely bound stemmed points in war (Figure 3.2). Similarly detachable projectile heads were recorded as being utilized in warfare by numerous South American tribes. Marquesan war spears had weakened tips that were designed to break off in the wound, as did those of the Guanche tribesmen of the Canary Islands. The Mae Enga sheathed their war arrows and spear points with a hollow cassowary claw that would remain in the flesh after extraction of the main projectile point and cause the wound to fester. The war arrows of the Dani of highland New Guinea, unlike the arrows they used to kill pigs or to hunt game, were barbed to increase the difficulty of extraction, daubed with mud or grease to enhance infection, or wrapped near the tip with orchid fibers to contaminate the wound. Poisoned arrows were employed in warfare by many African groups—for example, the Meru of Kenya, the San of southern Africa, and the Tiv of Nigeria (although the Tiv used them only when fighting non-Tiv enemies). A large number of North and South American groups poisoned their war arrows, as well. The South American poisons included plant alkaloids (of which curare is the best known) and were also used in hunting. In North America and among the ancient Sarmatians of the Russian steppes, snake venom was a common ingredient in arrow poisons; other constituents were sometimes crushed red ants, spiders, scorpions, and poisonous plants such as hemlock.

Figure 3.2 Stemmed war points (left and middle) and side-notched hunting point (right) of Wintu tribe, northern California. (Redrawn after DuBois 1935: 124)

Still other "poisons" could have acted only by inducing infection, since they consisted entirely of putrefied flesh or blood. For example, some Nevada Shoshoneans drained blood from the heart of a mountain sheep, placed it in a section of intestine, and buried it in the soil to rot before smearing it on their arrowheads. Septic poisons of this type, unlike the toxic ones, were used exclusively in warfare. No advantage would be gained from inducing death in a prey days or weeks after it was initially wounded; the same was not true, however, with regard to human enemies. The widespread use of such nasty weapons directly contradicts the commonly held idea that primitives took pains to ameliorate the deadliness of their combat.

It is difficult to document the use of poisoned arrows in prehistory because poisons tend not be preserved for very long in most soils. In certain special circumstances where traces of poison might survive, such as in dry caves, no oneseems to have tested for it. Some Chinese archaeologists have argued, based on circumstantial evidence involving one male skeleton, that poisoned arrows were in use in the Chinese Neolithic period. This particular middle-aged male appears to have been killed by a minor wound in the thigh, implying that the arrow that wounded him was unusually potent.[24] This conclusion would be more convincing if many similar cases could be identified. At any rate, some prehistoric parallels for the "improved" projectiles noted by ethnographers do exist, and many others may well have been overlooked by archaeologists oblivious to prehistoric violence.

Primitive fire weapons were almost as effective at killing as most modern hand-held weapons and, as we saw earlier, were more effective than earlier gunpowder arms. In a recent comparison of casualty rates from ancient and modern battles, it has been calculated that an average of 70 percent of men engaged in ancient battles were killed or wounded, whereas only 60 percent of combatants in the bloodiest modern battles have become casualties.[25] Since the weapons used in ancient civilized battles (except perhaps the sword) were the same devices as were used in primitive and prehistoric combat (sling-stones, spears and arrows), the effects of the latter were probably equally severe.

This is not to argue that muskets had no advantages over bows and slings, but their advantages were in very narrow areas. Initially, the musket's great advantage over the bow was that, once drilled volley fire was instituted, it required less skill, briefer training, and little strength to use. The smooth-bore musket also delivered a missile with greater impact force, which at short range inflicted very damaging wounds. But its effective range was no greater than the bow (80 to 100 yards), it had a slower rate of fire, and it was incredibly inaccurate. Indeed, the command given to infantry until the rifled musket appeared in mid-nineteenth century was "Level!" and not "Aim!" because aiming was useless. And one late-eighteenth-century viceroy of New Spain ordered that Indians be given muskets and provided with plentiful ammunition so that they would "begin to lose their skill in handling the bow," which he recognized as being a more effective weapon than the contemporary musket.[26] The decisive advantage of hand-held gunpowder weapons over the bow came only with the breech-loading rifle, which added tremendously increased accuracy, range, and rate of fire to the musket's capacities. Until the late nineteenth century, civilized soldiers were at a slight disadvantage in fire weaponry when facing primitive bowmen.

With regard to prehistoric fire weapons, archaeologists have seldom considered whether any of the point types they study might originally have functioned as war points.[27] One case in eastern North America involves an uncommon type of Archaic (ca. 4,000 to 5,000 years ago) flint projectile point with a short stem that would have been able to slip easily from its haft. This almost certainly represents a specialized war point because it is primarily found embedded in the bones, chest cavities, and skulls of homicide victims from several Archaic cemeteries in Kentucky and Alabama. The Danubian point used by colonizing farmers of the Linear Pottery culture of northwestern Europe (ca. 5000 B.C.) may be another such example. It has a triangular shape and would easily have slipped from its haft when the latter was withdrawn from a wound. Its makers apparently rarely hunted, judging from their food refuse, so it was probably not used in the chase. Danubian points are common only in areas where some villages were fortified; they are rare where settlements were undefended. In the Talheim mass grave and in a nearby Linear Pottery cemetery, several male skeletons bear wounds from such points. In fact, there is no evidence to suggest that Danubian points were anything other than war points.

As in civilized warfare, aside from incendiary devices such as torches and fire-arrows (which were used mostly against structures and not against people), chemical weapons seem to have been rarely used in prestate warfare.[28] A few South American groups poured or threw boiling water on their foes, invariably in siege situations. In a few areas of South America, chili powder was thrown into pots containing burning coals to produce a noxious smoke that the wind carried to the enemy. But there was a difficulty with all such weapons: they either could be used only at very close range from fortifications or had to be delivered by an undependable means (such as the wind) that did not discriminate between friend and foe.

Artillery is usually a great killer on modern battlefields and had no counterpart on primitive ones. But until the latest generation of electronically assisted artillery, its poor accuracy has demanded enormous expenditures of shells per casualty. The accuracy problem was only exacerbated when rifled cannon moved the effective range beyond the sight of gunners. For example, during the battle of Verdun, the greatest artillery battle of artillery-dominated World War I, approximately 200 artillery rounds were fired for every casualty inflicted.[29]

Besides fortification, the best defenses against artillery are dispersion and mobility, two of the primary characteristics of primitive warfare. As a matter of fact,
in the fights with western Indians, the U.S. Army was able to employ artillery
very rarely, for the simple reason that the Indians refused to concentrate or stay
put long enough for it to be used. In many instances where it was employed, as
in the Modoc War battles in the lava beds or at the Grattan fight, it was
singularly unsuccessful. The narrowness of the conditions under which artillery
is genuinely lethal were well observed by a party of Sioux visiting Washington,
D.C., in 1870. To emphasize the White Father's might, government officials
took them to see a huge coastal artillery gun firing into the Potomac. The Sioux
were unimpressed: it was a monstrous weapon, all right, but "nobody with any
brains would sit on his pony in front of it."[30] Artillery, even of the ancient
catapult type, was not used by tribes and bands because it works only against
large fixed targets, such as fortifications or large compact formations of enemies.
Artillery also demands highly skilled specialists to construct and operate it and
prodigious quantities of special ammunition, both of which were beyond the
social and economic capacities of tribal societies. As the Sioux understood,
artillery also depends on considerable cooperation from its victims to be
effective—the kind of cooperation that tribal warriors were unwilling to provide.

FORTIFICATIONS

In denigrating the poor security and supposedly defective defensive techniques
of primitive warriors, Turney-High pointed to the common neglect of fortification by nonstate peoples. He claimed that if groups "erected good fortifications,
they are on the threshhold of the state."[31] This pronouncement is contradicted
by the existence of many groups that did employ fortifications and yet were
politically organized as small tribes or weak chiefdoms. Although only a few
states have not built them, fortifications have commonly been constructed by
nonstate societies.[32]

Yet fortifications are the costliest and largest-scale pieces of preindustrial
military technology, and some features of social life constitute necessary preconditions for their construction. Because of the large input of labor necessary
to construct even the simplest log palisade around a small settlement, the requisite labor can seldom be mustered for the whole period of construction by very
egalitarian societies whose leaders have little power. Moreover, fortifications are
stationary fixtures and protect only a small point in the landscape. Therefore,
people with very nomadic life-styles and very portable possessions do not waste
their time on such labor-intensive projects that they will soon abandon. The
variable sufficient condition for the construction of defenses is the relative
intensity of the preceived threat. Groups that are only infrequently attacked or

that can easily absorb the losses suffered from small raids may have little impetus to fortify themselves.

The principal tactical function of fortifications is as an extension of the hand-held shield. Fortifications shield defenders, their noncombatant dependents, their property, and their livestock from enemy weapons. Because they must be scaled or torn down by attackers, fortifications also increase the amount of time during which assailants are vulnerable to defenders' weapons. Fortifications are a barrier to easy infiltration or flanking by attackers, and they make surprise attacks more difficult to accomplish. They tend to force attackers to concentrate on specific points such as gates, mitigating any advantage in numbers an attacker might otherwise enjoy. Fortifications also provide a "screen of manuever," preventing attackers from observing directly the defenders' strength and movements. Depending on how they are constructed, they can include elevated platforms to fight from; they also provide defenders with a better view of the battle and enable them to use gravity to increase the force of their missiles. Obviously, fortifications are militarily very advantageous, but their immobility and substantial cost of construction may outweigh these benefits for many small social units.

But fortifications also have some significant strategic functions. They can offer extra protection to settlements on frontiers, which are often thinly settled or otherwise geographically exposed. Judging from ethnographic records, fortifications are most commonly located on hostile borders or frontiers. Where the territories of sedentary social units are small, nearly every settlement is only a few hours' walk from a hostile frontier, and in such circumstances nearly every village is fortified. This has often been the case in areas of tropical South America and highland New Guinea. It was also the case for the Mandan, Arikara, and Hidatsa villagers of the Upper Missouri River who farmed the floodplains and restricted their settlements to a narrow band along the river. With such a lineal settlement pattern, every village was on the "frontier," subject to raids by the more nomadic tribes of the surrounding plains. Where tribal territories are larger, only frontier settlements may require fortification and then only if the neighbors are hostile.

Because wealth and population—that is, potential booty and captives—are usually concentrated in one or a few large centrally located settlements in chiefdoms and states, these attract the unwelcome attentions of raiders and invaders more often than do the poorer peasant villages. Fortification of such "central places" is often useful and may even be necessary.

Concentration of fortified settlements on frontiers and fortification of central places with elite residents have been documented in the prehistory of several well-studied regions.[33] In northwestern Europe, fortified settlements of pioneer Early Neolithic farmers (ca. 7,000 years ago) were clustered along the limits of their settlement zone, presumably to defend against the Mesolithic hunter-gatherers living beyond the frontier (Chapter 8). On the Missouri River in South Dakota, between A.D. 1300 and 1500, fortified villages clustered along the fluctuating boundary between Middle Missouri and Coalescent prehistoric cultures, ancestors of the historic Mandan and Arikara tribes, respectively. In the American Southwest, fortified or defensively situated farming settlements often appeared in pioneering periods or at the limits of major cultural provinces. Indeed, at Spanish contact, the "border" pueblo of Pecos was heavily fortified with an outer wall enclosing defensible buildings without ground-floor windows or doors. In prehistoric Europe, by the end of the Early Bronze Age (ca. 1800 B.C.), fortified regional centers had become common. Remains found in them often give evidence that they were centers for metal production and for distribution of high-status goods, and they probably were the residences of chiefs.

Few human artifacts do not acquire at least some symbolic functions and attributes, and fortifications certainly have their symbolic aspects. At the most prosaic level, they symbolize their owners' military sophistication, military power, and determination to hold occupied territory. More abstractly, they demarcate the boundary between defenders and attackers, "owners" and "usurpers" (although the owners are often the newcomers, and the usurpers are indigenous). In chiefdoms and states, fortifications symbolize the importance and manifest the power of a leader.

But all these symbolic functions derive from and depend on the practical military functions of such constructions. A house designed by a famous architect may be a status symbol, but it remains a habitation, too. Furthermore, occupation of a fine house is much more symbolically valuable than absentee ownership (otherwise the mortgage clerk would enjoy a status superior to the occupant). Similarly, fortifications must be capable of withstanding attack, and the most symbolically useful of these are ones that have actually done so on occasion. The medieval castle lost much of its symbolic cachet when the modern monarchy and its artillery rendered them militarily useless. The nobility—and even royalty, which needed no permit to fortify residences—then displayed their importance by building unfortified Renaissance mansions and palaces, often on the newly razed sites of their by then purely symbolic and comparatively uncomfortable castles.

There are four general types of fortifications (which are not mutually exclusive): fortified settlements, fortified refuges, fortified elite residences, and purely military fortresses. Fortified settlements are by far the most common type ethnographically, especially among nonstates. Indeed, these are usually the only type found among village and tribal societies. They are not situated in locations with any special military advantages, but appear where villages and towns are normally located for economic reasons. They enclose otherwise normal settlements in which all the common activities of daily life take place. Fortified refuges or fortresses proper are located at sites chosen for their military advantages, such as at high points or places difficult to reach. They do not normally serve as residences, except briefly during crises. This type of fortification seems to occur most frequently in chiefdoms or petty states such as those on the Pacific Northwest Coast and in Polynesia. In one case, some small Indian bands in northern California and Washington State were so continually raided by their neighbors that they eventually built small stone fortresses to use as refuges.[34] During the obviously troubled period between A.D. 1200 and 1300 in the American Southwest, many large tribal settlements were relocated to defensible locations and served as refuges for smaller hamlets located on valley floors.[35] The most infrequently encountered type of fortification in nonstates is the fortified elite residence or castle. In its purest form, it is little more than a fortified "household" (which can include as many as several thousand people) belonging to a paramount chief or petty king. The royal kraals of many African kings and paramount chiefs are of this type. In the eastern woodlands (especially the Southeast) of North America and in the large chiefdoms of South America, the chief or principal chiefs resided in the largest town, which was also fortified. Purely military fortresses occupied primarily by soldiers or warriors are found most frequently in states and occasionally in high chiefdoms, usually on frontiers. The military kraals occupied by young age-set warriors of some African chiefdoms are examples of the latter. These are small settlements—sometimes defended by walls, but often open—where members of an age-grade serve for several years, guarding the tribal frontiers and cattle herds, as well as raiding hostile neighbors, before being permitted to marry.

Small-scale societies do not "neglect" fortification, but the social and economic conditions requisite for undertaking such constructions are seldom met by bands and tribes. Even when the necessary social conditions exist, the level of threat may be too low to justify the cost. When tribal and village societies do construct fortifications, these are merely less specialized and elaborate than the ones erected by chiefdoms and states.

FOUR

Imitating the Tiger

Forms of Combat

The forms of combat used by nonstate peoples have varied tremendously, but they can be divided roughly into formal battles, small ambush raids, and large raids or massacres. For most primitive groups, small raids have been the most and massacres the least frequent form of combat.

BATTLES

Because battles are the largest-scale, most prolonged, and most dramatic kind of warfare, both primitive and modern, much ethnographic attention has focused on them at the expense of the other types of fighting. Much of the traditional view of primitive warfare as sportive and ineffectual comes from the direct comparison of primitive and civilized battles. Many primitive battles were arranged—that is, a challenge or warning was issued to the enemy, and a battle site was named or understood.[1] For example, early on the day chosen for formal battle, the Dugum Dani sent a herald

59

to the enemy border to shout a challenge, which might be accepted and a battle site agreed on. If the challenge was not accepted, the challengers returned home and tried again another day. Among the Maring of New Guinea, if the challenge was refused, the challengers immediately invaded enemy territory, killing anyone they caught and destroying property. The Kalinga of Luzon, the Nguni tribes of southeastern Africa, and several California Indian groups also prearranged battles. Usually—on both sides in a challenge battle and on the aggressor's side in an encounter (or unarranged) battle—the warriors are painted and dressed in special decorative or nonfunctional paraphernalia: war paint, headdresses, armbands, and so on. Such battles are typically preceded and accompanied by considerable taunting and exchanging of insults. Many primitive battles consist of little more than two lines of warriors armed with throwing spears or bows, firing at one another at about the maximum effective range of their weapons. For example, the bows of the Huli of New Guinea have a maximum range of about 150 yards but are really only effective within 50 yards. During a battle, the contending parties exchange arrows and skirmish at a distance of between 50 and 100 yards (just beyond effective bow range).[2] Throughout the world, primitive battles—whether they last a few hours or a few days—are commonly terminated by agreement after each side has suffered a few serious casualties. These various features of prearrangement, elaborate dress, catcalling, long-distance skirmishing, and low casualties give primitive battles their ritualized allure.

Of course, it is essential to recognize that *all* battles take place by mutual agreement, although such agreement is usually informal in the modern era. The military historian John Keegan notes that battle "requires, if it is to take place, a mutual and sustained act of will by two contending parties" and that one party's refusal to accept battle can "inflict a very serious frustration on its enemy's plans."[3] Among the most important decisions made by military leadership involve deciding when and where to offer or accept battle. Armies and war parties consist of concentrations of men, and the area covered by these concentrations is invariably small in comparison to the territories in which they operate. Fabian strategies that simply avoid battle by yielding space, used successfully by the Romans against Hannibal, by the Russians against Napoleon, and by guerrillas everywhere, are based on this fact. For any battle to take place, the contenders must cooperate with one another: they must agree to fight. Thus the arranged battles of primitive groups and of medieval European armies merely formalize an inherent aspect of battle.

Other features of primitive battle have been cited as evidence of its particularly stylized or sportive nature. One of the most commonly cited was the Plains Indian custom of "counting coup." When a Plains warrior "counted coup," he committed an act of bravery or daring. The French word *coup* (mean-

ing "blow," "stroke," or "deed") attached to the custom. Customs varied somewhat among tribes, but a number of different acts committed in combat could be
counted as a coup, including stealing a horse from an enemy camp, killing an
enemy with a hand-held weapon, saving a wounded comrade, and charging
alone into a group of enemies. Relatively few countable coups—being one of the
first three or four braves to touch a dead enemy with the hand or with a hand-
held object, touching a live enemy, or being first to sight the enemy—were at all
unusual. Nevertheless, all these deeds carried a serious risk of death—even that
of touching a dead enemy, since Plains warriors would fight furiously to recover
fallen comrades and save them from scalping and other mutilations. Merely
killing an enemy with a projectile was considered useful, but it was not counted
as a coup. There is every evidence that Plains warriors tried and often succeeded in killing large numbers of one another, but a warrior's reputation as a
brave man depended on the number of coups he could recount.[4]

This attitude is not terribly different from the civilized concept of military
courage—and the reward of honors for it; in both cases, the personal risk
involved, and not the effect on the enemy, is deemed the paramount consideration. Nation-states award soldiers decorations and promotions not for killing but
for conspicuously risking death in combat. The main divergence of coup counting from civilized customs is related to the specific acts rewarded (such as
stealing a horse or touching an enemy versus tending wounded comrades under
fire or volunteering to go for help through a gauntlet of enemies).[5] The Classical
Greeks, for example, awarded honors for maintaining order in the ranks under
extreme difficulty and for being the first to reach an enemy camp.[6] Counting
coups no more ameliorated the deadliness of combat than does the civilized
custom of awarding medals. Moreover, equally important to Plains warriors was
the custom of taking scalps, and these were decidedly difficult to obtain from
living enemies.

In some areas, modern warfare is far more ritualized than the primitive
variety. One of these areas involves surrender—by both individuals and units.
For individuals, this ritual entails raised hands, white flags, weapons proffered
or tossed out, shouts of key words, and so on. The surrender of units requires an
even more involved choreography: the white-flag approach of emissaries; the
discussion of terms; an arranged cease-fire at a prescribed moment; and, for
very large units, a formal signing of "instruments." Thus individuals and groups
that have made every effort to kill their enemies can, by the enactment of
appropriate rituals, preserve themselves from immediate harm at the hands of
their adversaries. Additional niceties of prisoner exchange and *parole* (that is,
release after a promise not to bear arms again) have practically disappeared from
warfare, but they were common until the nineteenth century.[7] Other conventions govern sparing and even rescuing enemy sailors and airmen who have

abandoned their ships and planes. Ritual battles prior to a foregone surrender are not absent even from quite recent wars. Several times during World War II, commanders of some Allied and Axis positions requested that their adversaries fire briefly at their position so that they could surrender "with honor." Even the German commander of the citadel at Cherbourg asked that investing American forces "fire artillery at the main gate, to give him a pretext for surrender."[8] As we shall see, these civilized rituals of submission have few counterparts in primitive warfare.

Many other irrational conventions are peculiar to modern civilized warfare. Killing of enemy civilians by bombardment or by systematic starvation via blockade is to some degree acceptable under international law, but murdering them with small arms is considered completely vile. In modern warfare, the more personal the cruelty or destruction, the more likely it is to be regarded as reprehensible. Historically, some weapons (such as Greek fire, boiling oil, napalm, and shrapnel) have been countenanced despite the horrible suffering they inflict, while equally brutal items (such as serrated swords, square and dum-dum bullets, and poison gas) have been officially banned. International conventions and customs also tend to outlaw or eschew use of weapons that kill with certainty (for example, poisoned bullets and nerve gas). Customary civilized laws of war and the Geneva Conventions (and their historical predecessors) manifest the ritualized nature of modern warfare.

Until the end of the nineteenth century, civilized soldiers exhibited in battle an extraordinary preoccupation with protecting their own and seizing their enemy's regimental colors, imperial eagles, and the like. Terrible dishonor was associated with losing these symbols (which were nevertheless carried in the front ranks, at the point of maximum exposure, during combat) to the enemy. When combat became close, especially fierce struggles developed around these standards as men fought to seize or retain them. Perhaps the clearest evidence of their purely symbolic nature was that two British officers were posthumously awarded Britain's highest award for valor, the Victoria Cross, for *flight* in the face of the enemy, because they were attempting to save the colors of their regiment from capture by victorious Zulus.[9] The men were staff officers of the British units that were defeated at Isandlwana in 1879, and they had fled several miles from the battlefield before being caught and killed. Behaviors that would therefore normally be regarded as cowardly and irresponsible in an officer—abandoning a command and fleeing from battle—were transmuted into acts of extreme courage because their purpose was to save a useless symbol. Compounding the irony of this incident, the Zulus showed no interest in these British colors and left them on the spot. The curious focus of civilized soldiers on capturing such gewgaws is surely no less stylized and impractical than the desire of Plains Indian warriors to count coups.

As far as decorative regalia worn by warriors is concerned, only in the past fifty years have the field uniforms, aircraft, and ship colors of civilized societies become truly practical (that is, camouflaged). The last war fought by British soldiers in their famous red coats was the Zulu War of 1879. The French army entered World War I dressed in light blue, and initially some German troops in that war wore the preposterous *pickelhalbe* helmet. The "flying circuses" of the German air force in World War I are the most extreme modern example of impractical, assertive coloration, but the famous squadron art of American aircraft (and tanks) in World War II continued, in a more subdued fashion, this supposedly primitive fashion. Even as recently as the Persian Gulf War, American A-10 Warthog ground-attack aircraft were decorated with shark's-mouth motifs on their noses.

The practice of taunting the enemy before a battle has also not entirely disappeared from modern warfare, but the greater distance between contending front lines that modern weaponry imposes means that loudspeakers, leaflets, and radio broadcasts must be employed. Such devices are devoted to issuing appeals to surrender (usually in vain) and to propagating elaborate taunts or boasts prepared by psychological warfare and propaganda services. Where front lines lie close together and where linguistic knowledge is sufficient, the more concise and ethnographically familar form of taunting will occur. For example, during the War in the Pacific, Japanese soldiers tried to unnerve their adversaries at night by screaming taunts in broken English (in Burma, they used Hindi) that ranged from the banal "Marine, you die!" to such infuriating insults as "Joe DiMaggio, no good!" The retorts of Allied soldiers were mostly in their native tongues and scatological in nature.[10] In terms of content and intent, there is little difference between a Tokyo Rose broadcast and a tribal prebattle harangue.

If modern battles are thus not free of rituals and stylized or impractical behaviors, are they more deadly than their primitive counterparts? Many ethnographers vaguely note that primitive battles tend to be called off after a few casualties, but they seldom actually count the number of warriors engaged or lost. In Figure 4.1, some of the few available casualty figures for specific or "average" tribal battles have been compiled and compared with various high-casualty civilized battles (Marathon, Zama, Gettysburg, the first day of the Somme, and a battle lost by the Aztecs in Michoacán). The lowest proportion of total casualties (killed, wounded, and missing) is registered by those of the Union and Confederate forces at Gettysburg; the highest rates are those attending the Aztec invasion of Michoacán, the Carthaginians at Zama, and the Assiniboin raiders. In several instances involving formal primitive battles begun or terminated by agreement (the Mtetwa, Cahto-Yuki, and Mae Enga confrontations), the proportion of warriors killed in action is below 2 percent, a rate that

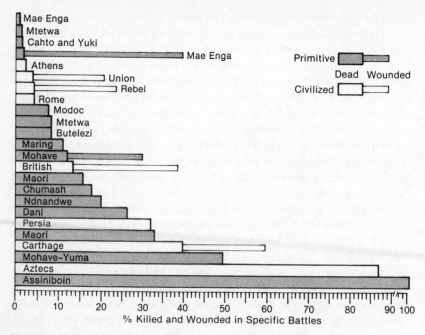

Figure 4.1 Casualties in various tribal, ancient, and modern battles (see Appendix, Table 4.1).

tends to confirm the impressions of ethnographers and their informants. There are many descriptions of such battles with no fatal casualties, although the fighting would often then be renewed after brief intervals until fatalities did occur. However, the phenomenon of low casualties in arranged battles is not universal in prestate warfare. Sources among the Yokuts of central California insisted that half of the participants in one formal battle involving three "tribelets" were killed.[11] Furthermore, the casualties in primitive encounter battles were often heavy. For example, as in the case of the Assiniboin raiders, when a war party of Plains Indians was caught and heavily outnumbered by its enemies, the smaller party was usually completely wiped out.[12] The safest conclusion to draw from such a small and mixed sample is that no evidence consistently indicates that primitive battles are proportionately less lethal or less injurious than civilized ones.

The preceding figures, moreover, are for single sustained encounters of one to four days and do not account for the frequency of battle. For example, in the Cahto-Yuki case, battle was resumed twice with similar losses after ten-day truces. The Cahto fought six separate battles during that summer. By comparison, the armies of the Potomac and of Northern Virginia did not have another minor engagement after Gettysburg for three months, and the next full-scale battle (the Wilderness) occurred ten months later.[13] The cumulative effect of frequent but low-casualty battles will be discussed in Chapter 6.

When one of the contending parties in prestate warfare was routed, the subsequent rampage by the victors through the losers' territory often claimed the lives of many women and children as well as men.[14] One Maring clan of 600 people in New Guinea lost 2 percent of its population in the rout that followed its loss of 3 percent of its people in the preceding battle. This total may not seem very severe, but to produce equivalent figures France (with a population of 42 million) would have had to lose over 1.2 million soldiers in its 1940 defeat and some 840,000 civilians in the immediate aftermath (or five times the total number of war-related French deaths during the whole war). Victorious Tahitian warriors killed so many people in a loser's territory that an "intolerable stench" of decaying corpses "pervaded defeated districts for long periods after battle." Similarly severe slaughters attended battlefield defeats among the chiefdoms of Fiji and Cauca Valley of Colombia. These examples illustrate the most important and universal rule of war: do not lose.

In several ethnographic cases, formal battles with controlled casualties were restricted to fighting within a tribe or linguistic group. When the adversary was truly "foreign," warfare was more relentless, ruthless, and uncontrolled.[15] Thus the rules of war applied to only certain "related" adversaries, but unrestricted warfare, without rules and aimed at annihilation, was practiced against outsiders.

RAIDS AND AMBUSHES

The most common form of combat employed in primitive warfare but little used in formal civilized warfare has been small raids or ambushes. These have usually involved having a handful of men sneak into enemy territory to kill one or a few people on an encounter basis or by means of some more elaborate ambush. Women and children have commonly been killed in such raids.[16] The Cahto-Yuki war mentioned earlier was started when some Yuki, angry over Cahto use of a disputed obsidian quarry and some plant-gathering territory, killed a gathering party of four Cahto girls. One common raiding technique (favored by groups as diverse as the Bering Straits Eskimo and the Mae Enga of New Guinea) consisted of quietly surrounding enemy houses just before dawn and killing the occupants by thrusting spears through the flimsy walls, shooting arrows through doorways and smoke holes, or firing as the victims emerged after the structure had been set afire. During hard winters, the Chilcotin of British Columbia would attack small isolated hamlets or family camps of other tribes, kill all the inhabitants, and live off their stored food. The East Cree of Quebec slaughtered any Inuit (Eskimo) families they encountered, taking only infants as captives. Neither age nor sex was any guarantee of protection during primitive raids.

Because the victims were unprepared or unarmed and because raids were so frequent, a predictably high cumulative fatality rate resulted.[17] One Yanomamo village was raided twenty-five times in just fifteen months, losing 5 percent of its population. In just one summer (1823), two Yellowknife raids killed eight Dogrib (four men and four women), representing 3 percent of the population of the two victimized Dogrib bands; similar raids had been endured for years. Even when formal battles occurred frequently, more deaths were inflicted by raids. Among the Dugum Dani, in fewer than six months, seven ritual battles killed only two men, but nine raids over the same period killed seven people. Figures cited in Chapter 2 indicate that nearly all western North American Indian groups were raided at least twice each year. A careful and open-eyed reading of ethnographies, early historical accounts, and recorded tribal traditions for some supposedly pacifistic Plateau tribes in British Columbia leaves no doubt that raiding and other forms of combat were both frequent and persistent in this area. The numbers killed as a result of these raids were sometimes extremely significant, as in the case of 400 Lilloet (approximately 10 percent of the tribal population) slain in the course of a week-long raid by a neighboring tribe.[18] Many groups, such as the Yanomamo of Venezuela and Koaka of Guadalcanal, never resorted to formal battles at all. Raids and ambushes have been the most frequent and widely employed form of nonstate warfare because they are terribly effective at eliminating enemies with a minimum of risk.

Raids characteristically kill only a few people at a time; they kill a higher proportion of women than do battles or even the routs that follow them; they kill individuals or small groups caught in isolated circumstances away from major population concentrations; and because the victims are outnumbered, surprised, and often unarmed, their wounds are often inflicted as they try to flee. Archaeologically, this pattern will thus be evidenced by four corresponding characteristics: burials of individual or small groups of homicide victims; women as a high proportion of the victims; burials sometimes located away from the major habitation zones (although raid victims were recovered and buried in the usual cemeteries); and evidence that most wounds, even on adult males, were inflicted from behind.[19] Several isolated prehistoric burials in central Washington State fit this pattern precisely, and radiocarbon dates indicate that raiding went on in this region for over 1,500 years. Projectile points found embedded in these skeletons indicate that in some cases the killers were "foreigners." Interestingly, the usual ethnographic descriptions of the tribes in this area—indeed, in the whole culture area of the Plateau—depict them as exceptionally peaceful. At a cemetery site in central Illinois dating to about A.D. 1300, 16 percent of the

264 individuals buried there met violent deaths and also fit the patterns expected for raid victims. Similar attritional violence is documented in prehistoric cemeteries in central British Columbia and in California, where burials of probable raid victims were accumulated over several hundred years. The homicide victims at the 13,000-year-old Gebel Sahaba cemetery in Egypt do not quite fit this small ambush–raid pattern: more victims were buried at one time; adult males' wounds were commonly left frontal, indicating that they were wounded while fighting with their bows; and children were common among the victims. In this case, the attacks seem to have been on a larger scale—perhaps against small encampments rather than against isolated work parties. These burials accumulated over at least two generations. In each of the cases cited, the proportion of violent deaths is quite high. For example, the homicide rate of the prehistoric Illinois villagers would have been 1,400 times that of modern Britain or about 70 times that of the United States in 1980![20] There can be little doubt that the frequent, sustained, and deadly raids recorded for ethnographic tribal groups were also practiced in many prehistoric cases.

MASSACRES

A gradual scalar transition in primitive warfare leads from the small raid to massacres. The latter are larger surprise attacks whose purpose is to annihilate an enemy social unit. The simplest form involves surrounding or infiltrating an enemy village and, when a signal is given, attempting to kill everyone within reach.[21] Such killing has usually been indiscriminate, although women and children evidently escape in the confusion more often than adult males. In one case of massacre in New Guinea, the victim group of 300 lost about 8 percent of its population. In a case from a different area, a tribal confederation of 1,000 people lost nearly 13 percent of its population in just the first hour of an attack by several other confederacies. Surprise attacks on California Pomo villages usually killed between 5 and 15 percent of their inhabitants. When the first Spanish explorers reached the coastal Barbareño Chumash of California, the latter had just had two of their villages surprised, burned, and completely annihilated by raiders from the interior, representing a minimum loss of 10 percent of their tribal population. After enduring years of raids by the Yellowknife tribe of northern Canada, several Dogrib bands combined to wipe out a Yellowknife camp, killing four men, thirteen women, and seventeen children who accounted for 20 percent of the victims' population. The Yellowknifes never recovered from this blow, and the descendants of the demoralized survivors were gradually absorbed by neighboring groups. The seldom-achieved goal of another subarctic tribe, the Kutchin, was to surround and annihilate an encampment of their traditional enemies, the Mackenzie Eskimo, leaving only one male alive. This male, called "The Survivor," was spared only so he could spread word of the deed. The Upper Tanana or Nabesna of Alaska massacred most of one band (numbering perhaps 100 people) of Southern Tutchone. Similar slaughters have been recorded in South America, as in the case of a treacherous attack on guests at a Yanomamo feast in which 15 of 115 people were killed in a single day. The approximate average loss in these various instances was 10 percent. To put such massacre mortalities in perspective, this level of population loss would be equivalent to killing over 13 million Americans in 1941 or over 7 million Japanese in 1945 in a single air raid. The results of intertribal massacres could be devastating, especially to a social unit already decimated by battles and raids.

Such explosive slaughters seem to have occurred infrequently.[22] For the Dugum Dani of highland New Guinea, it is estimated that such massacres happened only once every ten or twenty years. Over a period of half a century, the Sambia of the same region fought six neighboring tribes in wars involving massacres. The Yellowknife tribe of northern Canada had been raiding the neighboring Dogribs for no more than twenty years when, as we have seen, the latter annihilated one of their camps. These few cases hardly suffice to support a generalization; but in a number of other ethnographies, such slaughters were recalled by older informants born a generation before colonial pacification, suggesting that massacres once a generation were not an unusual experience in many nonstate groups.

Contrary to Brian Ferguson's claim that such slaughters were a consequence of contact with modern European or other civilizations, archaeology yields evidence of prehistoric massacres more severe than any recounted in ethnography.[23] For example, at Crow Creek in South Dakota, archaeologists found a mass grave containing the remains of more than 500 men, women, and children who had been slaughtered, scalped, and mutilated during an attack on their village a century and a half before Columbus's arrival (ca. A.D. 1325). The attack seems to have occurred just when the village's fortifications were being rebuilt. All the houses were burned, and most of the inhabitants were murdered. This death toll represented more than 60 percent of the village's population, estimated from the number of houses to have been about 800. The survivors appear to have been primarily young women, as their skeletons are underrepresented among the bones; if so, they were probably taken away as captives. Certainly, the site was deserted for some time after the attack because the bodies evidently remained exposed to scavenging animals for a few weeks before burial. In other words, this whole village was annihilated in a single attack and never reoccupied.

A similar massacre occurred in the historic period (ca. 1785) at the fortified Larson site, where the dead had been similarly scalped, mutilated, and finally buried under the collapsed roofs and walls of their burned houses. This example clearly shows that except for introducing some new weapons (in particular, muskets and iron-headed arrows), contact with Western civilization caused no significant change in the tenor of warfare in this area. In other words, anthropologists are not justified in dismissing or discounting the ethnographic descriptions of Middle Missouri warfare since they apply equally well to the precontact period. Evidence of a similar slaughter and burning of a whole village, dating to the late thirteenth century, has been uncovered in southwestern Colorado at Sand Canyon Pueblo, where (as at the Larson site) the bodies of the victims were buried under the collapsed roofs of their burned houses.

After surveying a large number of prehistoric burial populations in the eastern United States, archaeologist George Milner concluded that the pre-Columbian warfare of this whole region featured "repeated ambushes punctuated by devastating attacks at particularly opportune moments."[24] From North America at least, archaeological evidence reveals precisely the same pattern recorded ethnographically for tribal peoples the world over of frequent deadly raids and occasional horrific massacres. This was an indigenous and "native" pattern long before contact with Europeans complicated the situation. When the sailing ship released them from their own continent, Europeans brought many new ills and evils to the non-Western world, but neither war nor its worst features were among these novelties.

Similar massacres are also documented for the prestate peoples of prehistoric western Europe (Chapter 2).[25] At the time of the Talheim massacre 7,000 years ago, neither civilizations nor states had yet developed *anywhere*. At Roaix in France, 4,000 years ago, more than 100 people of both sexes and all ages were killed by bow-wielding adversaries and then hastily buried in a mass grave. When this French massacre occurred, the nearest civilization was 1,000 miles away in Minoan Crete. In both cases, the number of victims conforms closely to the average number of inhabitants estimated by archaeologists for the average Early Neolithic hamlet and the average Late Neolithic village—respectively, the most common size of settlement in each period. Before any possible contact with civilizations, the tribesmen of Neolithic Europe, like those of the prehistoric United States, were thus wiping out whole settlements.

1 Dani formal battle, highland New Guinea. The bowmen hoped to wound and immobilize a foe who could then be killed with a thrown spear or lance thrust. The
front lines are well within the lethal range of these weapons, yet no shields are used;
warriors were expected to dodge missiles. Most casualties occurred when men had
their backs turned to the enemy as they moved to the rear or when they thought they
were safely out of range at the rear and were less attentive to incoming arrows.
(Copyright © Film Study Center, Harvard University)

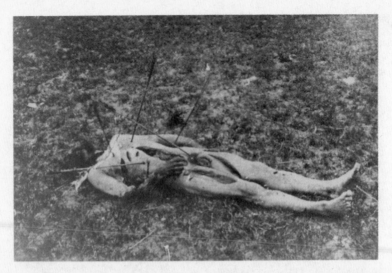

2 Corpse of a U.S. cavalryman (Sgt. Frederick Wylyams) killed and mutilated by Southern Cheyenne in 1867. These mutilations were meant to cripple the victim in the afterlife. Notice also the overkill with arrows. (Courtesy of Fort Sill Museum, Fort Sill, Oklahoma; neg. no. P-2692)

3 Obsidian projectile point embedded in vetebrae of a prehistoric woman eighteen to twenty-one years old from central California (site: ALA-329). The arrow passed through her abdominal viscera before becoming embedded in her backbone. The absence of observable healing or inflammation of the bone around the point indicates that the victim died immediately or soon after being shot. (Courtesy of Robert Jurmain)

4 The "bone bed" in the prehistoric (A.D. 1325) fortification ditch at Crow Creek, South Dakota, containing the remains of nearly 500 men, women, and children. These victims had been scalped, mutilated, and left exposed for a few months to scavengers before being interred. (Courtesy of P. Willey)

5 Surviving log palisade at the Tlingit village of Hoonah in southeastern Alaska. The entrance at the left has been modified with a European-style stairway, but the entrance at the right retains the original "notched-log" that could be drawn up into the palisade like a drawbridge. At this village, only the houses of the Raven clan were protected by the fortification; hence, the carved Raven totem (upper middle). (Courtesy of Canadian Museum of Civilization, negative no. 78-6041)

FIVE

A Skulking Way of War

Primitive Warriors Versus
Civilized Soldiers

The general claim that the difference between civilized and primitive warfare is analogous to that between serious business and a game is invariably bolstered by the observation that civilized soldiers can always defeat primitive warriors. But while it is true that European civilization has steadily and dramatically extended itself to the utmost parts of the earth during the past four centuries, it is by no means clear that this expansion is a consequence of superior weaponry or specialized military technique. In fact, civilized soldiers have often lost to warriors in combat despite superior weaponry, unit discipline, and military science. But they have seldom lost campaigns or wars.

A review of the history of warfare between tribal warriors and civilized soldiers uncovers a number of interesting general features that are not very flattering to Western military bombast. For one, when civilized soldiers have been caught in the open by superior numbers of primitive warriors, they often have been defeated, whereas if the soldiers have been fortified, even behind wagons or in shallow rifle pits, they could hold off many times their number until they could escape or be rescued. Let us consider a few examples.

In the many struggles between the Roman legions and undisciplined barbarian hosts of Celts and Germans, the latter inflicted some notable annihilations on the former, usually when they caught or enticed the Romans far from their fortified encampments, as in the case of Sabinus's reinforced legion in 54 B.C. and Varus's three legions in A.D. 9. Whatever Julius Caesar's excuses, it is clear that the blue-painted barbarians of Britain defended their island vigorously and effectively against the cream of the Roman army. The raid and ambush tactics the Britons quickly adopted after being defeated in formal battles were so troublesome for the Romans that a century passed after Caesar's retreat before Rome made another attempt at conquest.

The Norsemen, or Vikings, of Scandinavia were among the most fearsome fighters in medieval Europe. When Vikings were defeating every fighting force worthy of the name in Europe and conquering England, warriors from a few bands of Newfoundland Indians drove them out of their North American (Vinland) colony.[1] In one battle, the Vikings, armed with their swords and shields, were routed by Skraeling (the Norse word for the North American natives) arrows and an unnerving native weapon that seems to have been an inflated bladder on the tip of a pole that "made a frightening noise when it fell." They were saved from this flying whoopie cushion and ignominious defeat only when one of the Viking women alarmed the Skraelings by uncovering her breasts and slapping them with a sword. Despite a better climate, richer pastures, and more plentiful natural resources than in Greenland, the colonists decided they had seen enough of North America's dangerous natives and abandoned their colony. During their prolonged journey back to Greenland, the colonists revenged themselves by killing a few more Indians they surprised along the way. Historian Samuel Eliot Morison emphasizes the key role that native hostility played in the Viking decision to abandon Vinland, especially the Skraelings' "ability to deliver surprise attacks at will" (in other words, their expertise at the tactics of primitive war).[2]

Until the nineteenth century, Europeans in most parts of sub-Saharan Africa were restricted to fortified places on the coasts. The Portuguese in Mozambique, for example, could not penetrate the interior during the seventeenth century because the "natives with their assegais were normally able to destroy the small groups of Portuguese as soon as they strayed outside of their few fortified bases."[3]

During the Indian Wars in the United States, when U.S. Army units were caught in the open and outnumbered, they usually suffered severe defeats.[4] The series of victories engineered by the Seminoles in late 1834, the annihilation of the artillery-equipped Grattan command in 1854, and the destruction of Fetterman's unit in 1866 are examples of defeats in the open. The Battle of the Little Bighorn clearly illustrates the general character of primitive and civilized clashes. Colonel Custer, with 200 men, was caught in the open by 1,800 Sioux and Cheyenne warriors and destroyed. Custer's subordinates, Major Reno and Captain Benteen, hastily fortified a small hillock with 400 men and survived the attacks of the same warriors for another day and a half. With their food and grazing exhausted and more soldiers approaching from the north, the Indians abandoned their siege. Thus behind breastworks, however flimsy, soldiers could repulse many times their number of warriors.

The same strictures apply to their tribal foes.[5] Fifty Modoc braves ensconced in the natural fortifications of the Lava Beds in northern California withstood the assaults and artillery of 1,200 U.S. soldiers for almost five months, while inflicting heavy casualties on the besiegers. Only dissension among the Modocs and a shortage of water led to their ultimate surrender. When Indians were caught in the open, especially by surprise attacks on their villages by more numerous U.S. cavalry, they were defeated. When numbers were approximately equal and the Indians were not encumbered by women and children, however, victory could go to either side. United States soldiers were defeated at Rosebud Creek in 1876 and Big Hole in 1877; the Indians lost at Four Lakes and Spokane Plains in 1858 and at Bear Paw in 1877. The supposed tactical superiority of the civilized soldier was not especially obvious. In several instances, however, outnumbered fortified Indians were defeated—including at Horseshoe Bend in 1814, Apache Pass in 1862, and Tres Castillos in 1880—as a result of U.S. and Mexican artillery and mass assaults.[6] One disadvantage the Indians faced when fortified was that, unlike the whites, they seldom had anyone available to ride to their relief. In addition, logistical superiority, artillery, and other aspects of nonmilitary engineering (for example, tunneling and bridging) gave Europeans a very marked superiority in siege operations over any primitive warriors, however well fortified they might have been.

European soldiers and military historians have sometimes impugned the discipline and fighting qualities of American and Mexican soldiers.[7] But the proudest armies of Europe did not avoid debacles against African tribesmen in the late nineteenth century. During the Zulu War (1879), when caught in the open, the redcoats of the British Army—with their breech-loading rifles, artillery, and Gatling guns—were soundly defeated at the battles of Isandlwana, Myer's Drift, and Hlobane by superior numbers of Zulus armed primarily with thrusting spears. When they were behind fortifications, the British survived, as at the famous battle of Rorke's Drift where 140 soldiers held off 4,000 overaged and unfed Zulus for two days. Only at the last battle of Ulundi did a huge British "square" with shrapnel and Gatling guns defeat a larger but dispirited Zulu force in the open.[8]

In the 1890s, the French fighting the Tuareg of the Sahara met similar disasters in the open and survived attacks when behind solid walls. For example, at Goundam, 150 French soldiers, with artillery and behind a filmsy stockade of thorn bushes, were destroyed by an equal number of Tuareg.[9] Germany's army, too, met embarrassing reverses when it fought the Hehe in Tanganyika (1891–1898) and Herero and Nama tribesmen in Southwest Africa (1904–1907). In the latter case, the outcomes of fights were predictable: "Against stone walls and machine guns, the Hereros lost; when the Germans were caught in the open, the Hereros defeated them."[10] As with the Modocs in America, when African tribesmen could fight behind fortifications, they could hold off superior European forces for long periods and inflict grievous losses on the attackers. In 1879, for example, 300 Pluthi tribesmen in a hilltop fortress held off 1,800 soldiers and artillery for eight months.[11] Again, we find no clear evidence of the *tactical* superiority of civilized over primitive methods, only the eternal advantages of fortifications and superior numbers.

In most cases, civilized soldiers have defeated primitive warriors only when they adopted the latter's tactics. In the history of European expansion, soldiers repeatedly had to abandon their civilized techniques and weapons to win against even the most primitive opponents. The unorthodox techniques adopted were smaller, more mobile units; abandonment of artillery and use of lighter small arms; open formations and skirmishing tactics; increased reliance on ambushes, raids, and surprise attacks on settlements; destruction of the enemy's economic infrastructure (habitations, foodstores, livestock, and means of transport); a strategy of attrition against the enemy's manpower; relentless pursuit to take advantage of civilization's superior logistics; and extensive use of natives as scouts or auxiliaries.[12] In other words, not only were civilized military techniques incapable of defeating their primitive counterparts, but in many cases the collaboration of primitive warriors was necessary because civilized soldiers alone were inadequate for the task.

Several historians of Indian Wars of colonial times in the northeastern United States note that the borrowing of military techniques was rather one-sided: the Indians were the "military tutors," and the Europeans were the "trainees."[13] One grateful New Englander wrote in 1677, "In our first war with the Indians, God pleased to show us the vanity of our military skill, in managing our arms, after the European mode. Now we are glad to learn the skulking way of war."[14] Similarly harsh tutorials were administered by tribal warriors to civilized soldiers in many regions of the world. Frontier militias, composed of men who had learned the "skulking way of war" by direct and prolonged experience, were thus usually more effective at fighting tribesmen than were European regulars. And when these "tribalized" colonial militiamen fought European regulars, they proved to be extremely tough and frustrating opponents themselves, as the American Revolutionary and the two Anglo-Boer wars illustrate.

Primitive (and guerrilla) warfare consists of war stripped to its essentials: the murder of enemies; the theft or destruction of their sustenance, wealth, and essential resources; and the inducement in them of insecurity and terror. It conducts the basic business of war without recourse to ponderous formations or equipment, complicated maneuvers, strict chains of command, calculated strategies, time tables, or other civilized embellishments. When civilized soldiers meet adversaries so unencumbered, they too must shed a considerable weight of intellectual baggage and physical armor just to even the odds. Once soldiers match their tactics to those of their primitive adversaries, their superior manpower, economic surplus, transportation technology, and logistical expertise—if vigorously exploited—enable them to win most such campaigns and wars. By attrition, they gradually erode the primitives' small and inelastic manpower pool; by destruction of food and matériel, they exhaust the slim economic surpluses of the warriors, often inducing them to surrender to avoid starvation. These are precisely the techniques of primitive war, as well as those of civilized total war. The only difference is that civilized societies can apply vastly greater resources to their efforts to execute these techniques. Thus by exploiting their logistic superiority, civilized soldiers could continue harrying and abrading primitive social groups, especially during the harshest seasons, giving them no time to rest, recuperate, or replenish supplies of food and ammunition. To a great extent, the superior transportation and agricultural technology of Europe and its efficient economic and logistic methods made possible its triumph over the primitive world, not its customary military techniques and advanced weapons.

The U.S. Army campaigns against the Plains tribes and the Apaches illustrate these points. In 1865, General Pope sent large units attended by the usual slow supply trains on great sweeps through the Plains, with the result that, as historian Robert Utley put it, "only the most careless Indians failed to get out of the way."[15] Like so many other similar civilized campaigns, it failed to bring tribal enemies to battle and only exacerbated their raiding and other depredations. A similar excursion by General Hancock in 1867 did little more than provoke subsequent raids against settlers. Relative calm reigned for a few years, after a number of "peace policy" treaties (which neither side fully observed) separated the contending parties. But the anger of the Indians over pioneer incursions into their treaty territories and the settlers' mounting irritation at the continuing Indian raids reached the boiling point in the early 1870s. By this time, Generals Sherman and Sheridan were in charge and were prepared to visit on the "hostiles" the total war they had so brilliantly and ruthlessly inflicted on the Confederate rebels during the Civil War. The U.S. Army won the Red River War against the southern Plains tribes almost without combat, by relentlessly pursuing the hostile bands during the winter of 1874/1875. Exhaustion, hunger, and worry over the ever-present danger of an army attack broke the tribes' resistance. In the northern Plains, after the defeats of traditional columns at the Rosebud and Little Bighorn in the summer of 1876, the army, aided by Indians scouts, pursued the scattered Sioux and Cheyenne bands throughout the following autumn and winter, burning tipis and food stores and killing ponies whenever it caught a hostile band. By the end of spring, except for a few who went to Canada, almost all the Sioux and Cheyenne were on the reservations.[16] These successful campaigns coincide almost exactly with the final destruction of first the great southern and then the great northern herds of bison, which were central to the life of the defeated tribes.

Various Apache bands had defied the power of local agricultural tribes, the Spanish, the Mexicans, and the United States for three centuries, raiding and pillaging at will. During the Civil War, an extremely ruthless campaign involving a "general rising" by troops, citizens, and the settled tribes failed to end Apache raids. The Apache "scourge" was a fact of southwestern life until the eccentric General Crook mounted campaigns in the early 1870s and early 1880s using small mobile units consisting mostly of Indians (specifically Apaches) and supplied by mule rather than wagon trains. His units' excellent scouting, relentless pursuit, and surprise attacks on encampments broke first the resistance of the Yavapai and Western Apaches and then the last "wild" bands of the Chiricahua. Thus, in all its successful western campaigns, the U.S. Army employed primitive methods (and tribal warriors) backed by civilized resources to defeat natives who could match them only in the former.

Even so, as we have already seen, not all civilized campaigns against primitives succeeded. For example, it was the most primitive portions of Celtic Europe that gave the Roman army the most difficulty.[17] Despite being subjected to repeated military campaigns by one of the finest civilized armies of any era, Scotland was never conquered; Ireland was simply left alone. The Roman conquest of interior and northern Spain demanded 200 years of almost constant warfare, during which the native Celtiberian tribes first demonstrated the Spanish genius for small-scale warfare. These two centuries of extremely bitter and often unsuccessful "pacification" campaigns occupied the full-time attention of four to six of Rome's twenty-eight legions—as many as were posted to guard against encroachment by the populous and aggressive Parthian (Persian) Empire. Similarly, for over a century, the small predatory tribes of the Alps survived periodic pacification campaigns by the very same Roman armies that had rapidly defeated the more civilized societies around and beyond them. The nomads of North Africa also gave Rome considerable trouble and ruined many military reputations. In general, the Roman legions performed much better against civilized opponents who "fought fair" than against the more barbarous tribesmen and provincial guerrillas who did not.

Although it did not hinge on anything that could properly be called a campaign, the fate of the Norse colonists in Vinland and Greenland provides no support for the notion that civilized people possessed inherent military superiority. Viking accounts (discussed earlier) record that they were driven from Vinland by the hostile natives. But three centuries later something even worse befell them, when southward-migrating Thule Inuit (Eskimo) reached a long-established but declining Norse colony in southwestern Greenland. The last written Norse records recount attacks by the Skraelings, and an expedition mounted from the Eastern Settlement to reconquer the Western Settlement from the Inuit found it completely deserted. The unequivocal traditions of the Inuit, not recorded until 1850, claim that their ancestors administered the coup de grâce to the fading Norse colonies in the course of mutual raids and massacres. Archaeology also suggests that the Inuit may have played a role in the final disappearance of the Eastern Settlement.[18] In these first military conflicts between the warriors of the New and Old Worlds, all the spoils belonged to the Americans.

Also in the fourteenth century, the Neolithic Gaunche tribesmen of the Canary Islands, armed only with wooden spears and stones for throwing, repulsed several French, Portuguese, and Spanish campaigns of conquest.[19] The Gran Canaria Guanches held out against these various conquistadors for almost a century and a half (1342–1483). Tenerife resisted until 1496 after pushing two invading Spanish armies into the sea. The prolonged resistance of these Stone Age tribes compares very favorably with the swift defeats suffered by the highly civilized Aztecs and Incas at the hands of Spanish invaders a few decades later. Similarly, the "wild tribes" of tropical South America defeated many Inca, Spanish, and Portuguese campaigns of conquest, as often as not, by completely annihilating the armies sent against them.[20]

The story was no different in North America. In one case, an early Spanish expedition sent from New Mexico to overawe the ever-troublesome Plains tribes (and detach them from any connection with French traders) was wiped out by the Pawnees in eastern Nebraska.[21] The Seminoles of Florida were never completely conquered by the U.S. Army, and it is hardly hyperbole to claim that tourists, armed only with tasteless clothing, have done a better job. One of the biggest American successes was obtained in 1839 when a corrupt Indian agent "bought out" a tough Seminole chief named Billy Bowlegs; when he left for exile in Oklahoma, he was reconciled to his defeat by fifty slaves and $100,000 in gold. A century after the Seminole War petered out in the early 1840s, Florida Seminoles plausibly (but unsuccessfully) claimed exemption from conscription during World War II because they belonged to a sovereign and never subjugated enemy "nation." After several years of dogged raiding by Chief Red Cloud's Sioux and Cheyenne warriors, the United States conceded the Bozeman Trail and the Powder River country it transited in the Treaties of 1868, admittedly because there was an alternative (but longer) route to the Montana mines. If not every civilized campaign in the New World was a success, it must be conceded that the great majority were. But the reasons for these victories had little to do with tactics, and even logistics and economics may have been irrelevant to the results.

As the ecological historian Alfred Crosby points out, European conquerors of the "brave new worlds" of the Americas, Australia, the Pacific islands, and the isolated extremities of the Old World were aided by invisible but overpowering allies.[22] These silent partners included viruses, bacteria, seed plants, and mammals that disseminated death and triggered ecological transformations that decimated native manpower and disrupted traditional economies. These insidious conquistadors spread far more rapidly and were many times more deadly than the human conquerors who followed in their wake. The deaths meted out by measles, influenza, and (especially) smallpox far exceeded in magnitude the deaths inflicted by the weapons of the Europeans. For example, the highest estimates for the number of Aztecs killed in combat during the Spanish Conquest (mostly by the Spaniards' Indian allies) are about 100,000, whereas in the decade following, introduced diseases killed at least 4 million and perhaps more than 8 million central Mexicans.[23] Many groups in these new worlds commonly lost a third to half of their populations just in the initial epidemic. Certainly, far less effort was needed to defeat adversaries who had just watched half of their comrades and families die of an alien and untreatable disease or had seen the mainstays of their economy choked out by the weeds and feral animals of the invaders. Crosby concludes that the celebrated victories of the small armies of Cortez and Pizarro over the populous Aztec and Inca civilizations were "in large part the triumphs of the virus of smallpox." The Yukaghir hunter-gatherers of Siberia had no doubt about why the Russians had been able to overpower them. They claimed that the Russians had brought with them a box containing smallpox, which, when opened, filled the land with smoke, and "the people began to die."

Crosby makes several historical comparisons that illustrate how essential these biological weapons were to European military success.[24] Despite using very primitive military technologies and tactics, possessing resources (such as spices, gold, and ivory) that excited the greed of Europeans, and being far closer to Europe than to temperate South America or Australia, many tribal areas were not conquered by Europeans until the late in the nineteenth and early in the twentieth century. What distinguished these resistant regions (the prime example being tropical Africa) from those rapidly subdued by Europeans during the previous four centuries was the natural immunity of their populations to Eurasian diseases and, in some areas, endemic diseases to which Europeans were especially susceptible. Also, European commensal species (such as rats and cattle) either were already native to these regions or could not survive there (such as rabbits and many weeds). Where disease-resistant tribal populations were established in the New World—for instance, the "Bush Negroes" of the Guianas—they were victorious over their seventeenth- and eighteenth-century European foes.[25] In other words, where Europeans were deprived of their biological advantages, their supposed military superiority was useless. Only the advent of modern medicine and public hygiene, the steamship, repeating rifles, and machine guns gave Europeans overwhelming advantages in health, logistics, and firepower over all tribal adversaries. In the face of these facts, the claim that the superior tactics and military discipline of Europeans gained them dominion over primitives in the Americas, Oceania, and Siberia is so inflated that it would be comic were not the facts that contradict it so tragic.

Primitive warriors often more quickly appreciated the military potential of civilized weapons than did soldiers long familar with them. The Indians of New England, in contrast to the first European colonists, preferred the flintlock to the matchlock musket, loading and using the flintlock in such a way as to much improve its accuracy and deadliness in combat.[26] In a more recent example, whereas civilized soldiers took a decade or more to translate powered flight into a means of inflicting death and destruction, some New Guinea tribesmen grasped its possibilities in only a matter of minutes.[27] The Eipo of highland Irian Jaya were first contacted by an ethnographer (Wulf Schiefenhövel of the Max Planck Institute) and his pilot, who landed their small plane among the tribesmen. Despite never having seen an airplane before, the tribal leader immediately asked for a ride, a request that was granted. When finally seated, he said that he wanted to bring a few heavy stones with him on the the flight. Asked what the rocks were for, he replied that if he were flown over the village of his enemies, he would drop these rocks on them. Although his request for a bombing raid was not granted, this tribal Billy Mitchell had immediately recognized the military value of aerial bombardment—far more quickly than the military leaders of the civilized nations that created and developed the airplane. These leaders assigned the first military aircraft to unarmed observational roles.

In the present day, the tactics, objectives, and practices typical of primitive war survive in civilized contexts under another name: guerrilla warfare. Like their tribal counterparts, guerrilla units are part-time, weakly disciplined bands of lightly armed volunteers. They prefer hit-and-run raids and ambushes to formal battles, and they rely heavily on their mobility, excellent intelligence, and knowledge of terrain to exploit the advantages of stealth and surprise. Guerrillas gain territory by harassing and terrorizing their enemies into abandoning it. Because of the lightness of their weapons and the weakness of their logistics, they are usually thwarted tactically by fortifications that they cannot take by either assault or siege. But they can sometimes maintain a strategic siege by harassing a fort's supply lines, as Chief Red Cloud did against Fort Abraham Lincoln on the Bozeman Trail. Antiguerrilla warfare requires exactly the same tactical adjustments by conventional armies as were adopted to counter tribal warriors. Defeating guerrillas is virtually impossible by purely military means; almost invariably, political and economic methods must also be employed.

American GIs in Vietnam acknowledged the similarity between tribal raiders and guerrillas when they ruefully termed their own fortified encampments "Fort Apaches" and Viet Cong–controlled areas "Indian country." The connection was even more direct for the Soviets in Afghanistan, who could not do any better against actual tribesmen than the British had a century before. Since guerrilla wars have long been recognized as especially destructive, prolonged, costly, and murderous, it is very curious that primitive warfare, being almost identical in means and methods, could ever be regarded as frivolous.

Indeed, every successful guerrilla campaign, however rare, is a demonstration that there is nothing contemptible about primitive military techniques. The nineteenth century witnessed some notably successful guerrilla campaigns, including the "Spanish Ulcer," which Napoleon could not cure, and the defeat of the best units of Maximilian's army (mostly French) by the Juaristas in Mexico.[28] In this century, guerrillas have been victorious over conventional forces more often than they have lost.[29] The fact that most guerrillas who lost either lacked or were cut off from logistical support by a larger and more modern economy highlights the only real weakness of primitive warfare and the decisive advantage of the civilized version. As the military truism asserts, "Amateurs discuss tactics while professionals discuss logistics."

The elaborate tactics, complex organization, and strict discipline of civilized armies are not just irrelevant rituals or irrational customs. But the techniques of civilized war are focused on winning battles, whereas those of tribesmen and guerrillas are devoted to winning everything else, especially wars. In many cases, primitive warfare requires long periods of time—even generations—to gain its ends, whereas the goal of civilized war is the extremely elusive "knock-out blow."[30] Civilized techniques are much more effective when the fighting is between civilized foes who field large formations of more or less equal size and employ heavy and complex weaponry. This fact is demonstrated by the success of European and European-led armies over those of Asian states during the eighteenth and nineteenth centuries.[31] But in World War II, the superior weaponry and tactics of the Germans and the suicidal courage and superior discipline of the Japanese were eventually ground into powder by the overwhelming weight of the Allies' manpower and industrial productivity. These twentieth-century cases, as well as those of the American Confederacy and of Napoleonic France in the nineteenth century, demonstrate that faith in "superior" (civilized) military techniques, élan, and discipline as a substitute for a larger population and a stronger economy is criminally insane.

The superiority of the disciplined mass formations and arcane military techniques of civilization over the looser methods of primitives is elusive, if not illusory. A broad survey of warfare indicates that (in the short term or tactically) superior numbers or fortifications and (in the long term or strategically) a larger population and better logistics are the keys to victory. In fact, primitive tactics are superior, since civilized forces must adopt most of them—despite already possessing an often stupendous superiority in weapons, manpower, and supplies—in order to triumph over primitive or guerrilla adversaries. Remarkably, the armies of civilization inevitably suffer some severe and embarrassing defeats before these truths dawn on their commanders. In two full decades of determined fighting, neither the French nor the Americans could defeat the guerrillas of Southeast Asia. But together in the Persian Gulf War, with but a fraction of the strength they employed in Indochina, they decimated one of the largest and best-equipped *conventional* armies in the world in just three months.[32] In contrast to the Iraqi army's performance in the Gulf War, the Apaches survived civilized military pressure for almost 300 years and were defeated only by primitive methods—literally by other Apaches wearing U.S. Army uniforms. Where is Tactic's sting and Discipline's dominion?

SIX

The Harvest of Mars

The Casualties of War

Although anthropologists have paid some attention to the actual conduct of primitive warfare, until very re cently they seldom documented or examined its direct effects. Like those Soviet planners who believed that one big factory was always better than a host of smaller ones, Westerners have a tendency to equate size with efficiency. But efficiency is a ratio, not an absolute. Effects are most profitably assessed in relation to the effort invested in obtaining them. Viewed in proportionate terms, how effective is precivilized warfare in wreaking death and destruction on enemies or in exacting profits from victory? This is the question to which we now turn.

PRISONERS AND CAPTIVES

It is extremely uncommon to find instances among nonstate groups of recognizing surrender or taking adult male prisoners. Adult males who fell into the hands of their enemies were usually immediately dispatched.[1] The Mae Enga tribesmen of highland New Guinea provide a typical example. When a Mae Enga warrior was seriously wounded by an arrow or a javelin, his adversaries would charge forward to chop him literally to pieces with their axes. To save their wounded from such a gruesome and culturally humiliating death, comrades would surround them so that they could be guided or carried to the rear. But the usual eagerness to dispatch enemy wounded was such that slightly wounded warriors would sometimes feign greater debility in order to draw their reckless opponents forward into flanking crossfire.[2] Armed or unarmed, adult males were killed without hesitation in battles, raids, or the routs following battles in the great majority of primitive societies. Surrender was not a practical option for adult tribesmen because survival after capture was unthinkable.

The reasons for this no-prisoners policy were seldom articulated by its practitioners. In many cases, it was simply tradition, a practice so common and universal that it needed no explanation. For example, during the 1879 Anglo-Zulu War, a British officer asked some Zulu prisoners why he should not kill them, as Zulus always killed British who fell into their hands. One prisoner answered, "There is a very good reason why you should not kill us. We kill you because it is the custom of Black men but it isn't the White men's custom."[3] Impressed by this appeal to the power of custom, the officer spared these Zulu prisoners. Overall, however, British soldiers were quick to abandon civilized constraints with regard to Zulu captives when it became evident that no reciprocity was forthcoming. Beyond the proximate cause of convention, one can only speculate about the ultimate reasons that male prisoners were seldom taken in primitive warfare. The most likely reason is that enemy warriors were unlikely to accept captivity without attempting violent escapes or revenge; thus holding them captive required levels of vigilance and upkeep that most tribal societies were unable or unprepared to provide.

A few cultures occasionally took men captive only to sacrifice them to their gods or torture them to death later.[4] Among the Iroquoian tribes of the Northeast, captured warriors were often subject to preliminary torture during the return journey of a war party. When the party arrived at the home village, the prisoners were beaten by running the gauntlet into the village. At a council, the warrior prisoners who survived these initial torments were distributed to families who had recently lost men in warfare. After these prisoners were ritually adopted and given the name of the family's dead member, they were usually tortured to death over several days. The victim was expected to display great fortitude during these torments—taunting his torturers and expressing contempt for their efforts. When the prisoner was dead, some parts of his body were eaten (usually including his heart) by his murderers. Archaeological finds of human bones in prehistoric Iroquoian kitchen middens indicate that it was also a pre-Columbian practice.[5] Similar treatment was inflicted on captives by various

Tupi groups in South America; in some tribes, the tortured prisoner was dispatched by children using arrows or axes, and the boys' hands were then dipped in the victim's blood to symbolize their duty to become warriors. Later destruction of male captives by ritual torture, sacrifice, or cannibalism (Chapter 7) has been recorded for the Maoris and Marquesans of Polynesia, Fijians, a few North American tribes, several South American groups, and various New Guinea groups.[6] This fate was usually reserved for only a few enemy warriors—usually chiefs or other men of renown. The majority of captured foes were simply executed without further ceremony. These elaborate customs, however gruesome, merely delayed or prolonged the inevitable destruction of enemy males.

In some societies, of course, blood kin and in-laws who met one another in combat would try to avoid harming one another. In highland New Guinea, for example, a warrior who spotted a relative on the other side might move to another part of the battle line or might point this relative out to his comrades, asking them to spare him (a protection that was usually only temporary).[7] The underlying motive was to avoid having a relative's or in-law's blood on one's hands—not necessarily to save him from harm. In most primitive combat, adversaries neither gave nor expected quarter from anyone.

However, some East African tribes did recognize surrender because the practice of ransoming prisoners with cattle was common. Among the Meru herdsmen of Kenya, a warrior wishing to surrender lifted his spear above his head and shouted "Take cattle!" But if his opponents had deaths to avenge, acceptance of his capitulation was by no means a foregone conclusion. The custom of capturing adult males and incorporating them into a tribe was extremely rare anywhere.[8] The Shawnee and Fox tribes of the United States (and very occasionally a few other tribes in the Northeast) spared only those male captives who had survived the hardships and tortures inflicted during their journey to their captors' village and who were immediately claimed by families who needed replacements for war casualties. A few South American petty chiefdoms saved some captive young men and married them to the daughters of their captors, in order to incorporate them as a despised "servile" class. The Nuer of Sudan adopted boys captured from their enemies (the Dinka), and women of marriageable age and girls were incorporated less formally. On the other hand, old women and babies captured in Nuer raids were clubbed to death and their bodies burned with the Dinka huts. Dinka adult males were simply killed.[9] Groups that used or sold war captives as slaves usually preferred to subjugate women and children and therefore immediately dispatched all adult male captives.[10] In general, the primitive warrior had only three means of surviving combat: an arranged truce, victory, or (in defeat) fleetness of foot.

In some primitive societies, women were spared injury or capture by enemy warriors.[11] Even in societies where women were often slain in the small raids and rare wild slaughters attending massacres and routs, they could enjoy remarkable immunity from harm on formal battlefields. In Kapauku battles in New Guinea, for instance, married women wandered freely about the battlefield collecting arrows to resupply their men, "as if they were harvesting potatoes or cucumbers," and even acting as scouts or lookouts. Unmarried Kapauku girls had to be more circumspect because if caught by the enemy, they might be raped. When Tuareg tribesmen of the Sahara were defeated near their encampments, they bolted, leaving their women and children in the hands of their enemies. This behavior reflected the Tuaregs' expectation, given their own customs, that women and children were inviolable in warfare.[12] Such chivalrous behavior toward women and children was, however, not the norm among non-state groups.

The capture of women was one of the spoils of victory—and occasionally one of the primary aims of warfare—for many tribal warriors. In many societies, if the men lost a fight, the women were subject to capture and forced incorporation into the captor's society. Most Indian tribes in western North America at least occasionally conducted raids to capture women.[13] The social position of captive women varied widely among cultures, from abject slaves to concubines to secondary wives to full spouses. In a few cases, female captives could be ransomed or, of course, escape.[14] In situations where ransom or escape were not possible, the treatment of captive young women amounted to rape, whether actual violence was used against them to enforce cohabitation with their captors or was only implicit in their situation.

Sometimes the number of captive women held by a group represented a considerable proportion of its female population. According to their traditions, the Island Caribs of the Lesser Antilles had conquered these islands a century before Columbus by exterminating the resident Arawak men and taking the women for wives. After a few generations, there developed a peculiar linguistic situation in which the women and children spoke Arawak to one another, but the men spoke a corrupt form of Carib among themselves and to the women.[15] Although the loss of even a large percentage of males will have no direct influence on a group's demographic fortunes (whatever the effect on its military viability may be), the loss or gain of fertile women can mean the difference between population decline and growth.[16]

Female captives were also very valuable economically. In many societies, women's labor provided the greater part of staple food. In California, acorns (a dietary staple) were gathered and processed by women. On the Pacific Northwest Coast, women performed the time-consuming but essential work of cleaning and drying salmon, which could be caught only during brief annual runs but were a staple food year-round. Since salmon were not difficult to locate or to catch, one man could supply several women with full-time work. Throughout Melanesia, gardening and pig rearing were female specialties. The widespread practice of polygamy indicates that many societies found that having several adult women in a household was not burdensome but was usually an economic boon. It became even more of an advantage if the additional women could be acquired without the costs of a bride-price or interfering in-laws.

Of course, many tribal societies took no prisoners and retained no captives of any sex or age.[17] The Chemehuevi of the Southwest and several tribes in California spared no one. Perhaps the harshest treatment of captives was meted out in Polynesia. The Tahitians are described as leaving enemy children pinned to their mothers with spears or "pierced through the head and strung on cords." The Maoris sometimes disabled captive women so that they could not escape, permitting the warriors to rape, kill, and eat them when it was more convenient to do so. Even in societies where captives were taken, once general killing started it could be difficult to stop. For example, in an Asmat head-hunting raid in New Guinea, anyone interested in saving a woman or child as a captive (something rarely done) experienced considerable difficulty in preventing his overexcited comrades from dispatching his chosen prisoners.[18]

In general, nonstate groups preserved the lives of captives only when some material benefit would accrue; this approach generally limited the persons spared to women and children. States, by contrast, often have a strong material interest in preserving the lives of defeated enemies—even adult males—because they can become tax- and tribute-paying subjects, serfs, or slaves. The life-preserving rituals of formal surrender and widespread official distaste for killing noncombatants are expressions of this interest. Economically, the state is usually best served by the submission of its enemies, not by genocide. The atrocities that do occur in civilized warfare usually happen when commanders lose control of their soldiers, whose primary motive may be the primitive one of avenging combat losses or previous real or fictive enemy atrocities. And slaughters of noncombatants can occur as a matter of policy, when the policymakers themselves are consumed by ethnic hatred or when they make a calculated attempt to use state terrorism to cow a conquered populace.

The reaction of the German government during the Herero-Nama uprising in Southwest Africa in 1904 is an example of the self-interested mercy of states and of the conditions under which it fails. The local military governor, General von Trotha, issued an extermination order against the Hereros. The imperial chancellor and the German colonial office successfully demanded that this order be countermanded by the Kaiser: it was inhumane, was bad for public relations, and (perhaps most important) would "undermine the potential for development" by eliminating native labor. The governor, his troops, and the German colonists paid little heed to the Kaiser's order, however. When the fighting ended several years later, only one-half of the Nama and one-sixth of the Herero had survived.[19] Precisely this weakness of state control over frontier "militias" made massacres of native peoples more common by such agents than by the "regular" forces of the state. Indeed, the most notorious massacres of North American Indians, such as those at Sand Creek and Camp Grant, and the only actual genocides (that is, complete extinction of a tribe primarily by homicide) during the European conquest were all inflicted by local militias.[20] In many respects, these frontier struggles played out as tribal wars in which one tribe happened to be composed of European colonists. In general, though, the prospects for the defeated were slightly brighter (if still dim) if they were vanquished by a state than by a nonstate society.

Only the "rules of war," cultural expectations, and tribal or national loyalties make it possible to distinguish between legitimate warfare and atrocities. Is there any behavioral difference between Caesar's extermination of the Bituriges at Bourges, the slaughter of Minnesota settlers by the Sioux in 1862, the massacres by the U.S. Army at Wounded Knee and My Lai, the Allied air strikes at Dresden and Hiroshima, the massacres committed by Japanese soldiers in Nanking and Manila, and the similar accomplishments of primitives described earlier, except the body counts and the assignment of our sympathies with the perpetrators or the victims? Apologists for such massacres always claim that their perpetrators were "provoked." But war always seems full to overflowing with provocations. At any rate, the treatment of captives and prisoners by nonstate groups has usually and literally been atrocious.

WAR DEATHS

Citizens of modern states tend to believe that everything they do is more efficient and effective than the corresponding efforts of primitives or ancients. Given the neo-Rousseauian tenor of the present day, this expectation about modern civilization finds ready acceptance in relation to distasteful or harmful behavior. Therefore, it comes as a shock to discover that the proportion of war casualties in primitive societies almost always exceeds that suffered by even the most bellicose or war-torn modern states.

Actual casualty figures from primitive warfare are scarce, and only in the past few decades have ethnographers attempted to collect such information. Figure 6.1 compares these casualty rates with those of the most war-torn modern states. Following the practice of several ethnographers, to facilitate comparison, these war death rates are expressed as annual percentages of mean population. Another measure of the deadliness of warfare is the proportion of all deaths caused by war; these figures are given in Figure 6.2. By either measure, primitive warfare was much deadlier than its modern counterpart.[21] The death rates

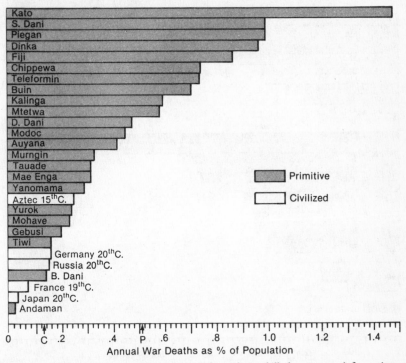

Figure 6.1 War fatality rates (percentage of population killed per annum) for various prestate and civilized societies (see Appendix, Table 6.1).

shown for civilized states overestimate the deadliness of combat, since most war deaths were caused by disease until very recently. For example, two-thirds of the deaths suffered by the Union armed forces during the Civil War were due to disease.[22] Such disease casualties are included in the war death rates for civilized states but not in those of primitive groups. Moreover, many civilized war deaths were the result of accidents involving horses, vehicles, and weapons. For example, approximately 20 percent of British deaths in the Crimean War and 14 percent in the Boer War were accidental.[23] The deaths recorded for the primitive groups were all the direct result of wounds suffered in combat and inflicted by the enemy. Were such noncombat deaths deleted from the civilized rates given in Figure 6.1, the terrible deadliness of primitive compared with modern combat would be even more one-sided.

But what of civilian deaths from disease or starvation resulting from the disruptions and dislocations caused by war? Again such deaths are included in the civilized rates but not in those of the primitive groups. These are difficult to

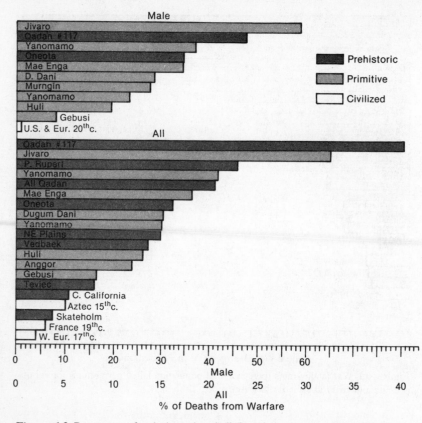

Figure 6.2 Percentage of male (upper) and all (lower) deaths caused by warfare in various societies (see Appendix, Table 6.2).

calculate for modern states, and no figures are available for any primitive society. However, they were probably just as common in primitive warfare as in the civilized variety. For example, the ethnographer of the Mae Enga of New Guinea describes the wartime consequences of the "sudden and forced movements of women and children, the elderly and the ill, over difficult terrain in bleak and often wet weather":

> We simply do not know how many infants and old people succumb to pneumonia in these flights, how many refugees are drowned when trying to cross boulder-strewn torrents, how many already sick and weak people die because food supplies are interrupted. These less obvious costs of war, I believe, accumulate significantly through time and . . . have played their part in effecting a relatively low rate of population growth in the recent past.[24]

One may also quickly dispose of the argument that these high casualty rates only reflect contact between tribal peoples and Westerners by citing the very similar proportions of violent deaths documented in several prehistoric populations (Figure 6.2).[25] My own first excavation training was on a prehistoric village site on the San Francisco Bay in California. Thousand-year-old skeletons with obsidian arrowheads embedded in the bones, missing heads, and other signs of violent death were so common that our excavation crew referred to burials as "bad sights." As a matter of fact, one distinctive characteristic of this period in central Californian prehistory is that about 5 percent of all human skeletons contain embedded arrowheads—which, of course, represent only the most obvious evidence of death in warfare. The actual percentage of violent deaths must have been much higher. Indeed, several of these prehistoric cases seriously underestimate the number of violent deaths because only individuals with projectiles in their bones are counted as war deaths. Judging from the Gebel Sahaba cemetery, where only 25 percent of the skeletons that show signs of arrow wounds have the points so embedded, the real proportion of war deaths in the California and Scandinavian cases in Figure 6.2 probably ranged from about 7 percent to as much as 40 percent of all deaths. Contrary to arguments that tribal violence increased after contact with Europeans, the percentage of burials in coastal British Columbia bearing evidence of violent traumas was actually *lower* after European contact (13 percent from 1774 to 1874) than the very high levels (20 to 32 percent) evidenced in the prehistoric periods.[26] It is clear from these archaeological examples that the casualty rates recorded by ethnographers are neither improbable nor exceptional. Tribal peoples needed no instructions or inducements from Europeans to make real war.

But how can such high losses be reconciled with the low casualty rates generally observed in primitive battles, where action is often broken off when both sides have suffered a few dead? Part of the answer lies in the higher sortie rate of primitive warriors. As was noted earlier, warfare occurs much more frequently in most primitive societies than in civilized ones. Thus a relatively low loss rate per war, battle, or raid can cumulate very rapidly to catastrophic levels. Suppose that a tribe with 100 warriors breaks off fighting or arranges a truce in a battle after the loss of just 5 percent dead or mortally wounded. If such battles occurred about four times a year, the cumulative loss in just five years would be 64 percent, leaving only about 36 warriors alive to defend the group. Given a high frequency of warfare, likely losses due to small raids and ambushes, and other sources of losses to warrior strength from accidents or disease, no small group could afford to accept losses in battle exceeding 2 percent. Even that loss rate per fight, if battles take place four times a year, would reduce the group's fighting strength by a third in just five years. When debilitating wounds that do not result in death are also taken into account, it becomes clear why warriors from small societies were so prone to end battles after just a few casualties. At issue was not just their personal survival but literally that of their group.

Restricting the number and severity of casualties can be done only in the context of formal battles. Small raids and ambushes, which are more frequent than battles and more indiscriminately deadly, are less subject to control. Larger-scale surprise attacks, not uncommon in primitive wars, can cause extremely high levels of casualties. The uncontrollable violence and frequency of such raids and massacres thus make primitive warfare deadlier than modern wars.

The usual primitive practices of not recognizing surrender and of dispatching all male captives also contribute to the lethality of such warfare. Despite the great difficulties inherent in successfully surrendering in the heat of battle, this life-saving option is often resorted to by civilized soldiers; as we have seen, however, it is unavailable to his primitive counterparts. Wounded soldiers who fall into the hands of civilized foes may receive very poor care or may be killed to prevent them from becoming a burden to their captors, but a similar misfortune for a primitive warrior meant certain death.

As for women, even when the ritual conventions of civilized war are not observed by modern states, their female mortalities do not exceed those usually inflicted over time by tribal warfare. The Allied "strategic" bombing of Germany killed more women than men; but compared with Germany's total male losses, these deaths still represented a ratio of only one female to every sixteen to twenty males.[27] Of course, the Nazi death squads and death camps killed so indiscriminately that the sex ratio of Germany's victims must be much closer to unity.[28] The corresponding ratios for the prestate groups range from about 1:1 to 1:15 (with a median of 1:7)—in every case a higher proportion of female deaths than that caused by the Allies and in a few cases little better than the proportion inflicted by the Nazis.[29]

The cumulative effects of all these forms of violence can decimate a small clan or tribe.[30] One small New Guinea community began a war with twenty-two married men. After just four and a half months of fighting, six men (27 percent) had been killed, eight men had moved away to safety, and the group had been forced to merge with another unit in order to survive. In a war between two Papuan village confederacies (each with populations of 600 to 700 people) that lasted for more than a year, over 250 people were killed, and one side was left with almost no adult males. At the beginning of the nineteenth century, the Blackfoot tribe of the northern Plains was 50 percent deficient in adult males— presumably because of combat deaths since the deficiency disappeared rapidly after intertribal warfare ended later in the century. These percentages equal or exceed the decimations suffered by any modern state in its wars.[31]

Even complete annihilation of enemy social units has not been unknown in primitive wars. Instances of tribes or subtribes being driven to extinction by persistent tribal warfare have been recorded from several areas of the world.[32] Such genocides were sometimes accomplished by a single surprise massacre, on other occasions by longer-term attrition from repeated raids, or by a combination of both. The case of the Woriau Maring of New Guinea illustrates one method by which such annihilations were accomplished, and it also indicates why such occurrences tend to be rare. As was mentioned in Chapter 4, a favorite raid tactic in highland New Guinea consisted of stealthily surrounding the men's houses of an enemy, settting them afire, and killing all those who emerged. Usually, one Maring clan had insufficient manpower to attack all of an enemy's men's houses simultaneously and had to retreat in the face of counter-attacks from the unattacked houses after killing a few men. In the Woriau case, two enemy clans allied themselves for the attack and were able to cover every house, annihilating the Woriau's manpower in a single day. The defenseless survivors then dispersed and ceased to exist as a collective group. Indeed, social extinction in tribal societies seems not to have entailed the killing of every person in the victimized group; rather, after a significant portion of the group (including most of its adult men) was killed, the surviving remnants were incorporated into the societies of the victors or into friendly groups with whom they sought refuge. Thus a social or linguistic entity was destroyed, if not necessarily the whole of the biological population that composed it. These may be social versions of "the death of a thousand cuts," but they are extinctions just the same.

The high war death rates among most nonstate societies are obviously the result of several features of primitive warfare: the prevalence of wars, the high proportion of tribesmen who face combat, the cumulative effects of frequent but low-casualty battles, the unmitigated deadliness and very high frequency of raids, the catastrophic mortalities inflicted in general massacres, the customary killing of all adult males, and the often atrocious treatment of women and children. For these reasons, a member of a typical tribal society, especially a male, had a far higher probability of dying "by the sword" than a citizen of an average modern state.

One author has very liberally estimated that more than 100 million people have died from all war-related causes (including famine and disease) on our planet during this century.[33] These deaths could be regarded as the price modern humanity has paid for being divided into nation-states. Yet this appalling figure is *twenty times smaller* than the losses that might have resulted if the world's population were still organized into bands, tribes, and chiefdoms.[34] A typical tribal society lost about about .5 percent of its population in combat each year (Figure 6.1). Applying this casualty rate to the earth's twentieth-century populations predicts more than 2 *billion* war deaths since 1900. Unlike a nuclear holocaust, such "back-to-nature" scenarios are certainly imaginary, but so is the idea that primitive war is not lethal.

WOUNDS AND THEIR TREATMENT

At what rate have nonfatal wounds been inflicted in primitive combat? Are these rates higher or lower than those suffered in civilized warfare? Unfortunately, such figures for primitive groups are very scarce.[35] In one inconclusive New Guinea battle, by actual count, one Mae Enga clan suffered 40 percent of its warriors killed and wounded—which the clan regarded as a normal casualty rate. The large number of wound scars generally borne by Mae Enga men demonstrate that they were often wounded. Over half of the wounds suffered were on the limbs, however, and were not considered very serious. Similarly, a Mohave Indian war party was expected to suffer about 30 percent casualties in an average battle. Of course, victims caught by small raiding parties were very unlikely to survive the encounter, since they were usually outnumbered and often unarmed. In contrast, in an average Civil War battle, only 12 to 15 percent of the combatants were killed and wounded; even at Gettysburg, the Union forces engaged lost only 21 percent and the Confederates 30 percent to death or wounds.[36] On the terrible first day of the Somme battle in 1916, about 40 percent of the thirteen attacking British divisions became casualties.[37] The scant available evidence, then, indicates that, at least in formal battles, tribal warriors were wounded about as often as soldiers in the bloodiest modern battles.

Although just as high a proportion of those engaged in primitive battles may be wounded, fewer in proportion are killed outright than is usually the case in modern battles (Figure 4.1). For instance, in Mae Enga formal battles, which were primarily firefights, only one man was killed for every ten to thirty wounded. Approximate ratios of killed to wounded for some modern battles are 1:5 at Gettysburg and in the battles for Atlanta, 1:3 for one particular British battalion at Waterloo, and 1:2 for the British at the Somme.[38] The casualness with which Mae Enga warriors viewed most of their wounds suggests that those inflicted by unpoisoned missiles (which many tribes used exclusively) were seldom immediately serious. Only wounds to the neck, chest, belly, and groin were greatly feared.[39]

Of course, some primitive and ancient battles were exceptionally deadly. The Mohave, who closed with the enemy and fought with deadlier shock weapons (lances and clubs), suffered an estimated two wounded for every battlefield death. Casualty estimates for the losing side in several Macedonian and Roman battles identify the number of killed as equaling or exceeding the number of wounded.[40] As statistics for the Mohave case and for ancient European battles indicate, wounds from shock weapons tend to be much more deadly than wounds from untainted missiles. In the same way, a single hit from a bullet, bomb blast, or shell fragment is much more likely to mortally wound or kill outright than is a single strike from an unpoisoned javelin or arrow. Thus the higher ratios of dead to wounded noted for modern and ancient civilized battles reflect of the greater lethality of modern gunpowder and ancient shock weapons.

But if modern gunpowder weapons are more deadly, how is it that even in hardest-fought modern battles the casualty rates (about 30 to 40 percent) are generally no higher and sometimes even lower than those inflicted with primitive fire weapons? The main difficulty is that the enemy in modern warfare usually refuses to cooperate by exposing himself in large concentrations where he can be found, aimed at, and killed en masse by the deadly but ponderous weapons of modern war. To put it bluntly, soldiers have a natural tendency to "duck." Only when modern soldiers cooperate through gross stupidity (as they did during the first few months of World War I, by charging in mass formations into machine guns and rapid-firing artillery), does the latent lethality of modern weapons become manifest.[41] Whatever the potential destructiveness of such weapons, against even a moderately uncooperative enemy, thousands of shells and bullets must be fired just to wound a single person. Against thoroughly unobliging enemies who fight in the primitive fashion, including modern guerrillas, the stupendous paraphernalia of modern war is often useless.

One possible explanation of the high war death rates of primitive societies is that because of their poor medical practices, a greater proportion of primitive warriors subsequently died of wounds. But first consider that nineteenth-century France, which suffered most of its war casualties during the Napoleonic Wars, was used in comparison with primitive groups in Figures 6.1 and 6.2. This was a period when medicine practiced neither antisepsis nor anaesthesia. Military surgeons actually contributed to the fatality of wounds by "bleeding" wounded men, routinely amputating wounded limbs, probing uncleaned wounds with unsterile instruments, and immediately binding them tight with unsterilized bandages. All these standard early-nineteenth-century practices induced shock or increased the chances of infection. The wholesale prescription of powerful laxatives at the slightest provocation, often for soldiers already suffering from dysentery, can hardly have aided convalescence. With modern medical hindsight, it is clear that military medicine during the nineteenth century was worse than ineffective: it was positively harmful.

In contrast, most primitive healers merely extracted the projectile, sometimes bathed the wounds, and commonly covered them with poultices of plants known to have healing properties. A recent pharmocological study of over 2,000 plant extracts found that 61 percent had some antibiotic effect, lending support to the idea that these poultices would have been more helpful than the tight, unsanitary bandages of pre-twentieth-century military medicine.[42] Another shamanistic treatment, common at least in North America, involved sucking blood from the wound; where arrows were poisoned, this would have been a necessary precaution, but it would have helped to clean the wound in any case. The only surgical advantage that Western military doctors of the nineteenth century possessed over their primitive counterparts was their ability to stop massive bleeding from major arteries and veins. On the other hand, a number of prehistoric and recent chiefdoms practiced trepanation—removal of small pieces of the skull to treat cranial fractures—an operation that Western surgeons did not master until the late nineteenth century. Archaeological finds of skulls with multiple healed trepanation scars indicate that this operation often had a high rate of success.[43] Thus shamanistic treatments were, in many cases, harmless at worst and very efficacious at best.

Evidence also shows that the patients of nineteenth-century military doctors feared their incompetence. Civil War soldiers, for example, often concealed their wounds, preferring their own home remedies to the army surgeons' excruciating, fearsome, and often fatal treatments.[44] Seriously wounded soldiers seldom had any choice in the matter, but others were somewhat luckier. In 1876, a Cheyenne brave, whose leg bones had been shattered by a bullet, was told by a U.S. Army doctor that his leg would have to be amputated to save his life. He refused and was instead treated by a Cheyenne medicine man. Both he and his leg survived, with the only lingering effect being a certain stiffness in his walk.[45] One may dismiss this case as a fluke; but overall, the limited surgery and salutary herbalism of shamans may well have saved more wounded men than the septic interventions and the shock-inducing amputations of nineteenth-century civilized surgeons.

In addition, civilized soldiers often had to wait a long time for first aid. For example, after Waterloo, many of the British wounded were not collected until the following morning, and some live French wounded remained on the field two days later. By contrast, many (if not most) primitive warriors could obtain treatment minutes after suffering their wounds. As we have seen, tribal warriors made special efforts to protect wounded men and to move them out of danger in order to save them from certain death and mutilation. In New Guinea, older men and women, located immediately behind the battlefield, were available to dress wounds. In North America, shamans often accompanied war parties to work favorable magic and to treat wounds.[46] Furthermore, convalescing wounded warriors enjoyed the interested care of family and friends, whereas civilized soldiers were subjected to the impersonal, often overburdened, and indifferent ministrations of personnel at military hospitals. Surely the former offered superior intensive care and psychological support.[47]

The medical care given to wounded tribal warriors was thus no worse, and in some cases better, than that given to civilized soldiers until this century. It is unlikely, then, that the high warfare death rates of primitives can be explained by their supposedly inferior medical practices.

SEVEN

To the Victor

The Profits and Losses of Primitive War

In war, various possessions, representing wealth and the means of production, can be seized or destroyed to benefit attackers and harm defenders. Even from the corpses of the vanquished, the victors can extract gains and inflict losses on their foes. Both civilized and uncivilized adversaries experience the spoils and horrors of war in ways that extend far beyond the numbers of dead, wounded, and missing.

MUTILATION AND TROPHY TAKING

In Tahiti, a victorious warrior, given the opportunity, would pound his vanquished foe's corpse flat with his heavy war club, cut a slit through the well-crushed victim, and don him as a trophy poncho.[1] This custom was extreme only to the extent that most tribal warriors were seldom so surreal in their mutilations or so unselective in their choice of trophies from the bodies of their dead enemies. There are both anthropological and archaeological reasons for discussing this type of behavior in the context of costs and gains.

People in many cultures believe that improper treatment of a corpse can adversely affect the fate of the soul or spirit it once housed. For such people, deeply felt injuries could be inflicted on them by mutilation of their dead. Trophies such as scalps and heads were often included among the spoils of war because they were important tokens for reckoning male status or were thought to enhance a warrior's spiritual power. The gains from such trophies could include elevation to manhood and the right to marry, higher status, greater favor from gods and spirits, increased spiritual power, and general well-being. In certain systems of belief, then, these gruesome practices inflicted real costs and exacted real benefits. From an archaeological perspective, mutilated skeletons provide compelling evidence of prehistoric war, since few societies would mutilate their own dead. These pathetic remains are among the most enduring effects of war.

By far the most common and widely distributed war trophy was the head or skull of an enemy. The custom of taking heads is recorded from many cultures in New Guinea, Oceania, North America, South America, Africa, and ancient western Europe.[2] The popularity of this practice is probably explained by the obvious fact that the head is the most individual part of the body. For warriors the world over, the prestige or spiritual power accruing to the victor depended on the personal qualities and reputations of his victims. More than any other body part, the head of a vanquished foe was an unequivocal token of the individual that had been overcome. Such trophies were so representative of the individual from whom they were taken that victors often spoke to their trophy heads by name, reviling and exulting over them. For example, an early missionary in New Zealand heard a Maori warrior taunting the preserved head of an enemy chief in the following fashion:

> You wanted to run away, did you? but my meri [war club] overtook you: and after you were cooked, you made food for my mouth. And where is your father? he is cooked:—and where is your brother? he is eaten:—and where is your wife? there she sits, a wife for me:—and where are your children? there they are, with loads on their backs, carrying food, as my slaves.[3]

In Maori warfare, decapitation marked the beginning, not the end, of a vanquished warrior's humiliation.

The taking of trophy heads certainly occurred prehistorically in several areas of the world.[4] The 7,500-year-old caches of trophy heads found in Ofnet Cave in Germany have already been mentioned in earlier chapters. Several headless skeletons with cut-marks on their neck vertabrae indicating decapitation were recovered from a late prehistoric site in Illinois. Prehistoric chiefdoms in Central and South America left depictions of warriors taking and displaying trophy heads, as well as the heads themselves.

The native North American custom of taking scalps is well known, although historical revisionists have popularized the notion that Indians only learned scalping from Europeans. Undoubtedly, the "scalp bounties" offered by some colonial authorities did much to encourage scalping and helped spread the custom to a few tribes that had previously disdained the practice (such as the Apaches) or that instead took the whole head as a trophy (such as the Iroquois). Nevertheless, the custom of scalping enemy dead was observed at first contact among tribes ranging from New England to California and from parts of the subarctic down to northern Mexico.[5] Scalps and scalping were embedded in the myth and rituals of so many tribes that the custom's indigenous roots in North America are beyond serious question. For example, among the Pueblos of the Southwest, "warriors' societies" or "scalp societies" performed important cere-monial, social, and military functions; membership in them was restricted to men who had taken an enemy scalp. By contrast, the custom was unknown in ancient, medieval, and early modern Europe, where the preferred trophies were usually whole heads. Here again, archaeological evidence provides the decisive and unequivocal proof. Because the skin of the scalp is so thin, removing it from the skull leaves characteristic cut-marks on the cranial bones; such cut-marks have been found frequently on pre-Columbian skulls from many regions of North America.[6] Indians were plainly the scalpers, and it was from them that the colonists learned the custom. However, it was the "civilized" Europeans who turned human scalps into an item of commerce.

Less common trophies taken by tribes in various areas of the world included hands, genitals, teeth, and the long bones of the arms or legs.[7] These long bones were made into flutes in South America and New Zealand. Several chiefdoms in Colombia kept the entire skins of dead enemies. Often the women who accom-panied their men to the battlefield flayed the victims. One group even stuffed these trophy skins, modeled the features of the victims in wax on their skulls, placed weapons in their hands, and set the reassembled trophy "in places of honor on special benches and tables within their households."[8]

The symbolic significance of trophies varied enormously from one culture to another. In some, they merely provided a tangible numerical measure of a warrior's prowess. In others, they possessed magic powers that strengthened their possessor or transferred the victim's spirit to the victor's benefit. They might be necessary paraphernalia for rituals honoring deities, initiating youths, or cleansing their taker of the spiritual pollution of homicide. These items might degrade the victim, injure his afterlife, or enrage his survivors, as was the intention of the Paez of Colombia, who displayed the trophy penises of their enemies in order to "shame the foe." Body-part trophies have meant some combination of all of these things to various societies. As is so often the case in an ethnographic survey, a fundamentally similar behavior pattern displayed by many diverse groups conveys a huge range of meanings to its exhibitors.

Even if no trophies were taken, mutilations were commonly inflicted on victims' corpses—eyes removed, bellies slit, genitals severed, features defaced, and so on—with a similar variety of significances.[9] For example, the Zulus of South Africa slit a victim's belly to release his spirit, thereby saving the killer from pollution and insanity. To express their contempt for the social group of an enemy, the Mae Enga of New Guinea mutilated his corpse by stuffing his severed penis in his mouth or, in the heat of battle, chopping him to pieces with axes. Different Plains tribes mutilated their foes' corpses in characteristic ways as a kind of "signature": the Sioux by cutting throats, the Cheyenne by slashing arms, the Arapaho splitting noses, and so on (Plate 2). In the aftermath of the Battle of the Little Bighorn, Indian women used marrow-cracking mallets to pound the faces of dead soldiers into pulp. Perhaps the most common mutilation was "overkill," which involved shooting so many arrows into an enemy's body that he looked like a "human pin-cushion." In these cases, the disfigurements expressed hatred for the enemy and were meant to enrage surviving foes.

Similar mutilations practiced on the bodies of the victims at Crow Creek in 1325, at the Larson site in 1785, and at Little Bighorn in 1876 show that the Plains' traditions of mutilation and scalp taking persisted for over 500 years.[10] Over 11,000 years ago, overkill with arrows was practiced by the enemies of the victims buried in the Gebel Sahaba cemetery in Egypt. Several adult skeletons—male and female—bore evidence of having been shot with between fifteen and twenty-five arrows. Another type of overkill involving ax blows was found on the Mesolithic trophy skulls at Ofnet, dating to 7,500 years ago. Several skulls had between four and seven ax holes, any one of which would have sufficed to cause death. Identical multiple ax traumas were found on the skulls of the Talheim Neolithic victims, dating to 7,000 years ago.

Of course, mutilation and body-part trophy taking have hardly disappeared from modern civilized warfare.[11] The Third Colorado Cavalry, recruited from the dregs of Denver's populace, took scalps from the Cheyenne they massacred at Sand Creek in 1864 and displayed these immediately after the action to general acclaim in Denver. The human-hide lampshades produced at Nazi death camps are perhaps the modern era's preeminent symbol of evil. During the relentless fighting in the Pacific theater of World War II, Japanese mutilated Allied dead, and Americans soldiers extracted gold teeth as well as other trophies from the bodies of their enemies. Marine veteran E. B. Sledge, in a harrowing memoir of that war, compared such behaviors to scalping and felt that they were motivated by a savage mutual hatred and thirst for revenge. Both sides in the Vietnam War occasionally mutilated enemy corpses, and there are accounts of American and Australian soldiers keeping Vietnamese ears as trophies. The impulse toward such behavior clearly has not disappeared in civilized warfare, even though it is no longer morally or legally acceptable.

CANNIBALISM

The most extreme mutilation inflicted on dead enemies is cannibalism. Anthropologists usually make a distinction between ritual and culinary cannibalism. *Ritual* cannibalism, which is the more common type, involves the consumption of only a portion of a corpse (sometimes after it has been reduced to ashes) for magical purposes. *Culinary*, or gastronomic, cannibalism consists of eating human meat as food. Some scholars also distinguish *starvation* cannibalism, which may occur in famine conditions, from the culinary type. Since culinary cannibalism is strongly tabooed by many cultures, it has been a favorite propaganda accusation against unfriendly neighbors or distant strangers. Anthropological views of this phenomenon stretch from the neo-Hobbesian acceptance of almost all such accusations in the nineteenth century to the recent neo-Rousseauian denial that culinary cannibalism ever existed anywhere, except briefly under conditions of extreme starvation.[12] Certainly, it appears that many of the societies accused of culinary cannibalism either were being slandered by their enemies or, at most, practiced ritual cannibalism.

The diversity of opinion concerning the existence of culinary cannibalism exists because most anthropologists have had to rely primarily on the testimony of interested witnesses, such as missionaries, colonial administrators, and native propagandists. That wholesale consumption of humans would necessarily leave forensic circumstantial evidence for the archaeologist—in the form of human bones treated in the same fashion as the bones of nonhuman food mammals—seems to have escaped most students of cannibalism; archaeologists, with a few exceptions, have ignored the problem.[13] However, there do seem to be some well-attested and self-admitted ethnographic instances of culinary cannibalism (or at least ritual cannibalism on such a large scale that it is indistinguishable from the former). Many of these cases are also supported by archaeological evidence.[14]

Many tribes and chiefdoms in southern Central America and northeastern South America reputedly consumed large numbers of their dead foes and captives.[15] Notwithstanding some kind of magical or religious justification for cannibalism, several of these groups seemed to have positively relished human flesh. One record reports that a Colombian chief and his retinue consumed the bodies of 100 enemies in a single day following a victory. In another chiefdom, war captives were kept in special enclosures and fattened before consumption. Many of these groups smoked or otherwise preserved human meat to be eaten later. The Ancerma of western Colombia reportedly lighted their gold mines with lamps fueled by human fat and sold captives to their neighbors for use as food.

Enemy corpses and captives were eaten on a similar scale in a few places in Oceania.[16] On Fiji, one chief kept a tally of the number of bodies he had consumed by placing a stone for each victim in a line behind his house; the line stretched nearly 200 meters and contained 872 stones. Maori war parties supplemented their logistics and extended their campaigns by consuming enemy bodies and captives taken in battle. Several groups in New Guinea admitted to having conducted raids motived by the desire for human flesh. In many of these Oceanian cases, consistent archaeological data support the ethnographic descriptions.

Culinary cannibalism was often attributed to West African tribes. But as with similar accusations elsewhere in the world, most cases proved to be exaggerations of ritual cannibalism or misinterpretations of customs that had nothing to do with cannibalism, such as preserving enemy skulls as war trophies or sharpening the front teeth for aesthetic or erotic purposes. Still, some tribes in the eastern Congo seem to have consumed the bodies of those killed in battle. Indeed, some Belgian colonial officers resigned themselves to tolerating the practice, even going so far as to claim it was useful and hygienic. None of the usual reasons for skepticism about these Congolese accounts are present, since they were recorded only in confidential diaries or in letters to discreet intimates (because the cannibal tribes were military allies of the Belgians).[17]

Other instances of culinary cannibalism have been documented by archaeology in places where, according to ethnographic sources, it was supposedly absent. In the American Southwest, for example, twenty-five sites containing cannibalized human remains have been found.[18] These assemblages of disarticulated human bones share a number of features: butchering cut-marks, skulls broken, long bones smashed for marrow extraction, bones burned or otherwise cooked, and disposal with other "kitchen" refuse. At these sites, the treatment of the human bones suspected to represent the remains of cannibal consumption are comparable in almost every respect with the remains of nonhuman food animals. Almost all these occurrences are dated to Pueblo II and III times (A.D. 900–1300), which were periods when droughts appear to have been frequent. The intensively studied remains from Mancos show various pathologies indicative of nutritional deficiencies. Cannibalism in the prehistoric Southwest involved too thorough a consumption of bodies to be merely ritual; instances seem to be too common to represent simple survival cannibalism, and yet they seem to occur when other foods might well have been scarce. Given the very fragmentary condition of the skeletons and the numerous traumas inflicted on them in the course of their consumption, it is usually difficult to tell whether violence accompanied the victims' deaths. At one site, the rib of one victim had a projectile point embedded in it; at several sites, the cannibalism and some destruction of structures seem to have been contemporaneous. No one analyzing these bones has uncovered any evidence that the victims died nonviolently, and most analysts accept these cases as indications of intergroup violence.

Another unexpected case comes from the Early Neolithic (3000–4000 B.C.) of southern France.[19] Several concentrations of disarticulated human bones were found at Fontébregoua Cave, showing all of the characteristics noted for the American Southwest cases. Several other plausible cases in Europe date to the Bronze Age and the Early Iron Age. Thus, except perhaps for material from Oceania, the best documented and most unequivocal archaeological evidence of culinary cannibalism comes from two areas—southern France and the American Southwest—never suspected of the practice on historical or ethnographic grounds. Perhaps this very absence of suspicion impelled the archaeologists working there to be exceptionally thorough in their documentation and arguments.

Finally, there is the celebrated controversy over cannibalism in the Aztec empire, which Marvin Harris refers to as the only "cannibal state." The argument of some cultural materialists is that the primary goal of Aztec warfare was to capture enemy soldiers for sacrifice and cannibal consumption because densely populated central Mexico had few other sources of animal protein.[20] Their critics claim variously that Aztec warfare was motivated only by a religious desire to capture victims for sacrifice to the gods, that cannibalism was only of the ritual variety and made an insignificant contribution to the diet, or that other sources of sufficient protein did exist. There can be little doubt that the Aztecs annually sacrificed large numbers of war captives in their great temples and that parts of these victims' bodies were eaten. There were even special recipes for human stews. But the number of such victims, even if they had been completely consumed (which they were not), would not have yielded much protein for such a large population. And if obtaining meat was the object of Aztec warfare, why were only sacrificed captives eaten, and not the bodies of enemies killed on the battlefield? Archaeological excavation of the central temple complex in Mexico City has uncovered ample evidence of human sacrifice but none yet of cannibalism—perhaps because the temple precincts were not where the bodies were consumed.[21] Even if future excavations should turn up abundant evidence of cannibalism, the debate will probably continue, since it principally concerns the motive for Aztec warfare: Did the Aztecs go to war because they were obeying the dictates of their religion to capture victims for sacrifice or because they needed meat?

Both sides in this debate seem to have ignored the fact that during the century before Cortés, the Aztecs created their great conquest empire by using a very familiar form of warfare leading eventually to the seizure of land and subjugation of enemy societies as tributaries. The most useful spoils the Aztec empire gained by war were an enlarged territory and more taxpayers. As Barry Isaac concludes, the capture of sacrificial victims was "secondary or even incidental" to the political and economic goals of the Aztec ruling elite—however important it may have been to the prestige of the individual Aztec soldier.[22]

Ritual consumption of parts of a foe's body was very widely distributed, if not exactly common. The parts consumed included brains, hearts, livers, bits of flesh, and the ashes from various parts mixed with a beverage.[23] The purposes given are highly various, but common ones include to humiliate the enemy, to absorb his courage or spirit, to take spiritual as well as corporeal revenge. For example, Zulu warriors drank a soup made from selected "powerful" parts (penis, rectum, right forearm, breastbone, and so on) of a victim as a "strengthening" for battle. In the Solomon Islands, warriors drank blood from the severed head of raid victims to increase their spiritual power, or *mana*. Many groups in the Americas ate the hearts of slain enemies to absorb the latters' courage or to achieve an extended form of revenge. The frequency with which similar practices have been reported around the world is evidence that, while hardly the norm, ritual consumption of some part of enemy corpses was by no means rare in prestate warfare.

The case of Polynesians of the Marquesas Islands offers a warning that distinctions among ritual, culinary, and starvation cannibalism may sometimes reflect only the difference between the natives' distorted memories and the more objective circumstantial evidence recovered by archaeology. According to the accounts given by Marquesans to missionaries and ethnographers, they ate only small pieces of enemy flesh or merely mixed the juices from these pieces in other food, and did so purely for revenge. In ethnographic terms, the Marquesans would then be classified as ritual cannibals. But archaeological data from several Marquesan sites indicate that the scale of cannibalism was large and that its practice increased as certain other sources of animal protein declined and the human population expanded.[24] This evidence strongly suggests that, rather than being consumed in token quantities for ritualistic purposes, human meat was replacing overexploited and disappearing sea mammals, birds, and sea turtles in the Marquesan diet. In this case at least, the lines between starvation, ritual, and culinary cannibalism seem indistinct.

It is clear, then, that the consumption of enemies corpses has occurred in the warfare of several tribes and chiefdoms. Yet, to paraphrase Harris, victorious *states* may have ruthlessly exploited the vanquished, but, with the exception of the Aztecs, they have never actually consumed them.

LOOTING AND DESTRUCTION

Besides lives, property and means of production are lost in wars. In this regard, prestate warfare differs not a whit from its civilized counterpart—invaders the world over have commonly plundered portable food stores, livestock, and valuables; burned houses and crops; destroyed fences and field systems.[25] Plunder of food stores and gardens was very widespread practice in the Americas, Polynesia, New Guinea, and Africa and could leave an enemy facing starvation. When livestock was plundered, it was usually the species that—whatever its practical functions—symbolized or represented wealth: horses among the Plains tribes; pigs in highland New Guinea; camels among the Bedouin; cattle among East Africa tribesmen and among the ancient Germans and Celts of Europe. Often what could not be carried away was destroyed. When the Nuer of the Sudan raided Dinka villages, besides stealing cattle, they destroyed grain stores and standing crops; severe famine could result. In New Guinea, Tahiti, and the Marquesas, invaders would even girdle or chop down the nut and wild fruit trees in an enemy's territory. In a typical Mae Enga interclan war, about 5 to 10 percent of the total housing of either side was destroyed. Mae Enga houses were substantial productions, so the destruction of so many represented a severe blow. Very valuable and difficult-to-replace canoes would be smashed or burned by raiders on the Pacific Northwest Coast and in Polynesia. The destruction of villages and gardens was so thorough in the Cauca Valley of Colombia that warfare there was described as "a fight for annihilation, carried out by every available means." Such looting and vandalism commonly rendered the afflicted territory temporarily uninhabitable.

In civilized wars, because modern states have larger territories, redundant transportion networks, and a broad margin of productivity above the bare subsistence level, years of destruction and blockade may be necessary to reduce one to starvation. But, as previously noted, prestate societies, had small territories and much slimmer margins of productivity. Primitive social units could be reduced to a famine footing by the consequences of a few days of raiding or even of a single surprise attack. Because the infrastructure and logistics of small-scale societies were more vulnerable to looting and destruction, the use of these methods was almost universal in primitive warfare. And the economic injuries inflicted tended to be more deeply felt and slower to heal.

Looting and vandalism are difficult to document archaeologically. For example, looted goods cannot be distinguished from similar items acquired by peaceful means. A burned dwelling leaves a very obvious archaeological signature, but vandalism is not suspected unless the destruction is accompanied by other evidence of violence. Despite these limitations, archaeologists have uncovered many examples of war-related destruction of settlements from the best-studied regions of the world.

The massacre of their inhabitants and burning of prehistoric villages along the Missouri River in South Dakota have been mentioned in a previous chapter. In some regions of the American Southwest, the violent destruction of prehistoric settlements is well documented and during some periods was even common.[26] These instances of destruction are often correlated in time and space with the fortification or relocation of settlements to more defensible positions and sometimes with evidence of cannibalism. For example, the large pueblo at Sand Canyon in Colorado, although protected by a defensive wall, was almost entirely burned; artifacts in the rooms had been deliberately smashed; and bodies of some victims were left lying on the floors. After this catastrophe in the late thirteenth century, the pueblo was never reoccupied. The pueblo of Kuaua in New Mexico was plundered and destroyed around 1400, and the site was abandoned about that time and not reoccupied until seventy-five years later. In addition to the stormed and burned British Neolithic causewayed camps mentioned in Chapter 1, a number of similarly destroyed settlements have been found in western Europe and the Near East, dating to the later Neolithic, Copper, and Bronze Ages.[27]

In the early days of World War II, Britain's air minister refused to let the Royal Air Force bomb German arms factories because they were private property. Obviously, prestate warriors had much more in common with General Sherman than this English ninny.[28] Except in geographical scale, tribal warfare could be and often was total war in every modern sense. Like states and empires, smaller societies can make a desolation and call it peace.

TERRITORIAL ACQUISITION AND LOSS

One of the most persistent myths about primitive warfare is that it did not change boundaries because it was not motivated by territorial demand. This whole question has become muddied by the propensity of "idealists" to transmute intentions or causes into effects—that is, if warriors said that they were not fighting for land or booty, then the spoils that accrued to them must be insubstantial and irrelevant. The idealists' opponents, the "materialists," make exactly the reverse mistake: they claim that because economic benefits were gained by victorious warriors, these gains must be what they were really fighting for, despite their declarations to the contrary. This amounts to mistaking an effect for a cause. Of course, few tribal groups ever admitted they were fighting for territory (the Mae Enga were a rare exception to this rule). Like modern and ancient states, they invariably claimed to be fighting to avenge or redress various wrongs: murders, broken trade or marriage contracts, abduction of women, poaching, or theft. But the victors nevertheless acquired more territory or choice resources with striking regularity, albeit (like the British Empire) "in a fit of absent-mindedness."

Indeed, several cross-cultural surveys of preindustrial societies found that losses and gains of territory were a very frequent result of warfare.[29] One study concluded that the victors "almost always take land or other resources from the defeated." In another study, almost half of the societies surveyed had gained or lost territory through warfare. In some cases, societies lost land to one enemy while gaining it from another. Over 75 percent of the wars of the Mae Enga of New Guinea ended with the victors appropriating part or all of their enemy's territory.[30] In other words, territorial change was a very common outcome of primitive wars.

Two wars fought by the Wappo hunter-gatherers of California illustrate both the intentional and the unintentional territorial windfalls resulting from tribal warfare.[31] Six village communities of the Southern Pomo occupied a portion of the Alexander Valley (now renowned for its wine) along the Russian River, but their upstream neighbors were a village community of tough Wappo (whose name is an Anglo corruption of the Spanish *guapo*, meaning, in this case, "brave"). About 1830, some Pomo made the mistake of stealing an acorn cache from a Wappo oak grove. The Wappo immediately retaliated with two raids, killing a large number of Pomo and burning the offending village. All of the Pomo from the six Alexander Valley villages fled to other Pomo settlements downstream. The headman of the Pomo village cluster later exchanged gifts with his Wappo counterpart and settled the dispute. The Pomo were then invited to reoccupy their villages, but they refused. These changes at least temporarily widened the distance between the nearest Russian River Valley Wappo and Pomo villages from one to about ten miles. In the few years remaining before their decimation by disease and war with Mexican settlers, the Wappo occupied two of the six abandoned Pomo villages and had begun seasonally exploiting much of the relinquished area.

More than twenty years earlier, another group of Wappo had established themselves, by unknown means, in Pomo territory farther north on a small creek flowing into Clear Lake. These Wappo were dissatisfied because a delectable minnow spawned from the lake up a Pomo-held creek whose lower course ran only a few yards from their own minnowless stream. After digging a canal to divert the waters of the Pomo's creek into their own, the Wappo dammed the latter, apparently hoping by these activities to force the spawning fish to use their stream. With this provocation, their Pomo neighbors determined to fight, and a battle broke out along the course of the deputed creek. After some losses, the Wappo were driven back to their still-minnowless creek.

In both cases, as was typical in aboriginal California, disputes over food resources precipitated the fighting. In one case, the Wappo were merely fighting to defend their rights to enjoy the produce of a particular acorn grove, but the fierceness of their response (and probably previous conflicts) convinced the Pomo to put some unoccupied territory between themselves and their fractious neighbors. The depopulated area was then exploited and slowly settled by the victors. This pattern of abandoning territory out of fear in order to widen a buffer zone, followed by gradually intensified use of the zone by the victors, illustrates the most common mechanism by which primitive warfare expanded and contracted the domains of prestate societies. In the Clear Lake case, the Wappo were obviously attempting to take control, if not actual possession, of a desirable stream and were driven back. Had the Wappo been victorious in the Clear Lake fight, the creek would undoubtedly have been added to the Wappo domain of exploitation. In neither case were the combatants fighting over land per se; rather they were fighting over spatially fixed resources.

As Figure 7.1 shows, the scale of such territorial gains and losses could be very significant—about 5 to 10 percent per generation in some instances involving hunter-gatherers. This would be equivalent to the United States losing or gaining California, Oregon, and half of Washington every twenty-five years. The rates of expansion and contraction among agriculturalists and pastoralists tended to be even higher. In one New Guinea case, the Telefolmin tribe more than tripled its territory in less than a century by means of ruthless warfare and

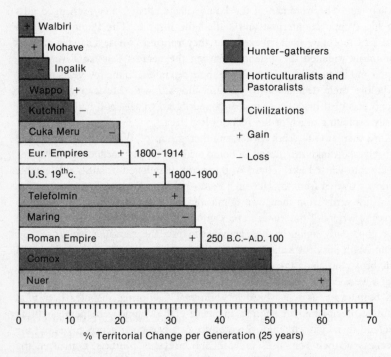

Figure 7.1 Relative territorial gains and losses per generation for various societies (see Appendix, Table 7.1).

virtual annihilation of the tribe's enemies. By relentlessly raiding its Dinka neighbors, rather than by pursuing any conscious campaign or plan, the Nuer tribe of the Sudan expanded its domain from 8,700 to 35,000 square miles in just seventy years. Comparable examples of territorial acquisition and loss as an effect of warfare are recorded from every major ethnographic region of the world.[32] These primitive rates of territorial change are proportionately similar to the extraordinary expansion rates of European empires and the United States during the nineteenth century, or of the growth of the Roman Empire. In this sense, tribal warfare against other prestate societies appears to have been just as effective as civilized war at moving boundaries and rewarding victors with vital territory appropriated from the losers.

Given the aversion of modern archaeology to the idea of migration and colonization (let alone conquest), the problem of documenting such processes in prehistory is difficult. One archaeologist who has given considerable thought to this problem, Slavomil Vencl, admits that annihilation or forced migration would be manifested in the archaeological record only by the "peaceful existence of winners on the territory of the losers."[33] He gives as an example the victory of the Germanic Marcomanni over the Celtic Boii (from whom the region became known as Bohemia), recorded by Roman historians. Archaeologically, this event is evidenced only by the expansion of Germanic settlements and cemeteries into regions previously inhabited by Celts. An additional difficulty, as we have seen in the ethnographic cases, is that many violent territorial exchanges involve social units that are nearly identical in culture and physique. Prehistory is replete with examples of very distinctive cultures (sometimes associated with distinct human physical types) expanding at the expense of others, but determining whether these expansions were accomplished violently or peacefully is usually no simple task. Several regions of the world offer evidence that at least some prehistoric colonizations or abandonments of regions were accompanied by considerable violence.[34] These most visible prehistoric cultural expansions, which involve the movement of a frontier, are discussed in more detail in Chapter 9.

As we have seen, even in situations where no territory exchanges hands, active hostilities along a border can lead to development of a no-man's-land, as settlements nearest an enemy move or disperse to escape the effects of persistent raiding. Such buffer zones have been reported from Africa, North America, South America, and Oceania.[35] As in the Wappo–Pomo case, encroachment on these zones by the stronger, more land-hungry, or more aggressive adversary was a common mechanism by which tribal warfare led to the exhange of territory, even in the absence of any clear design. The width of these no-man's-lands varied with population density.[36] High-density economies could afford to concede only a small amount of land to such low-intensity use and had a limited capacity to settle elsewhere refugees who fled such zones. Moreover, the higher the settlement density, the more eyes there were to watch for raids, the more rapid the communication of alarms became, and the more quickly local forces and allies could respond to incursions. Thus no-man's-lands tended to shrink with increasing human density because they became more costly economically to create and because the security belt they provided was less necessary.

Where population density was high, these buffer zones were measured in hundreds of meters, as in highland New Guinea. Where density was lower, their width stretched to tens of kilometers, as in the more lightly populated areas of the Americas or in the dry savannas of Africa. Although such buffer zones could function ecologically as game and timber preserves, they were risky to use even for hunting and woodcutting because small isolated parties or individuals could easily be ambushed in them.

Whatever their stated purposes in going to war, tribal groups, like civilized ones, were not averse to accepting the spoils of war—which usually included valuable goods and often land. Andrew Vayda, one of anthropology's most distinguished students of primitive warfare, decries the obscurantism of certain distinguished social scientists who (in contrasting primitive and civilized war) ignore the essential similarities—"as, for example, the fact that both types of warfare can result in territorial conquests and the redistribution of population."[37]

EIGHT

Crying Havoc

The Question of Causes

Not all societies are continually at war, nor are all wars equally terrible. As we have established, warfare is not a constant feature of human social life. It follows that explanations of these differences in warfare must focus on the *variable* characteristics and circumstances of human existence, not on constants of human biology and behavior.

THE MOTIVES FOR AND CAUSES OF NONSTATE WARFARE

As was noted in Chapter 1, some social scientists have asserted that the fundamental difference between primitive war and real, or civilized, war lies in the realm of motives and causes: real war is motived by economic and political goals (such as more territory or conquest), whereas primitive conflict is directed only toward fulfilling the personal and psychological aims of individual warriors (such as revenge or prestige). But the question of what motivates an individual or a group to engage in warfare is a vexing one. Should all of the individual motives expressed by active participants be considered? Should only the motives that are publicly declared by decision makers or deliberative bodies (kings, chiefs, councils, palavers, and so on) be taken into account? Should any motive *declared* by anyone be considered? Should motives be inferred from the operations, results, and effects of specific wars or acts of war? Are some causes of war independent of individual and collective motives—for example, droughts or crop failures?

A huge historical literature is devoted to the causes of modern wars and the explanations offered are often very complicated. For instance, many books have been devoted to the question of what caused World War I. Suggested factors include imperial and naval rivalries, diplomatic miscalculations and delusions, the Kaiser's withered arm, the conflicting ambitions of Austria and Russia in the Balkans, France's hunger to revenge its defeat in the Franco-Prussian War, and complicated alliances—all to explain how the murder of an Austrian prince by a Serbian terrorist could set off a global conflagration. Consider, too, the differences in opinion over rationalizations, causes, and motives for specific wars between adversaries such as the Union and the Confederacy, Japan and the United States, Iraq and the U.N. coalition. If civilized wars have multiple causes and mixed motives, why should we assume that wars in tribal societies, where there are no centralized governments or voluminous records, can accurately be reduced to a single and unmixed motive? Let us now turn to what ethnography tells us about the declared motives and causes of primitive wars.

No other aspect of primitive warfare has been the focus of more ethnological discussion than its causes.[1] But these discussions generally lead to quandaries like those that attend investigations of the causes of civilized wars. Confusion often arises between individual and collective motives, or among efficient, formal, and final causes. The declared motives and aims of participants often fail to conform to those inferred by external observers. The material or social conditions that invite conflict may exist for long periods of time, while outbreaks of war occur only at specific instants. Similar grievances or disputes between two parties may be resolved without violence in some instances but lead to war on other occasions. Given such ambiguities, it is difficult to understand why some anthropologists have so emphasized motive in distinguishing primitive from civilized war.

A schematic account of the antecedents of one war among the Jalemo of New Guinea, recorded by the ethnographer Klaus Koch, illustrates the problems inherent in specifying causes and motives.[2] Because the names of the two villages involved are so long, unpronounceable, and similar-sounding, I have replaced them with village A and village B. Village A owed village B a pig as reward for B's help in a previous war in which the latter had killed one of A's enemies. Meanwhile, a man from village A heard some (untrue) gossip that a man from village B had seduced his young wife; so, with the aid of a relative, he assaulted the alleged seducer. Village B then "overreacted" to this beating by making two separate raids on village A, wounding a man and a woman. The unpaid debt was acknowledged by both sides as the reason for village B's disproportionate reaction. These two raids by village B led to a general battle in which several warriors on both sides were wounded, but no one was killed. At this point, with casualties about equal, both sides agreed to suspend the fighting with an indefinite truce. The truce ended later that evening, however, when a warrior from village B, to avenge a wound suffered by one of his kinsmen during the battle, ambushed and wounded a village A resident. The following day battle was resumed, and a B villager was killed. After this death, the war became general: all the warriors of both villages, plus various allies, began a series of battles and ambushes that continued intermittently for the next two years. Now which of these grievances and injuries motivated or caused this war? Was it an unpaid debt, sexual jealousy, or revenge? Which of the series of injuries was the precipitating or proximate cause of the war?

Two of the cross-cultural surveys mentioned in Chapter 2 attempted to tabulate information on motives and causes, but exactly whose motives or views of cause are recorded is unclear.[3] Despite these ambiguities, the results of these two independent studies are remarkably similar. Both sets of data indicate that the predominant motives for prestate warfare are revenge for homicides and various economic issues.[4] The precise character of such economic motives differs tremendously, depending on the focal economies of the groups involved.[5] In New Guinea, for example, where gardening and pig rearing are important, thefts of pigs and of garden produce or pigs' depredations of gardens, figure prominently as causes of conflict. In California, where tribes depended heavily on gathering wild plant foods and on hunting or fishing, conflicts over resource poaching were very common. Horses were usually the focus of fighting among the historic Plains Indians for whom these became an essential means of transportation and hunting. On the salmon-dependent Pacific Northwest Coast, tribes not infrequently warred over river and ocean frontage. In Minnesota, the Chippewa fought for over 150 years with the Dakota Sioux over use of hunting territories and wild-rice fields. The cattle-herding tribes of East Africa usually fought over livestock. At every level of social organization and with every type of economy, there are instances of fighting over territory. For example, the Walbiri hunter-gatherers of Australia fought a neighboring group for possession of a water hole, and the Mae Enga horticulturists of New Guinea quarreled primarily over land. The impulse to enhance prestige and to serve other personal motives—supposedly especially characteristic of primitive war—figures much less commonly in the tabulations. Indeed, the data in one of the surveys show that the prestige motive is actually more commonly associated with higher levels of political centralization (that is, chiefdoms and states) than with band or tribes.[6]

The only motive completely absent from most tribal societies is that of subjugation and tribute. Polities that lack the physical power to subjugate their own populations or to extract involuntary tribute or taxes from them are extremely unlikely to make war against others for these purposes, since they lack the institutional and administrative means to convert victory into hegemony or taxation. Instead, decentralized societies focus on pacifying dangerous neighbors by intimidation, expulsion, or annihilation and on acquiring additional food, valuables, labor, and territory by the direct methods of plunder, capture, and physical expulsion. A complex chiefdom or state can accomplish all these goals simultaneously by conquest. For states, then, *subjugation* is merely a rubric that subsumes disparate goals of defense, revenge, economic, and territorial gain; but tribal societies, by their very nature, cannot fight for subjugation and all that it implies. Once this fundamental difference is taken into account, the cross-cultural studies indicate that the motives and goals in warfare of both states and nonstates are substantially the same and that economic motives predominate in both categories.

As we discuss in greater detail later in this chapter, tribal peoples have sometimes used continual military harassment to extract a kind of tribute from and even impose a weak degree of subjugation on another group.[7] For example, in pre-Columbian times, some nomadic Mbaya bands so harrassed Guaná farmers of the South American Gran Chaco that the latter bought peace by offering a kind of annual tribute. Every year at harvest time, a Mbaya band would spend a few days in its "subject" Guaná village, feasting and receiving its annual tribute. Since the Mbaya chiefs also gave "gifts" to their Guaná subjects, this interaction might be seen as a kind of enforced or extorted trade. The Mbaya also protected their "subjects" from inroads by other predatory semi-nomadic tribes. While none of these instances strictly qualifies as subjugation, they bear more than a passing resemblance to the protection schemes and extortion rackets exercised by urban gangsters, rural brigands, and pirates in civilized societies. Thus exploitative or unequal symbiotic relationships did arise among some tribal peoples, but whether this was the goal for which they initially fought is unclear.

The precipitating causes of most wars—primitive and civilized—are acts of violence that provoke further violence in immediate defense or subsequent retaliation. In preliterate societies, the original killing or attack that instigated a cycle of revenge may be lost in the mists of traditional enmities, but the latest violence by the other side provides ample immediate justification for further hostilities. In ethnographic accounts of the disputes that led to wars in nonstate societies, some nonviolent offenses—such as poaching, adultery, and theft—

prompted an immediate violent response. But other offenses—or the same ones under other circumstances—were resolved without bloodshed or at least without causing a war.[8] It was extremely rare, however, for an intergroup killing not to lead to warfare or feuding; the victim's group invariably held the perpetrator's group collectively responsible for the death and the latter invariably shielded the perpetrator from retribution.

It is interesting how commonly the grievances that provoked violence were economic in character. Even disputes over women often had an economic element—as we will see later. Declaring that primitive wars were fought primarily in defense or in retaliation focuses on only the most immediate or proximate causes and ignores the economic disputes underlying them. In contrast, similar economic and political disputes in civilized settings receive primary attention, whereas the "acts of war" that precipitate the fighting are treated as mere consequences.

Because archaeologists are constrained to infer human motives from circumstantial evidence, they are less likely than ethnographers and historians to become mired in hopeless efforts to extract from the statements and records of combatants the motives and causes behind wars and warfare. Perhaps the silence of archaeological evidence concerning this issue is a blessing, since it may liberate archaeologists from toiling at an impossible task. A more fruitful approach for all students of warfare may be to examine the subject using the more colorless archaeological concepts of context and association. The first of these involves isolating the general situations and circumstances in which wars are more common and warfare is more bitter. Associations are social, economic, and technological features that commonly co-occur (that is, are significantly correlated) with frequent, intense warfare. Such contexts and associations might include geographical or ecological circumstances, certain dynamics of human populations, technological change, social structure, and ideology.

POPULATION DENSITY AND PRESSURE

Since 1798, when Thomas Malthus published his famous *Essay on the Principle of Population*, it has been commonly assumed that violent conflicts must increase in frequency and intensity as human populations grow in size and density. The oldest and most direct argument supporting this idea is that of Malthus himself, who saw increasing population density as meaning more mouths to feed from a fixed or limited territory. In modern jargon, this dynamic process is called "population pressure on critical resources." As this pressure increases, more people must compete for the same resources and must fight to retain or acquire them, or starve. As we saw in Chapter 7, possession of such means of production is a typical spoil of war, whether the societies involved are civilized states or foraging bands. Along with famine and disease, Malthus saw war as one of the standard consequences of overpopulation.

Modern social scientists have suggested two other reasons why increasing population density should lead to more warfare. One is a proposition in social algebra: when human numbers increase arithmetically, potential disputes increase geometrically. More conflicts are likely to arise among a thousand people than among a dozen because there are more people to argue with. Even if only a tiny proportion of all such disputes lead to bloodshed, violence should increase as density climbs. An inexact analogy might be a table of moving billiard balls: the more balls, the more potential collisions. Some biologically inclined scholars have asserted a similarity between humans and other animals, especially rats, in their reaction to "crowding stress."[9] In some experiments, rats evidenced increased levels of fighting and killing as population densities increased, even though food remained plentiful. Whatever the precise mechanism envisioned, the idea that the intensity of warfare is a function of human numbers has become widely accepted.

Cross-cultural comparisons, however, do not support this proposition. Indeed, two cross-cultural samples of societies indicate that absolutely no correlation exists between the frequency of warfare and the density of human population.[10] Groups with densities of less than one person per square mile are just as likely to engage in warfare each year as groups whose densities are hundreds of times higher. The war death rates discussed in Chapter 6 likewise reveal no relationship between these measures of the intensity of warfare and the area's population density. For example, the Piegan Indians of the Great Plains, with a density of only one person per 30 square miles, had the same casualty rate as the Grand Valley Dani of New Guinea, whose population density was nearly 10,000 times higher. The proportion of male deaths due to warfare for the Murngin Aborigines of northern Australia was about the same as that of the Dugum Dani, whose population density was 3,000 times greater. Homicide rates also bear no obvious relationship to the density of humans. To give a civilized example, the homicide rate of Britain in the thirteenth century was thirty times greater than its present one, although its population density has increased by a factor of ten during that period.[11] In the broadest view, the frequency of warfare and violence is simply not a consequence of human density or crowding. However striking the images, human beings are neither rats packed in a cage nor irascible billiard balls jostling on a table.

But the type of population pressure that Malthus envisioned cannot be measured by simple density, since available food resources vary with ecology and technology. One person per 10 square miles may be an extraordinarily high population density in arctic tundra but an extremely rarefied one in tropical savanna. And the quantity of food produced from a given piece of ground by farmers who possess the technology to deep plow, fertilize with chemicals or manure, and irrigate exceeds that produced by dibble-stick, long-fallow, dry farming. Primitive farmers experienced land shortages and famines at far lower population densities than do their modern counterparts. Because so many factors—latitude, rainfall, soils, forest cover, biodiversity, energy input, and general technology—must be considered, making comparisons on the basis of "equivalent" population densities is extremely difficult.

Some limited comparisons can be made between societies with similar technologies and economies that live in the same general region, but since these focus on a few specific examples, they risk missing or misrepresenting the general pattern. In highland New Guinea, the percentages of deaths due to warfare of the more populous Dani and Mae Enga are significantly higher than those of the lower-density Huli. In northwestern California, the lower-density Yurok apparently had a lower annual casualty rate than did the higher-density Cahto. Among the Yanomamo peoples of South America, the higher-density Shamatari have had a significantly higher proportion of war deaths than the lower-density Namowei-teri.[12] In tropical northern Australia, though, the lower-density Murngin had a higher casualty rate than the more populous Tiwi.

As was noted in Chapter 2, some of the most peaceful nonstate societies in the world had very low population densities, as in the Great Basin of North America, the Western Desert of Australia, and the dense jungles of Malaysia and central Africa. Most of these peaceable groups prevented intergroup disputes and conflicts from escalating into armed violence by fleeing from their potential adversaries. But this option can be exercised only under conditions where possessions are portable and essential resources, however scarce, are widely distributed. Merely having a low population density is not sufficient—a fact underscored by our previous point that some groups living at extremely low population densities were quite violent. From such comparisons, it appears that some relationship may exist between population pressure and the intensity of warfare, but this relationship is either very complex or very weak or both. Because modern civilized states seem to go to war less frequently and to suffer proportionately fewer deaths as a result than did many primitive societies, it is at least theoretically possible that as human population density increases, the frequency of warfare and percentage of war casualties actually decline.

Admittedly, some sense of crowding may play a role in warfare, but it is usually relative—not only to the raw ecological productivity of a territory and to subsistence technology, but also to expectations and values. We have seen how commonly wars erupt when one group "crowds" another, by trespassing on its gathering plots, its fallow fields, its gardens or its women. The injured parties in such cases may fight because they feel the need to uphold their rights or because they regard such acts as representing the camel's nose in the tent—not because their survival or health is immediately threatened. For example, many California tribes often granted outsiders the right to exploit their gathering and hunting grounds when they were properly asked or rewarded with gifts; yet they would fight any group that poached (that is, hunted, gathered, or fished without permission or reciprocation). Conversely, the trespassers in many cases of crowding were not driven to commit their offenses by the cries of their hungry families or by sexual deprivation. For example, many Inuit murders and feuds focused on women, even though wife sharing was a common practice and a convention of Inuit hospitality. Of course, some wars were indeed undertaken by groups for whom a failure to fight would have meant famine or extinction; but many wars were fought to establish control over essential resources, rather than exclusive use or absolute possession of them. In some regions, the degree of ownership or control exercised over resource locations was correlated with population density.[13] Thus some higher-density groups were more likely to assert such rights and touchier about trespassing. But since conflicts over resource locations were not the only kind of war, and since groups for whom the concept of ownership did not extend beyond personal and household equipment also had frequent wars, increasing density may have changed the contexts for war but not necessarily its incidence. The only reasonable expectation to be drawn from ethnographic data is therefore that warring societies are equally common and peaceable ones equally uncommon at any level of population density.

Archaeologists, then, should be alert for signs of warfare whether the population density of their prehistoric subjects seems low or high. They should not assume (as many do) that violent conflicts could reach significant levels only when regional densities and social complexity increased to a certain threshold. In some notable archaeological cases, in fact, an increase in human density and social complexity has not been accompanied by any increase in violence.[14] The Near Eastern Levant sustained a large growth in both regional or local human density and the sedentism of foraging communities between 13,000 and 11,000 years ago—a change recorded as the development of Natufian culture from the earlier Geometric Kebaran. Not only is there no evidence of an increase in warfare during this period, but there are no indications of warfare at all. In a contrary case, the last Mesolithic hunter-gatherers of central Europe (ca. 7500 years ago), whose density is estimated to have been quite low and whose way of life was rather nomadic, seem to have been quite violent, perhaps even headhunters. Prehistoric examples such as these show that the association between human density and the intensity of warfare was as complex or weak in prehistory as in the ethnographic record.

Increasing human population densities are highly correlated with greater social and economic complexity, including such features as more complex labor-intensive technologies, labor specialization, concentration and redistribution of food surpluses by centralized leadership, and a host of other innovations that permit larger numbers to be supported from the same resource base.[15] The larger, more efficient social units that result develop social and political mechanisms for resolving or suppressing violent conflicts between their members. In a reversal of social algebra, the outcome is fewer social units and fewer possible violent disputes. To return to the billiard-ball analogy, it is as though when more balls are added to the table, they merely merge into larger balls so that the rate of collision remains constant or even declines. In addition, deciding to go to war, concentrating supplies, and mobilizing men are more difficult and complicated tasks for larger societies than for smaller ones. In a small tribe, mobilization for a raid may require no more than a dozen willing recruits, each equipped with a small supply of food, and can be accomplished in a few hours. Weeks or even months may be needed to mobilize and equip the army of a chief or a king. This may be one reason why states seem to resort to war somewhat less frequently than do smaller-scale societies. The issue of whether increasing human population density is the efficient cause or merely an effect of social and economic evolution is extremely controversial among anthropologists and archaeologists, but it is clear that these variables are very closely associated. In other words, increasing population density is the mother or handmaiden of organization and invention, not the father of war.

TRADING AND RAIDING

One common assumption made by many people concerning the contexts for war and peace is that if societies are exchanging goods and marriage partners with one another, relations between them are likely to remain peaceful. This assumption underlies the often-voiced opinion that increasing trade and "cultural exchanges" between otherwise hostile nations will lessen the chances of war. This attitude reflects some social anthropological observations about what has been called the trade–raid opposition. Following the lead of the great French structuralist anthropologist Claude Lévi-Strauss, anthropologists have characterized trading and raiding as structurally opposed forms of social relations: "war is exchange gone bad, and exchange is a war averted."[16] In a brief time frame, this statement is generally true: the exchange of goods or voluntary intermarriage cannot very well take place while active hostilities are in progress. But in the longer term, assuming that intertribal exchanges of goods or intermarriage preclude warfare is a mistake.

In the modern civilized world, exchange partners commonly become periodic enemies. Historical research has found that "disputes between trading partners escalate to war more frequently than disputes between nations that do not trade much with each other."[17] A classic twentieth-century example of this phenomenon is Japan. In this century, Japan's most important trading partner has been the United States—earlier in the century primarily as a source of essential materials for basic industry and, after World War II, also as a market for finished products. Yet it was against its largest prewar market for goods, China, and its most important source of raw material, the United States, that Japan embarked on its most disastrous war. In the same way, major shipments of grain, oil, and strategic metals poured into Nazi Germany from the Soviet Union right up to the moment the Wehrmacht invaded. Nor should we forget the close network of intermarriages and blood relationships that existed among the royal families of the belligerents in World War I. Countless examples from the primitive world demonstrate that these civilized instances are not just modern aberrations.

Ethnographers have frequently encountered tribes that intermarried and traded with one another but were also periodically at war.[18] For example, the several Eskimo tribes of the Kotzebue Sound region of Alaska took part each year in a cheerful midsummer "trade fair" at Sheshalik. Besides intergroup exchange, there were intertribal feasts, dances, athletic contests, and exhibitions of magic by shamans. But the trade and these festivities did not in any way lessen the chances of war between the participants: "some of the same people who participated peacefully in the Sheshalik Fair in July could be trying to annihilate one another the following November." Similar combinations of trade, marriage, and war between two groups within the same year also occurred in Canada and in other parts of Alaska, including relations between traditionally hostile Eskimo and Indian bands. The bellicose Tupinamba of coastal Brazil made periodic truces with their inland enemies, during which they traded coastal goods for inland commodities, such that one ethnohistorian speaks of "cycles of war and commerce" between hostile groups in this region. When the Sioux came to trade at Hidatsa villages along the Upper Missouri, a truce was in force only within sight of the villages; once the nomads passed out of sight by climbing over the bluffs, they might steal horses or kill Hidatsa and were themselves subject to attack. The Mae Enga of New Guinea asserted, "We marry the people we fight." Indeed, one very delicate battlefield task facing warriors in many New Guinea groups was how to avoid spilling the blood of in-laws fighting on the enemy side. Since intermarriage between hostile Kikuyu and Masai tribes in Kenya was not uncommon, women traded with their relatives on the other side, even during times of war. Except at the instant of trade, exchanges of marriage partners or commodities and war were by no means mutually exclusive forms of social interaction.[19] Structuralist anthropologists do seem correct in seeing exchange and war as being two sides of the same coin, but the coin could be (and was) flipped frequently.

The major reason why exchange partners and enemies have often been the same people is simple propinquity. We interact most intensely with our nearest neighbors, whether those interactions are commercial, nuptial, or hostile. More intense contact also increases the chance of disputes, some of which can turn violent. However, mere proximity cannot explain why some interactions are benign, why some are violent, or why they are so often both.

As previously mentioned, economic exchanges and intermarriages have been especially rich sources of violent conflict. Primitive exchange was subject to all the defaults and miscarriages that bedevil civilized commerce, as well as some others that were peculiar to premarket economies. In the absence of impartial third-party arbitration or adjudication, disputes involving exchange could and often did escalate into wars.

In most tribal economies, the great bulk of commodities were exchanged through various forms of reciprocity rather than by direct barter or purchase. These types of exchanges involved the mutual giving of "gifts" between individuals or groups. The giver expected a gift of similar value in return, either immediately or at some later time. Failure in this regard could engender a grievance that immediately escalated into warfare (if the commodity involved was especially crucial or valuable) or create a smoldering resentment that predisposed the aggrieved party toward violence at the next pretext or provocation. In tribal societies, failure to reciprocate or to reciprocate fully was equivalent to default or fraud in a more commercial system.

One common source of wars over trade arose when one social group held a monopoly over a particular commodity—usually because the only source lay within its territory.[20] Such monopolies could lead to a premercantile form of price gouging or to envy and resentment on the part of those groups less favored by geography. The two commodities that served almost universally as the foci of such tribal conflicts were hard stone (for tools) and mineral salt. Both were usually available only at rare locations; one was a technological necessity before metallurgy, and the other was a physiological necessity where the diet consisted primarily of plant foods.[21] The Salt Wars fought among several northern California tribes in the early nineteenth century provide a good example of this phenomenon. The territory of the Northeastern or Salt Pomo of northern California included a salt seep that produced a remarkably pure crystalized sodium chloride. Many nearby tribes came to this seep to obtain salt. But although special friends were occasionally allowed to gather salt without payment, the usual procedure was for the salt-gathering party to give gifts—in proportion to the salt taken—to the Salt Pomo for permission to use the seep. When one party of Indians from a neighboring tribe that usually brought gifts tried to gather salt surreptitiously, they were caught by the Salt Pomo and nearly annihilated. This incident and the Salt Pomo's high-handed treatment of some other "customers" touched off a series of wars that continued intermittently over a generation.[22] In the early stages of colonization, European trading posts and settlements constituted similar "point sources" of metal and other useful commodities that could be monopolized by the local tribes. In the Americas, many wars were fought against middleman tribes by "consumer" tribes for direct access to such outposts.[23]

Trade and warfare could also find intimate connection through the not un-common practice of killing and robbing traders or trading parties.[24] Traders could be waylaid by tribes whose territory they were transiting or even by those with whom they had come to trade. Parties to primitive exchanges who yielded to the lure of short-term profits over long-term gains by killing and robbing traders usually found that war had to be included in the balance.

Finally we come to systems of exchange referred to earlier in this chapter: extortion or forcible exchange.[25] For example, the Pueblos of the Rio Grande region of New Mexico "found it advantageous to trade with marauding Co-manches and Navajos, even when they were ill-provisioned, in an effort to avoid crop thefts and wanton destruction." Hopi farmers in Arizona never knew whether approaching Apaches were coming to trade or to raid and plunder. In their uncertainty, they relied on omens: if a rain cloud was sighted in the direction of the approaching Apaches, the Hopi expected trade; but if no clouds were observed, every precaution was taken against a raid. Since their pueblos were essentially oases in a desert and rain clouds were rare, the Hopi seldom must have admitted an Apache party to their mesa top until its peaceful inten-tions were completely established. This fearful expectancy of the Hopi and their relief at finding that their visitors came this time only to trade cannot have hurt the Apaches' chances of getting the corn they wanted at a reasonable price.[26] The implicit threat of raids by the nomadic Plains tribes may have given similar impetus to their trade for corn with the sedentary villagers of the Upper Mis-souri tribes, such as the Mandan, Hidatsa, and Arikara. In a fashion analogous to the relationship in South America between the Mbaya horsemen and the Guaná farmers of the Grand Chaco, the tough Teton Sioux were said to have held Arikara villagers "in a position approaching complete subjugation," obtain-ing gifts of corn from them at regular intervals. These cases and many others may reflect the consequences of the common imbalance between trading part-ners that bedeviled systems of barter. Often one group desperately needed some item from another party; but either it had little that the other party wanted, or the "sellers" had no surplus of the desired item to trade. The temptation to extort what was needed by the threat of violence or to seize it as plunder was very strong in such situations. When raiding became a frequent substitute for trade, as it often did when poorer nomads exchanged goods with richer villagers and townspeople, trade could verge on extortion.

Some rare tribes dropped the pretense of exchange altogether and simply took what they required in raids.[27] For some bands of Mescalero and

Chiricahua Apaches, plunder from raids was the primary source of certain basic commodities. The Tuareg tribesmen of the Sahara took what food they pleased from Arab oasis dwellers and acquired other useful or prestigious goods by raiding caravans. Acquiring some goods, because suppliers were loathe to part with them, necessitated forceful seizure. Slaves were the best example of such "commodities," since ultimately (wherever slavery was practiced) they were drawn from war captives. Few people were so desperate that they would trade away their children and kin, especially knowing the burdens and humiliations of slavery. But once forcibly extracted from the protection of their families and tribes, slaves were freely traded. The wholesale substitution of brigandage and piracy for exchange was unusual, however, probably because paying for goods with human lives was socially expensive and because any augmentations in the strength of one's victims could raise "prices" to unacceptable levels.

If trade often leads to war, marriage—which has usually been as much an economic transaction as a sexual or romantic one—can play a similar role.[28] In addition, intermarriages between social units mean that any difficulties that afflict such unions are likely to cause ill-feeling between the groups concerned. In cultures where young girls were promised to men in other social groups by their fathers, violent disputes occurred when (for various reasons) the bride was not "delivered" when she came of age. Disappointed suitors could take violent exception to their rejection, triggering a war. In situations where payment of the bride-price or dowry was made in installments, failure to deliver a payment as promised could lead to fighting. Spousal abandonment or divorce usually entailed refunding the bride-price or dowry; but since this had often been spent or distributed to others in the meantime, reimbursement was often refused and a war resulted. In some societies, a married woman's lover, when discovered, was expected to reimburse the husband for her bride-price and take the wife as his own. If the lover refused, homicide and war were the common outcome. Among some New Guinea tribes, divorce and adultery were the most usual occasions for war, and violence could erupt even at wedding ceremonies because the bride's family found fault with the bride-price collected. Mistreatment or killing of a wife might be avenged by the wife's brothers or male kinsman, actions that could start a spiral of revenge killings and escalation that ended in wholesale war. Intermarriage is thus no guarantee of peace; like trade, it can be an inducement to war.

The interchangeable character of exchange and war becomes clearer when we consider their ultimate physical results. Trade, intermarriage, and war all have the effect of moving goods and people between social units. In warfare, goods move as plunder, and people (especially women) move as captives. In exchange and intermarriage, goods move as reciprocal gifts, trade items, and bride wealth, whereas people move as spouses. In effect, the same desirable acquisitions are thus attained by alternative (but not mutually exclusive) means. If raiding and trading are two sides of the same coin, the goods and people acquired must be the coin itself.

The fact that exchange and war can have precisely the same results is often forgotten by archaeologists. When exotic goods are found at a site, they are almost invariably interpreted as being evidence of prehistoric exchange. That such items might be the spoils of war seldom occurs to prehistorians, who immediately proceed to plot "trade routes" and try to reconstruct the mechanisms of exchange. For high-volume exotic items with an everday use, like pottery or flakeable stone (for example, obsidian or flint) for tools, these assumptions are probably usually correct. But for rarer items, especially those that might have prestige value, or the bones of domestic livestock, archaeologists should at least consider the possibility that they represent plunder. In fact, archaeologists studying exchange between the Norse and the Inuit in Greenland and Canada have noted a peculiar imbalance in the evidence: finds of Norse goods at Thule Inuit sites are common, whereas finds of Inuit items at Norse sites are extremely rare. Since some of the Norse artifacts discovered at Thule settlements have been "precious items—ones not likely to have been traded" (for example, a bronze balance arm and chain-mail armor) by the metal-impoverished Greenland Norse—some scholars suspect that the Inuit plundered rather than traded for some of these goods.[29] It is also useful to recall that livestock-stealing raids were at least as important a method for acquiring horses (among the historic Plains tribes) and cattle (among many East African tribes) as any form of exchange.[30] Thus archaeologists doubly pacify the past by assuming that all exotic items are evidence of exchange and that exchange precludes war. The ethnographic evidence implies that both of these assumptions are invalid: war moves goods and people just as effectively (albeit sometimes in only one direction) as exchange, and exchange can easily incite warfare.

To varying degrees, then, many societies tend to fight the people they marry and to marry those they fight, to raid the people with whom they trade and to trade with their enemies. Contrary to the usual assumptions, exchange between societies is a context favorable to conflict and is closely associated with it.

NINE

Bad Neighborhoods

The Contexts for War

We have observed that increasing human density does not promote warfare and that increased trade and intermarriage do not inhibit it. What conditions (if any) promote or intensify conflict? As noted in Chapter 8, the most common "reasons" given for wars have been retaliation for acts of violence—that is, revenge and defense—and various economic motives. If this generalization is accurate, one might expect warfare to be more frequent in situations involving at least one especially belligerent party, severe economic difficulties, and a lack of shared institutions for resolving disputes or common values emphasizing nonviolence. These conditions are found in the "bad neighborhoods" that are created by proximity to a bellicose neighbor, during hard times, and along frontiers.

"ROTTEN APPLES" AND RAIDING CLUSTERS

In his statistical study of the Indians of western North America, Joseph Jorgensen noticed that raiding activity was clustered rather than uniformly distributed.[1] Warfare was more intense in certain regions than in others, apparently because of the presence of a few very aggressive societies that frequently mounted offensive raids. The tribes that were the foci of these raiding clusters were those of the northern Pacific Northwest Coast, the Klamath–Modoc of the southernmost Plateau, the Thompson tribe of the northernmost Plateau, the Navajo–Apaches of the Southwest, and the Mohave–Yuma of the Lower Colorado River. These groups frequently raided not only their immediate neighbors, but also much more distant tribes. Records indicate that the Tlingit from Alaska's panhandle raided as far south as Puget Sound, and the Mohave attacked groups on the coast of California. The booty acquired by these inveterate raiders varied widely: slaves on the Pacific Northwest Coast and for the Klamath–Modoc; food and portable goods for the Apaches, Thompsons, and Mohave; territory on the Northwest Coast and the Lower Colorado. Other especially bellicose groups in North America included the Iroquois, the Sioux of the northern Plains, and the Comanche of the southern Plains. During the historic period, the Iroquois raided as far afield as Delaware, the Great Lakes, and the Mississippi Valley. South American and Old World examples include the Tupinamba of Brazil, the Caribs of the Guianas, the Yanomamo of Venezuela and Brazil, some Nguni Bantu tribes (such as the Mtetwa–Zulu) in southeastern Africa, the Nuer of the Sudan, the Masai of East Africa, and the Foré and Telefolmin of New Guinea. The aggressive societies at the heart of these raiding clusters were rotten apples that spoiled their regional barrels.

An analogous pattern is recognizable in Western history—various peoples and nations that were especially belligerent for several generations. The list of such Western rotten apples could include republican Rome, Late Classical Germany, medieval (Viking) Scandinavia, sixteenth-century Spain, seventeenth-century France, revolutionary–Napoleonic France. During the nineteenth century, Canada, Mexico, and most Indian tribes west of the Appalachians had war-related reasons to regret that they were, in the words of a Mexican president, "so far from God, so near the United States." Certainly the twentieth century would have been far less bloodstained if Germany and Japan had been less quarrelsome and covetous societies.

Evidently, then, one factor intensifying warfare is an aggressive neighbor. Most societies that are frequently attacked not only fight to defend themselves, but also retaliate with attacks of their own, thus multiplying the amount of combat they engage in. Less aggressive societies, stimulated by more warlike groups in their vicinity, become more bellicose themselves, devote more attention to military matters, and may institutionalize some aspects of war making. The military sodalities or clubs of the Pueblo tribes of the American Southwest seem to have been an institutional response to Apache–Navajo aggressiveness since they declined in importance and membership (and in some tribes disappeared altogether) after the Apacheans were pacified by the Americans. With their long experience in defending against raids, the "peaceful" Pueblos were anything but peaceable. The Spaniards found them to be tough opponents initially and valorous and effective allies later in fighting with the nomadic tribes.[2]

Why some societies are more inclined than others to assume the offensive is both an anthropological and a historical puzzle. In most (but not all) of the cases mentioned earlier, the aggressive groups acquired territory at the expense of more passive ones. But whether the desire for more territory causes aggressiveness or whether expansion is merely an effect of bellicosity remains a contentious subject among scholars. Many expansionist nation-states experienced a higher rate of population growth than their less warlike neighbors.[3] In some tribal cases, such growth was partially due to the practice of incorporating captive women and children into the tribe, as in the case of the Sudanese Nuer.[4] Nevertheless, aggressive American Indian groups should have been experiencing population *declines* from introduced diseases during the early historical period. Although tribal population figures are usually little more than educated guesses, it often appears that these more bellicose groups either were being less rapidly decimated than their immediate neighbors or may even have had a period of increasing population during their offensive heyday.[5] For example, the estimated population of the aggressive Mohave was 3,000 in the 1770s but 4,000 in 1872—the dates that demarcate the period of their most intense raiding activity and territorial expansion. During the same period, the population of one of the Mohave's favorite enemies, the Maricopa, declined from 3,000 to 400, primarily because of disease.

Rapid population increases can create population pressure by increasing demand in the economy and stressing the capacity of social institutions. For instance, having greater numbers of young men and women in the society requires having larger amounts of valuable commodities available to pay brideprices or dowries. In societies where the number of achieved (that is, not inherited) leadership or high-status roles is limited, a population boom will lead to more competition for these few positions. Since these are often achieved on the basis of wealth and/or military prowess, the resulting internal competition will encourage more raiding and plundering of other social groups. For example, each new age-grade among several East African tribes could advance in seniority, toward marriage and "elderhood," only by raiding other tribes.[6] This kind of population pressure can occur at any population density, since it is the product of relative growth and not absolute numbers or density. Population increase not only encourages aggression, but also provides a larger manpower pool to absorb the losses that more frequent combat entails and allows formation of larger war parties that are more likely to be successful.

Another relatively common factor in such cases—and one that often accompanies population growth—is the development or introduction of new technology in food production, transportation, and weaponry. The relationship between maritime technology and European expansion is obvious. The introduction of the Old World horse had similar effects on the demography and militancy of many Indian tribes in North and South America. Likewise, the development of a special *assegai* (sword-spear) and some tactical innovations related to its use were instrumental in the Zulu expansion.[7] Although these correlations remain controversial, the relationship between the diffusion of iron technology and the Bantu expansion in Africa, or between horse riding and the spread of the Indo-Europeans in Eurasia, may be prehistoric examples of this phenomenon. Perhaps a rapid population increase provides the push and new technology the pull in making some groups more aggressive. But whatever the reason—land hunger, rapid population increases, or new technology—some societies are more aggressive than others and radiate intensified warfare within their immediate vicinity.

Of course, raiding clusters and the bellicose societies at the heart of them do not endure forever. The hyperaggressive Norsemen have become the pacific Scandinavians. Except for a small class of samurai who used only edged weapons, Japan had been a peaceful, demilitarized nation for almost 250 years before Commodore Perry released its combative genie from its self-imposed bottle. Two generations later, its bellicosity was extreme. But two generations after 1945, Japan is again demilitarized and has one of the lowest rates of violent crime in the world. Within a few generations, the fearsome Iroquois became peaceable yeoman farmers. After a traumatic defeat and temporary exile from their homeland in the 1860s, the Navaho quickly made the transition from rapacious raiders to peaceful pastoralists; the Navaho have since become world renowned for their rugs and silverwork. In time, then, aggressive groups may be pacified by defeat at the hands of equally aggressive but larger societies, or by the loss of their technological advantage when their adversaries also acquire them. Even in the absence of defeat, the zeal of expansionist societies tends to abate as they begin experiencing the diminishing returns of overextension or succumb to the attractions of consolidation and exploitation. Military ferocity is not a fixed quality of any race or culture, but a temporary condition that usually bears the seeds of it own destruction.

FRONTIERS

Some recent anthropological work argues that frontiers between different cultural groups, economic types, or ethnic stocks are among the most peaceful places on earth.[8] Rather than constituting zones of tension and competition between different systems, such boundary regions (according to these accounts) are "open social systems" where the exchange of goods, labor, spouses, and information between two social realms is the order of the day. Implicitly, the anthropologists responsible for this interpretation seem to assume that these mutually beneficial exchanges discourage conflict and prevent war. The only exceptions allowed in this idyllic picture relate to frontiers shared with civilized Europeans. All other frontiers—whether static or moving, whether between cultures or language groups, whether between farmers and foragers or nomads and villagers—are represented as realms of exchange and cooperation.

Certainly, these scholars are correct in noting that even the sharpest boundaries between major cultural units seldom represent solid walls; rather, they resemble permeable tissues through which considerable exchange occurs. But due to three oversights, many anthropologists are excessively optimistic about the peacefulness of such places.

The first problem, discussed in Chapter 8, is that exchange is an inducement to or source of war and not a bulwark against it. Precisely because frontiers display things that people need or want (such as land, labor, spouses, and various commodities) just beyond the limits of their own social unit and beyond easy acquisition by the methods normal within their own society (such as sharing, balanced reciprocity, and redistribution by leaders), the temptation to gain them by warfare is especially strong in these regions.

The second problem for the concept of peaceful frontiers is the fact that these regions necessarily lack the very social and cultural features that prevent disputes from turning violent. Independent societies have no overarching institutions of intersocietal mediation such as headmen, councils, and chiefs. Nor are there shared cultural values emphasizing group solidarity that treat bloodshed among fellow tribesmen or countrymen as especially horrifying and supernaturally disturbing. For example, God's Sixth Commandment to the Israelites applied only to themselves, as their later treatment of the Canaanites demonstrated. Indeed, the Sixth Commandment is more honestly and precisely translated into English in the modern Jewish Torah as "Thou shall not murder," since murder is the killing of a countryman, not the slaying of a foreigner in war. The social-solidarity values that oppose "us" to "them" help foment the collective violence of war from disputes between individuals of different societies. For this reason, much of the "information" exchanged across social boundaries and frontiers may be acrimonious and include uncomplimentary ethnic epithets (for example, "Filthy-Lodge People," "Nit-heads," "Grey Feces," "Spittle," "Bastards," "Ferocious Rats," or the common and unambiguous "Enemies").[9] It is not just in movie Westerns that frontiers are regions of cultural antagonism where the legal and cultural constraints on violence are lax.

Finally, frontier areas tend to be less peaceful than the interiors of social and cultural domains because they are the most exposed to raids, the first to feel the effects of enemy depredations, and the most inclined to retaliate. Because they are usually less densely settled, easier to surprise, and easier to retreat from if resistance proves too great, border regions attract raids. The greater vulnerability and volatility of frontiers explain why they have often been buffered by no-man's-lands and why their settlements have often been protected by fortifications.

There are three major kinds of cultural frontiers: civilized–tribal; pastoral nomad–village farmer; and farmer–forager. Because civilizations produce written records, the first type of frontier has been the object of some comparative studies.[10] These comparisons indicate that although warfare between civilized and tribal peoples is not inevitable (as some examples prove), it has almost invariably occurred when a frontier involving a settlement or political control has moved. Very few pastoralist–farmer frontiers have been described that were not also part of primitive–civilized boundaries or from which warfare had been eliminated by the power of a state. And such frontiers seem to have been especially tense, even after pacification. Certainly, the few unpacified herder–farmer frontiers described ethnographically—for example, that between the aggressive Masai herdsmen of East Africa and their settled Bantu neighbors—appear to have been plagued by raiding and warfare.[11] Because farmer–forager interactions have been the focus of considerable archaeological discussion, the ethnography and ethnohistory of such frontiers can be used to test the peaceful-frontier concept.

Anthropologists who consider uncivilized farmer–forager frontiers peaceful invariably use as examples the relationships commonly found between certain tropical-forest hunting peoples and their village farmer neighbors—especially the relationship between Pygmy hunters and Bantu (or other Negro) farmers in central Africa. But using this well-known example first of all requires discounting the Bantu's claim that the Pygmies are actually their dependent subjects, literally serfs or "servants."[12] It also means overlooking the implications of the Pygmies' occasional resort to crop theft when their Bantu "masters" are not forthcoming enough. Recent evidence on the diet of Pygmies indicates that they could not survive in the tropical forest without recourse to the substantial amounts of food (approximately 65 percent of their calories) they obtain from the agriculturalists.[13] This dependency is further evidenced by the fact that no Pygmy groups speak their own language but only those of their Negro patrons. Under the circumstances, it is hardly surprising that Pygmies remain at peace and socially subordinate to the Bantu; to do otherwise would result either in starvation or in destruction at the hands of the more numerous Bantu. Most, if not all, supposedly benign farmer–forager relations in the tropical forests are predicated on a similar dietary dependence of the foragers and on the social subordination that follows from it.[14]

Any ethnographic evidence of frequent hostilities between farmers and foragers outside the tropical forests is dismissed by peaceful-frontier advocates as
being a product of the disruptions that resulted from colonization by civilized
peoples. This dismissal, like others of its ilk, is difficult to refute since all
evidence of the hostilities comes from the supposed disrupters.

Yet it is difficult to dismiss the indications of frontier hostilities between the
hunter-gatherers of southern Africa and their pastoral or farming neighbors.[15]
The pastoral Khoikhoi (Hottentots) of the Cape region of South Africa at first
contact were already fighting with the San (Bushmen) hunter-gatherers, who
were raiding their livestock. Initially, the Khoikhoi welcomed Europeans as
allies in this struggle. The precontact provenance of these Khoikhoi–San hostilities is attested by rock paintings left by the San and by the derogatory
Khoikhoi term *San,* which means something like "no-account rascal." Moreover, when the Kalahari San of Botswana encountered expanding Bantu
Tswana herders, the oral histories of both sides show that fighting and mutual
raiding occurred. The Tswana term for the San was *Masarwa,* the *Ma-* prefix
designating an enemy tribe (now softened by the Botswana government to
Basarwa, using the *Ba-* prefix signifying friendly Bantu tribes). San hunter-
gatherers in southeastern Africa fought with the neighboring Nguni Bantu
tribes—again because of stock raiding. These San–Nguni conflicts are recorded
in prehistoric San rock paintings (Figure 9.1) showing small-statured bowmen
without shields (San) fighting large-statured warriors bearing shields, spears,
and knobkerries (Nguni). In one early recorded incident, a Xhosa (Bantu) chief
ordered his warriors to exterminate the local San because they had killed his
favorite ox. In wars fought between rival Bantu tribes or clans, women and
children were usually spared; but in raids on stock-stealing San bands, often all
were slaughtered, without regard to sex or age. San bows and poisoned arrows
fared very well in combat against Bantu shields, clubs, and spears, however, so
extermination was not easy to accomplish. As a result, a certain balance of power
was often established, especially in settings where rugged country gave the
elusive San tactical advantages. In mountainous Lesotho, relations between the
Sotho Bantu and the San were supposedly amiable until Sotho hunting with
guns made game scarce and San stock raiding created conflicts. In all these
cases, the dynamic behind this farmer–forager warfare was the same: Khoikhoi
or Bantu retaliation for San livestock raiding, which itself was often predicated
on or exacerbated by game shortages created by the hunting of the farmer-
herders and by the ecological transformations induced by tillage and grazing.
This hostile dynamic was finally transformed when the better-armed and horse-
mounted Boers arrived on the scene. They, like the Nguni and Khoikhoi, found
that the San were difficult to subdue because of their poisoned arrows and the
mobility of their small bands. Indeed, the hostility of the San in the Sneeuwburg

Figure 9.1 Prehistoric rock painting showing battle between San foragers on the left and Bantu farmers on the right. The San are armed only with bows, whereas the Bantu carry oxhide shields and spears (held in reserve behind the shield) and wield knobkerries (a wooden club that could be thrown). The tadpole shapes around the San bowmen may represent thrown knobkerries. (Redrawn from Wilson and Thompson 1983)

Mountains halted the expansion of the Trekboers in the northeastern Cape for thirty years and even forced the frontier back in some areas. In the end, though, when the Boers became numerous enough, their commandos (militia) simply exterminated the San.

In none of these cases were hostilities incessant, even after Europeans appeared on the scene; in fact, there is plentiful evidence of trade, intermarriage, and the incorporation of individual San as "clients" or serfs by the Khoikhoi and

Bantu tribes. However, being the clients of one Khoikhoi tribe did not prevent San bands from raiding other Khoikhoi groups, so clientship did not necessarily eliminate farmer–forager hostilities.

In recent descriptions of these patron–client relationships between farmer-herders and foragers by historians and anthropologists, the arrangement is depicted as benign, voluntary, and mutually beneficial. But a description of San clientship by a Bantu Tswana chief has a very different tenor:

> The Masarwa [that is, the San] are slaves. They can be killed. It is no crime. They are like cattle. If they run away, their masters can bring them back and do what they like in the way of punishment. They are never paid. If the Masarwa live in the veld, and I want any to work for me, I go out and take any I want.[16]

This quotation raises questions about another dynamic recognized by advocates of peaceful frontiers. Proponents of this theory argue that farmers and herders on thinly settled frontiers often experience labor shortages that can be intense at certain seasons (such as during the harvest) and that it was convenient for them to enlist the temporary help of the local foragers in exchange for surplus food. The Tswana chief's description implies that it can be just as convenient for the more numerous farmers to conscript foragers by force, keep them as involuntary servants, and "pay" them bare subsistence. For the farmers, this version of farmer–forager symbiosis has the additional advantage of simultaneously eliminating potential stock rustlers and crop thieves. In an account of the first contact between his tribe and the !Kung San, a Tswana claimed that the San accepted a servile status out of fear of the Tswana and that, had these San resisted, the Tswana "would have slaughtered them."[17]

But the San were not the only hunter-gatherers to harass village farmers, nor was stock theft the only torment raiders inflicted. Both foragers and pastoralists showed a propensity for stealing crops as well as livestock from settled farmers (although, when there was a choice, livestock seems to have been the preferred booty, probably because it can be taken away under its own power).[18] Such thefts, however, were seldom accomplished without combat or inciting retaliatory raids. One old story among the Navajo is that the first time they ever heard this name applied to them (they call themselves Diné, or "people") was when one band was robbing a Tewa Pueblo cornfield; the victims shouted "Navaho" when the thieves were discovered. Among the Western Apaches of Arizona, when the meat supply of a band began to run low, an older woman would complain publicly and suggest that a raid be mounted to obtain a fresh supply. The band leader would then call for volunteers, and a small party of no more than fifteen warriors would set off for an enemy settlement. Moving as unobtrusively as possible, they would attempt to drive off some of the enemy's herds and then beat a very rapid retreat back home. The party would fight if it was caught, but it tried to avoid any contact; the object was simply to obtain food, not to inflict damage. If any raiders were killed or the victims retaliated by killing a band member, a much larger war party—up to 200 warriors—would depart, surround the offending settlement, and kill as many of its inhabitants as possible. Similarly, the Mura of central Brazil preferred to raid neighboring sedentary farmers for manioc and other crops rather than cultivate these themselves. Since pastoral and foraging groups were usually highly mobile and had such large territories to hide in, they were very difficult to catch, either to reclaim lost goods or to exact retribution. To note that foraging or pastoral nomads made exasperating adversaries for settled farmers is an understatement; to claim that they were almost never enemies is wishful thinking.

While static frontiers were often hostile, moving ones presented an even greater potential for violent conflicts. since they added further explosives to an already volatile mix. A moving cultural boundary meant that one human physical type, language, culture, or economic system was expanding at the expense of another. Of course, such spreads were sometimes accomplished through the peaceful mechanisms of intermarriage, willing adoption of novelties, and voluntary annexation. But people tend to be attached to their traditional way of life, territory, and political independence and are seldom completely defenseless; consequently, warfare often accompanies the movement of a frontier and occasionally may be the only mechanism by which it can advance. When the movement of a frontier involves colonization by newcomers on a large scale, conditions favoring warfare reach their peak. The newcomers are at least intruding, if not trespassing; often compete with the natives for land, water, game, firewood, and other limited materials; commonly change the local ecology; are inclined to be cavalier about the property rights of the other but are fastidious about their own; and exhibit inscrutably odd customs and tastes. It is seldom long before the colonists' behavior convinces the aborigines that the newcomers should be encouraged to be "new" someplace else. This type of moving colonist frontier is documented historically only for literate civilizations; all others are the province of archaeologists and are subject to the vagaries of their interpretive fashions. The advance and retreat of most (but not all) of these civilized settler frontiers have been accompanied by frequent warfare, as between the Romans and the Celts or Germans in western Europe, the late medieval Spanish and the Gaunche tribesmen of the Canary Islands, the medieval Japanese and Ainu tribesmen on Honshū, the modern Japanese and the Taiwanese Aborigines, and the modern Europeans and almost everyone else.[19]

Comparable prehistoric frontiers do give evidence that violence was common or at least expected.[20] The conflicts already in existence at the dawn of historical records between the Khoikhoi or Bantu and the San in southern Africa and between the Navaho—Apache and the Pueblos in the American Southwest have already been mentioned. In eastern North America, the intrusion of Mississippian peoples into various regions between A.D. 900 and 1400 was marked by the fortification of almost all new settlements in these areas. The retreat of these Mississippians from northeastern Illinois in the face of the expansion of Oneota settlements was marked by a high level of violent death and fortified villages. A concentration of fortified settlements and the horrific Crow Creek massacre occurred on or near a fluctuating frontier between Middle Missouri (proto-Mandan) and Coalescent (proto-Arikara) farmers between A.D. 1300 and 1500. The abandonment of some areas in northwestern New Mexico by Anasazi farmers between A.D. 1050 and 1300 was immediately preceded by frequent fortification and destruction of settlements as well as other indications of violence. There is also considerable indication of violence on the periphery of the shrinking area of Hohokam occupation in Arizona during this same period. Hostile frontiers, then, are not unusual in the later prehistory of the best-studied regions of North America.

Far earlier in western Europe, some 7,000 to 6,000 years ago, colonizing Early Neolithic farmers appear to have encountered, or expected to encounter, a hostile reception from the indigenous Mesolithic hunter-gatherers.[21] The farmers of the Impressed Ware (or Cardial) culture founded settlements at favorable locations along the Mediterranean coasts and often fortified these sites with ditches. The local foragers, whose sites were less substantial and unfortified, adopted (perhaps by looting) ceramics and livestock from these settlers. At one Cardial site in southern France, archaeologists found a few skulls with cut-marks from decapitation. These skulls differed in physical type from that of the Cardial farmers, but resembled the type of Mesolithic foragers farther to the north. It therefore appears that the Cardial farmers at least occasionally killed foragers and kept their heads as trophies. The colonization of Germany and the Low Countries by farmers of the Linear Pottery culture was accompanied by fortified border villages (Figure 9.2) and, in Belgium at least, a 20- to 30-kilometer (12- to 18-mile) no-man's-land between these defended sites and the settlements of Final Mesolithic foragers (Figure 9.3). In one of these border villages, most of the houses had been burned, after which the village was fortified. As the trophy heads at Ofnet and the mass grave at Talheim demonstrate, neither the indigenous foragers nor the invading Linear Pottery farmers were peaceful among themselves; thus it is unlikely that they treated each other less violently. Because human remains from this period and area are extremely rare (the soils did not preserve them well), no direct evidence yet exists of farmers killed with Mesolithic weapons or vice versa. Nevertheless, the fortification of pioneer and border settlements does imply that hostilities were

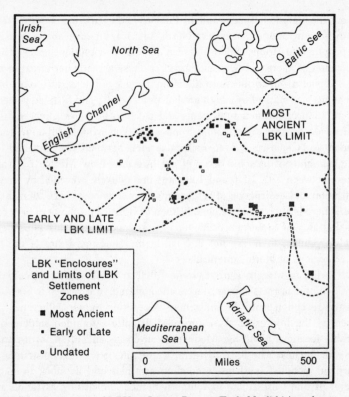

Figure 9.2 Distribution of LBK or Linear Pottery (Early Neolithic) enclosures relative to the limits of LBK expansion at two stages. The frontier distribution of the Most Ancient enclosures is very clear, while the pattern for the Early and Late periods is less clear because two periods are combined. (Hockmann 1990; drawn by Ray Brod, Department of Geography, University of Illinois at Chicago)

expected on these earliest European farmer–forager frontiers. From both the Old World and the New World, evidence suggests that prehistoric frontiers, like more recent examples, were far from placid.

HARD TIMES

In a recent cross-cultural study of the circumstances surrounding preindustrial warfare, Carol and Melvin Ember noted that the nonindustrial societies most frequently embroiled in warfare were those that "have had a history of expectable but unpredictable disasters" (droughts, floods, insect infestations, and so on).[22] These disasters do *not* include anticipatable chronic food shortages, such

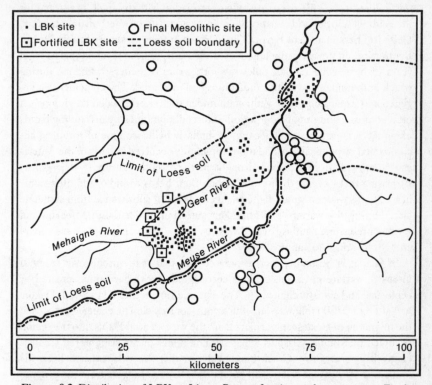

Figure 9.3 Distribution of LBK or Linear Pottery farming settlements versus Final Mesolithic foragers campsites, ca. 5000 B.C., in northeastern Belgium. Notice the no-man's-land to the north where no major geographical barrier (such as the deep valley of the Meuse) intervenes. (Redrawn after Keeley and Cahen 1989 by Ray Brod, Department of Geography, University of Illinois at Chicago)

as the "hungry season" endured by many hunter-gatherers and subsistence farmers in higher latitudes during the late winter and early spring. The clear implication is that the most war-prone groups go to war to recoup losses due to natural calamities, to replace deteriorating pastures and fields by means of territorial expansion, and to cushion the effects of expected future losses.

Droughts figure frequently in examples of disaster-driven warfare.[23] The various nomadic raiders who preyed on the Pueblos of the American Southwest were especially active during dry years. As noted earlier, the Hopi anticipated trading rather than raiding from approaching Apaches only if (rare) rain clouds were visible in the direction from which the Apaches were approaching. Offensive raiding by the Maricopa of Arizona was associated with low-water stages on the Colorado and Gila rivers. A similar correlation with dry spells is attested for the raids of Libyan and Asiatic Bedouin pastoralists on the Faiyum and Nile Delta frontiers of ancient Egypt. The increase in fighting among South African Bantu tribes in the early nineteenth century seems to have resulted in part from years of decreasing rainfall following forty years of better conditions during which both human and cattle populations had increased. The coincident emergence and expansion of the Zulu state under such overcrowded conditions set off a confused and sanguinary period of forced migrations by marauding bands of refugees known as the Mfecane. A similarly bellicose time of troubles, accompanied by political consolidation, apparently occurred in parts of the American Southwest during a long drought in the twelfth century.[24] It is hardly surprising that—seeing their crops wither, their herds dwindle, and their families go hungry—men would fight to obtain means of subsistence from someone else. During the warfare and attendant suffering of the Bantu Mfecane and various prehistoric southwestern droughts, some desperate people were apparently even driven to cannibalism.[25]

In fact, it is becoming increasingly certain that many prehistoric cases of intensive warfare in various regions corresponded with hard times created by ecological and climatic changes.[26] The extreme violence noted in South Dakota just after A.D. 1300 follows a late-thirteenth-century climate change that caused the migration of Coalescent farmers from the west-central Plains into the region occupied by Middle Missouri villagers. The bones of the slaughtered Coalescent villagers at Crow Creek bore evidence that the villagers had been ill-nourished for a prolonged period before their deaths. Judging from the proportion of skeletons with embedded projectile points, the most violent periods in the later prehistory of the Santa Barbara Channel region in California are related to "warm-water events" that disrupted the productivity of coastal waters and caused widespread dietary deficiencies. Certain pathologies (such as ricketts) possibly related to inadequate diet were also common in the Late Paleolithic Qadan cemeteries, including the often-mentioned one at Gebel Sahaba.

No type of economy or social organization is immune to natural disasters or to the impetus they give to warfare; foragers, farmers, bands, and states all can suffer them. Because of their smaller territories, slimmer subsistence margins, and more limited transportation systems, however, smaller-scale societies are more susceptible to injury from these disasters than are large states and empires. In the latter, a famine in one area can be ameliorated with supplies transported from more favored areas or taken from centralized food reserves. In a small society, the needed supplies may be too distant for practical transportation by human, animal, or canoe. Moreover, these supplements must be obtained by trade with outsiders who may not be particularly charitable, and trade itself (as we have seen) is a rich source of incitements to war. It should be said that larger, denser, and more technically sophisticated societies have a greater capacity to create their own disasters through deforestation, overgrazing, soil salinization, the introduction of new pests, and even foolish economic policies. But whatever their source, hard times create a very strong temptation for needy people to take—or try to take—what they lack from others.

What makes disaster-driven warfare especially bitter is that the defenders, while usually somewhat better off than the attackers, commonly are suffering to some degree from the same natural adversities. In such dire circumstances, any group that yields an acre of land or a bushel of corn may risk its own survival; war does become a struggle for existence. Of course, not all wars occur under these conditions, and sometimes people are simply too weakened by famine to fight. But natural disasters are clearly predicaments that increase the frequency and intensity of war.

TEN

Naked, Poor, and Mangled Peace

Its Desirability and Fragility

The other side of the question What contexts promote war? is What conditions favor peace? Indeed, answering the first question satisfactorily is impossible without addressing the second. However, the second question is much more difficult to answer on the basis of ethnographic data, simply because genuinely peaceful societies—as we have seen—are extremely rare. Both the historical and the ethnographic records display what frustrated social anthropologist Thomas Gregor called a "scarcity of peace."[1] Any attempt to look for the common circumstances and cultural features that encourage peace must proceed under this rather severe constraint.

ATTITUDES TOWARD WAR AND PEACE

Although warfare in many (if not most) nonstate societies was extremely frequent, deadly, and destructive, little evidence indicates that its practitioners and potential victims revelled in or harbored a special affection for it. Like people in civilized societies, tribal people responded to warfare with mixed emotions and contradictory social reactions. In most nonstate societies, as in our own, prowess and effective leadership in combat were granted high status and other rewards. The costs of defeat were so high and warfare was so frequent that the brave and skilled warrior was of immense social value. But warfare, whether primitive or civilized, involves losses, suffering, and terror, even for the victors. Consequently, it was nowhere viewed as an unalloyed good, and the respect accorded to accomplished warriors was often tinged with aversion.

For example, it was common the world over for the warrior who had just killed an enemy to be regarded by his own people as spiritually polluted or contaminated.[2] He therefore had to undergo a magical cleansing to remove this pollution. Often he had to live for a time in seclusion, eat special food or fast, be excluded from participation in rituals, and abstain from sexual intercourse. Because he was a spiritual danger to himself and anyone he touched, a Huli killer of New Guinea could not use his shooting hand for several days; had to stay awake the first night after the killing, chanting spells; drink "bespelled" water; and exchange his bow for another. South American Carib warriors had to cover their heads for a month after dispatching an enemy. An African Meru warrior, after killing, had to pay a curse remover to conduct the rituals that would purge his impurity and restore him to society. A Marquesan was tabooed for ten days after a war killing. A Chilcotin of British Columbia who had killed an enemy had to live apart from the group for a time, and all returning raiders had to cleanse themselves by drinking water and vomiting. These and similar rituals emphasize the extent to which homicide was deemed abnormal, even when committed against enemies.

Furthermore, even the most bellicose societies did not award their best warriors or captains their highest positions of status or leadership.[3] Instead, these rewards were reserved for men who, although they were often expected to be brave and skilled in war, were more proficient in the arts of peace—oratory, wealth acquisition, generosity, negotiation, and ritual knowledge. The six desired characteristics of a western Apache headman, for instance, were industriousness, generosity, impartiality, forbearance, conscientiousness, and eloquence; not one of these pertains directly to warfare. Cheyenne "peace chiefs" had more political influence, material wealth, and wives than the chiefs who led war parties. Among the militarily sophisticated and war-torn tribes of the Pacific Northwest Coast, chiefs and high-ranking males owed their status to inheritance and wealth, not to military prowess. The "Big Men" of highland New Guinea were seldom renowned warriors; rather, they were wealthy, generous, and persuasive. Among the Mae Enga, it was recognized that "rubbish men"—those with the least wealth and the lowest status—were often the most effective warriors. Civilized soldiers have often observed, with Kipling, that they are treated as saviors "when the guns begin to shoot" but are received with much less enthusiasm (and even with distaste) in peacetime. Evidently, tribal warriors were often regarded with similar reserve.

While men could acquire the spoils of victory or, even in defeat, the enhanced status of a warrior, women's share from warfare was mostly negative. Even if they and their children were less likely to suffer physical harm than adult males, women had a great deal more to lose and less opportunity to gain. The gardens they tended and the food stores they produced could be looted or destroyed, and their homes razed. The threat of capture, rape, and exile loomed if the men were defeated. In short, they shared many of the risks but few of the benefits of war. It is therefore not surprising to discover that in many societies women detested war. Representing the unanimous opinion of her sex in a society where land disputes were the most common cause of fighting, one Mae Enga woman protested, "Men are killed but the land remains. The land is there in its own right and it does not command people to fight for it."[4] Such feminine antipathy toward for war was neither universal nor eternal, however. The taunts of women often incited men to fight; women took an active role in the torture of captives, as among the Tupi and Carib of South America; and in a few cases, women participated in actual combat (Chapter 2). But in the more commonly encountered situation, where their opinions on political matters were discounted or ignored and where their expected role was to suffer in silence, women usually viewed warfare as an unredeemed evil.

At some level, even the most militant warriors recognized the evils of war and the desirability of peace.[5] Thus certain New Guinea Jalemo warriors, who praised and bragged about military feats and who took great pleasure in eating both the pigs and the corpses of vanquished enemies, readily confessed that war was a bad thing that depleted pig herds, incurred burdensome debts, and restricted trade and travel. Similarly, despite their frequent resort to it, Kapauku Papuans seem to hate war. As one man put it:

> War is bad and nobody likes it. Sweet potatoes disappear, pigs disappear, fields deteriorate, and many relatives and friends get killed. But one cannot help it. A man starts a fight and no matter how much one depises him, one has to go and help because he is one's relative and one feels sorry for him.

In small-scale societies, it is usually a matter of "my relatives, right or wrong" rather than "my country."

Even the fierce head-hunting Jivaro of South America regarded their incessant warfare as a curse. Additional evidence of the universal preference for peace is the ease and even gratitude with which some of the most warlike of tribal peoples accepted colonial pacification or, in the new conditions wrought by European contact, pacified themselves.[6] For example, Auyana men in New

Guinea declared that life was much better after pacification because now one could go out to urinate in the morning without fear of ambush and one could eat a meal without anxiety about raids. Whether one takes any of these protestations at face value or cynically, they are remarkably like the attitudes and platitudes expressed by civilized people, both military and civilian.

In a rare ethnographic mention of psychological reactions to combat, some New Guinean Auyana warriors with reputations for bravery—actually all who were asked—admitted to suffering nightmares about becoming isolated in combat. A somewhat comparable nightmare about engaging in solitary combat against a raiding party of spirits and being trapped was recorded from a New Guinea Tauade man.[7] Almost identical nightmares involving being left behind or otherwise separated from one's comrades and being surrounded or trapped by enemies have been a common symptom of "combat neurosis" or "delayed stress syndrome" among American combat veterans.[8] These examples provide tantalizing evidence that the fear and gore of combat are traumatic regardless of the cultural value placed on military prowess and that primitive combat is every bit as stressful and terrible as modern warfare.

On Tahiti, where warfare was especially brutal and merciless, "exhorters," called Rauti, circulated constantly among the warriors during combat, urging the latter to spare no enemy—even relative or friend—and to display the ferocity of "the devouring wild dog." When they were being browbeaten into doing something, Tahitian men would murmur, "This is equal to a Rauti."[9] This custom strongly implies that even when enemy atrocities to avenge were plentiful and where warfare was customarily exceptionally cruel, men had to be persistently nagged into committing acts of inhumanity.

Ethnographers have seldom asked individuals—men or women—about their attitudes toward and reactions to war, but the few available examples show that personal reactions in tribal societies varied as much as they do among civilized folk and that few people regarded war as more than a necessary evil. It was redeemed only by the opportunity it afforded for the display of courage and by the prospect of the profits of victory. In other words, tribal peoples were much like ourselves.

To judge from their mythologies, most cultural groups have invented many stories to account for the origins of warfare or for the warlike nature of aggressive neighbors, but they have created very few devoted to the genesis of peace. Although this seeming lack may be a consequence of the inadequate questions asked by ethnographers, it may also reflect a sense that war needs excuses (in the form of grievances, causes, mythological prescriptions by gods and ancestors, and so on), whereas peace requires none. From a similar survey, Harry Turney-High concludes that war and the killing it entails put men in a situation that they find at least uncomfortable and that peace is preferred "even in the minds of the most warlike peoples."[10] The clear implication is that peace is unexceptional, normal, and desirable to humans everywhere; and war is not.

Given that war is universally condemned and peace is everywhere preferred, it is very difficult to argue that values and attitudes play any significant role in promoting peace or war. As we have seen, even the most bellicose societies appear to regard their military heroes with mixed feelings—honoring their deeds but treating them in the short term as spiritually contaminated and denying them in the long term the highest rewards of wealth and status. Evidence also suggests that combat is just as psychologically traumatic for tribal warriors as for their civilized counterparts. People universally recognize that even for victors the practical effects of warfare are extremely unpleasant. It seems impossible that attitudes that are so widespread, realistic, and rational, that reflect direct experience and self-interest, are insincere or merely abstract. Yet if this worldwide revulsion had any real impact on social behavior, wars should be rare and peace common; instead the opposite is true.

This state of affairs is a paradox only for idealists, however. For materialists, values, beliefs, and attitudes are primarily epiphenomenal "superstructures"—that is, they either passively reflect or actively obfuscate economic and social reality. Negative attitudes toward war certainly reflect the unpleasant realities of warfare, but values and beliefs are slippery and changeable. Ironically (but often without the least trace of hypocrisy), a desire for peace has justified peacetime military preparations and the wartime use of very brutal methods. With bewildering rapidity, hated enemies can become respected allies, devout pacifists can become tigers on the battlefield, peaceable societies can become belligerent, and vice versa. The roots of war and peace clearly lie in certain social and economic circumstances that mold or override values and attitudes.

MAKING PEACE

By far the most common form of settlement concluding a tribal war involves having a leader on one side declare a desire for peace; this overture is then accepted by the opposing leader, followed by an exchange of gifts or the mutual payment of homicide compensation. This process may sound easy, but in practice the establishment of peace at any stage short of the utter defeat or annihilation of one party is as difficult and delicate a task as any arranged peace between contending nation-states.[11] Usually, peace negotiations are not even considered unless the fighting has reached an impasse and losses are approximately equal for both contenders. If the losses are not relatively even, there may be considerable resistance to a settlement on both sides: one group has suffered deaths that it must leave unavenged; the other must pay out a larger amount of "blood money" than it will receive.[12] Or one group may feel strong enough to push the fighting to a more decisive conclusion. Before any peace negotiations can even begin, there must be a general consensus for peace among the warriors on both sides, which may be difficult to obtain. Any "hawks" or "hotheads" dissenting from the consensus can easily sabotage the negotiations simply by committing further violence. Even with such a consensus, reaching a final settlement can be a laborious and precarious endeavor.

The peace-making process among the Central Enga of New Guinea illustrates the excruciating delicacy necessary to establish peace between small-scale societies.[13] When it is clear that neither side can defeat the other and when losses are nearly equal, the allies of the principal contenders will usually suggest that a peace be negotiated. Then the big men, or political leaders (who are not the war leaders), of the two principals will try to exhort a consensus for peace among their own warriors, with opposition expected from self-confident "fight leaders," hotheaded young bachelors, and bereaved relatives of the slain. If the necessary consensus can be obtained from each side, neutral go-betweens carry proposals and counterproposals concerning the composition of the peace delegations and the location of the peace conference. These are important issues because both sides may suspect a treacherous ambush and because the inclusion of hawks or hotheads in either delegation would increase the likelihood of violence erupting at the meeting. Even when a mutually agreeable meeting has been arranged, it remains "no easy task to create a setting for reasonable discourse, one that will not disintegrate into bloody violence." When meeting, the delegates lay aside their bows and spears (but not their axes), and both sides keep armed warriors lurking within earshot, ready to intervene if treachery is attempted or violence breaks out. As an opening, the opposing Big Men make prolonged speeches justifying their cause in a formal florid style, spiced with humor at the expense of their adversaries. Despite their conventionalized character and humor, these orations can fray tempers and lead to an explosion. When these harangues are finished, the crucial issue of blood-money payments is addressed. If this haggling is successful, down payments of homicide compensation are presented and divided among those due to receive them (the relatives of the slain). No one is ever really satisfied with these down payments, and it requires all of the Big Men's influence and powers of persuasion to have them accepted. It is very common for a brawl to break out at this point, as some warriors reject what they consider insultingly small payments. Should any blood be drawn, the war resumes. If this hurdle is successfully passed, however, more bombastic speeches follow, threatening dire consequences should the foes delay or default in making full payment of their reparations. In practice, Enga clans usually try to evade paying the outstanding blood money by resorting to delays, procrastinations, or token payments, so most of their "peaces" seldom endure for long.

As the Enga example shows, the custom of paying blood money or other forms of war reparations are almost as much a cause of subsequent warfare as of immediate peace. New disputes can arise or fighting can resume when compensation is not paid promptly or to the satisfaction of the recipients. Indeed, among the Huli of New Guinea, unpaid homicide indemnities have been identified as a very common cause of wars.[14] In addition, any wounded man who dies after the peace is concluded, even years later, requires new compensation. These belated claims are often refused, and the war begins again. Some New Guinea groups have even conducted autopsies to establish whether an old wound (or which of several old wounds) was the cause of death and represents a basis for a blood-money claim. In some cultures, compensation must be paid to families of allies killed in battle; if these payments are delayed or withheld, former allies can become active enemies. In general, reparations are a very weak mechanism for maintaining peace, and they often prove to be an impediment to reconciliation or an inducement to further violence.[15]

Other noncompensatory methods for establishing peace have been no more effective. For example, the Murngin of Australia would arrange very stylized and relatively harmless duels between the contenders in order to make peace. But these "peace-making fights" were often unsuccessful because the tribal elders could not control the tempers of their younger men; then one side would inflict a serious injury or death on the other, and wholesale fighting would resume.[16]

Just as with the Treaty of Versailles, the settlement of one tribal conflict could produce grievances leading to the start of another. Because these agreements were not enforced by a more powerful third party, peace settlements between nonstate societies, like those between nations, tended to be extremely brittle. The broken settlements, shifting alliances, smoldering grievances, and (in some instances) gross treachery displayed by nonstate societies led one ethnographer to remark that if records had been kept, the history of many such groups would be as complicated as that of any modern European nation.[17] Peace may thus have been more precious in the precivilized condition because it was so rare and fleeting.

States enjoy a slight advantage over nonstates with regard to peace making because they exercise a much greater degree of centralized control over their populations and economic resources. Because political decision making is in the hands of a tiny minority of a state's population, no complete consensus is needed from all citizens or soldiers before a peace can be negotiated. Hawkish dissenters can be controlled or even eliminated by the police institutions typical of states. States are then better able to enforce the peace from their own side. Where individuals have greater autonomy, as in small-scale societies or on colonial frontiers, almost anyone can commit acts (amounting to crimes) that bring their social units into armed conflict with neighbors. Of course, ambitious, greedy, treacherous, or faithless ruling elites can start wars without obtaining the consent of their subjects.

One of the apologies for imperialism during its heyday was *pacification*—the suppression of intertribal warfare by persuasion or force (usually the latter) and the substitution of legal means of resolving disputes or redressing wrongs. Had pacification and "the rule of law," wider trade, and improvements in transportation and communication been the only innovations introduced by imperial agents, imperialism might ultimately have been more of a boon and less of an ordeal for its native subjects. In fact, colonial pacification was not an end in itself but a means to achieve goals that almost invariably benefited the intruders as much as they harmed the native inhabitants: forced labor, loss of territory, economic exploitation, subordinate social and political status, and lack of legal redress against wrongs or crimes committed by colonists. The price of imperial peace was manifold indignity, dispossession, abject poverty, slavery, famine, and worse; and that price was surely too high. The peace that humans universally desire is not that of the grave or the chain gang, but imperial pacification often meant both.

MAINTAINING PEACE

As Gregor noted when decrying the scarcity of peace, the most common peaceable societies are ones that could evade the problem of intertribal relations by fleeing conflict, because they lived in very sparsely settled regions and were isolated from intimate contact with others by oceans, desert wastes, mountain barriers, unhealthful swamps, and dense forests. Unfortunately, preserving peace by flight from conflict has not been a strategic option available to most societies. Of more general and practical interest are ethnographic or historical instances in which peace was maintained even though contact between different cultural and social groups was close and sustained.

Gregor nominates as such an example the multitribal society of the Upper Xingu Basin in Brazil, comprising some 1,200 people of four different language groups living in ten politically independent villages.[18] For more than a century, aside from rare intervillage homicides and a few feuds, no wars or raids have occurred among these villages. But Gregor's descriptions of warfare with non-Xingu "wild" tribes and the frequent killing of "witches," which occasionally escalate into minor feuds, make what he calls a "negative peace" look anything but peaceful. He implies that deterrence primarily prevents these witchcraft killings from developing into wholesale feuding or even a Hobbesian state of war. He also notes that the Xingu region is geographically isolated, a situation that to some degree limits possible hostilities with non-Xingu tribes. But no matter how rarely they are met, these "wild Indian" enemies of the Xingu alliance are never far from its thoughts. They represent an external threat that binds the Xingu tribes together, and they serve as a moral example of the subhuman savagery that the Xinguanos could descend into should they abandon the principle of peace among themselves. Less extreme versions of ethnocentrism and negative ethnic stereotypes limit informal interaction among the allied tribes themselves. Formal interactions involve some intermarriage, considerable trade, and some participation in intervillage rituals; otherwise, the separate groups keep very much to themselves. It is also probable that the Xinguanos are all examples of a particular species of peaceable society we have previously encountered: defeated refugees. The Xingu tribes do seem much more harmonious than usual, but only with the aid of geography and on the basis of an uneasy but equitable social separatism.

The Xingu case does suggest that one form of monopoly exchange either promotes peace or is a symptom of it. Each of the Xingu tribes has what might be called an artificial monopoly.[19] Every tribe produces and exports goods that none of the other tribes makes, although there is no objective reason why these products can not be made by all. The tribal specializations include shell belts, salt produced by burning water hyacinth plants, hardwood bows, spears, and ceramic pots. None of these monopolies can be explained on geographic grounds, since clay for pots, water hyacinths, shells, and hard wood for bows are equally accessible to all. In other words, unlike monopolies that are accidents of geographic proximity to sources of materials (and can provoke war), these are arbitrary and maintained by tradition. When Gregor asked why the specialty of another village was not made "at home," he was told that to do so would anger the monopolists, perhaps leading them to bewitch the monopoly-busters. Allowing these arbitrary monopolies to remain in force has clearly helped to maintain peace.

A similar but less enduring association between arbitrary specializations and peaceful relations has been observed among the Yanomamo of the Upper Orinoco. For example, one of two allied Yanomamo villages made no pottery and obtained all its ceramics from its allies. When asked why they made no pots despite the availability of clay, the aceramic villagers claimed that the local clay was unsuitable and that they had forgotten how to make pots and so had to get them elsewhere. But when the alliance broke down, as frequently happens among the Yanomamo, the aceramic villagers immediately began making pots and exporting them to their new allies.[20] This instance shows that such patterns of specialization and exchange are an effect of peace, and not its cause. By contrast, the Xingu tribesmen seem to recognize that perturbing the trade among arbitrary specialists would disturb the peace.

A prehistoric example of similar arbitrary village specializations has been found among some frontier villages of Early Neolithic farmers in Belgium, some of which were fortified.[21] While all these villages raised their own grain and livestock, they appear (judging from finds of manufacturing debris) to have specialized variously in the production of stone axes, flint blades, some types of ceramics, and some special form of finished hide. These products were then exchanged among the villages, since all seem to have been equally well supplied with the finished products (except that no conclusion can be drawn as to the leather, which was not preserved). These specialties were arbitrary because the sources of raw material either were equally distant from all (as in the case of stone for axes) or were equally accessible (as with hides, flint, and clay). Moreover, most of these sites were separated from one another by distances of less than two miles. Given their frontier location and fortifications, these villagers, like the Xinguanos, appear to have been maintaining an alliance against the foragers beyond them.

One interesting "controlled" comparison that isolates the crucial conditions for war and peace involves the contrast between the nineteenth-century histories of western Canada and the western United States (and northern Mexico). These regions share a number of fundamental similarities in landscape, people, and final outcomes. During the nineteenth century, the arable and pasturable areas of North America west of the Mississippi and the Great Lakes passed from the possession of its native inhabitants into that of people of European origin. The prevailing subsistence economy changed from foraging or foraging supplemented by marginal agriculture to ranching and intensive farming. The Indians' numbers were severely reduced, their traditional economies were destroyed, and they were left in occupation of small and usually infertile reserves.

The tribes on both sides of the border were warlike. In many cases, in fact, they were exactly the same tribes because the forty-ninth parallel cut through their territory. The tribes of the prairie and plains of Canada were enthusiastic horse raiders and placed the same value on martial prowess as did those to the south. The tribes of the British Columbian coast were among the most aggressive and militarily sophisticated peoples north of central Mexico, and they did not hesitate to raid the Russians when they first appeared in the area. The westward-pioneering Euro-Canadians and Euro-Americans were likewise essentially the same people; they came from the same regions of Europe in the same waves, and their New World family histories often crossed and recrossed the forty-ninth parallel. Euro-Canadians displayed the same ethnocentrism as Euro-Americans concerning the Indian cultures and the conviction that because they would make "better use" of fertile land, they (and not the "feckless" Indians) deserved to possess it.[22] Francophone "Canadiens" and Métis ("mixed-blood" Catholics) played the same roles as traders, trappers, boatmen, and guides on both frontiers. Thus the plot, the scenery, the cast of characters, and the denouement were the same in both countries; however, the action and dialogue were very different.

South of the forty-ninth parallel, this drama was attended by frequent and bitter warfare. The Indians were, in the words of one of their foes, "fighting for all that God gave any man to fight for"—that is, for their homelands, for the safety of their families, and for preservation of their particular ways of life. The fertility, mineral wealth, and sheer magnificence of this huge territory made it a prize worth the risk to those who sought to seize it; and the settlers also fought, when war came, to protect their families and their way of life. Both the Indians and the settlers fought to perpetuate two incompatible ways of life so attractive (in retrospect, anyway) that they remain the objects of worldwide nostalgia. The Indian, Spanish, Mexican, and American bloodshed that stains the history of the West and littered its landscape with violent place-names (Battle Mountains, Massacre Lakes, and Bloody Islands) therefore appears to have been inevitable, a fated tragedy. It then comes as something of a shock to discover that in western Canada the same land-grab was perpetrated and the same subjugation of the Indians resulted but without a single war and with only one raid. North of the forty-ninth parallel, even though the stakes for both sides were every bit as high as in the south, peace reigned.

The Canadian peace was not absolute, nor was it maintained without the occasional use of force.[23] In British Columbia, before its Indian treaties were ratified when it joined Canada in 1871, a few minor incidents did occur, involving Indians killing a few whites or looting shipwrecks. One case, the "Chilcotin War," termed a "ludicrous 'campaign'" by one ethnohistorian, exemplifies the nature of these incidents. In 1864, some Chilcotin Indians murdered some whites in three separate incidents. A large party of Royal Marines and militia was sent up country to arrest the culprits. This "war" ended when the suspects were recognized and captured while they were nonchalantly visiting the militia camp. Another case of Indian–white conflict occurred in 1885 during the Second Northwest Rebellion in Saskatchewan. This was the second revolt by Métis; their first "rebellion" in Manitoba fifteen years earlier had been bloodless and involved no Indians. The Métis' principal grievance was that the parcels of land being granted to them were divided into grid squares rather than into long strips anchored on bodies of water. Despite the entreaties of the Métis and the hunger caused by poor government rations and the disappearance of the buffalo, only two small bands of Cree went on the warpath. The "hostile" Cree bands' military cooperation with the Métis was limited to murdering nine people captured at a small undefended trading post and repulsing a force of Canadian militia, killing eight militiamen. After a few dozen deaths on both sides and some surprising defeats of Dominion forces by Métis militia in several skirmishes, the Métis' "capital" was quickly overrun, their leader was arrested, and the rebellion ended.[24] More generally, of course, force was often used by the Mounties in capturing or killing Indian, Métis, and white law-breakers. But compared with what went on to the south, the Canadian colonization of the West was extraordinarily peaceful.

The reasons why western Canada's frontier history is so different from that of Hispanic northern Mexico and the American West are seldom addressed by historians. Extensive trade for furs preceded actual settlement on both frontiers, including trade in those inflammatory commodities, alcohol and guns.[25] Even if the Hudson's Bay Company's methods, calculated to create dependency, were less provocative than those of fly-by-night entrepreneurs in the south, it lost its trade monopoly before the agricultural settlement and railroad building began. In any case, the Canadian Plains tribes preferred to trade with cut-rate Métis and American independents. In the earlier fur trade in both countries, the Indians monopolized production of the furs, whereas whites and Métis played the role of traders. Later, whites and Métis eliminated this informal Indian monopoly when they began trapping and hunting directly, first in the 1820s in the Rockies and Pacific Northwest, and then on the Plains in the 1860s (when the focus of trade shifted to buffalo hides). In fact, the trade situation in western Canada was similar to that south of the border during the critical period between 1860 and 1890.

One crucial Canadian–U.S. difference was the role played by the central government in colonization.[26] In Canada, agricultural settlement occurred only after treaties had "extinguished aboriginal title," whereas in the United States, settlement usually preceded treaties. The Canadian government and its agents kept these agreements by regularly delivering the commodities and cash annuities promised and by preventing white encroachment. In the United States, such treaties were often not ratified by the Senate, nor were the necessary funds allocated by the House. If funds were available, they were often skimmed by corrupt officials and traders. The Spanish and Mexican governments, when they played any role at all, granted large land grants to settlers without paying any attention to native title. In the United States and Mexico, grazing or squatting on Indian land was ignored or even encouraged.

The reserves granted to Canadian tribes in arable regions were small and scattered but allowed each tribe or band to remain within its traditional territory, if only on tiny fragments of it. The Canadian government thus divided its potential enemies as it dispossessed them, but took pains to minimize other potential grievances. In the United States, reservations were much larger; but in these several tribes or bands (sometimes mutually hostile ones) were concentrated, often far from their homelands. Homesickness, intertribal rivalries, and the terrible living conditions made American reservations a constant fount of hostile excursions. Many army officers and settlers regarded these turbulent reserves as little more than temporary sanctuaries where the unpacified bands could receive food and be rearmed each winter after spending the warm season hunting and raiding. Although this view grossly overestimated the winter comforts of these places, in a few instances it bore a kernel of truth. The most outrageous case involved the Kiowas of Fort Sill (Oklahoma) who raided each summer into Texas but then received supplies and ammunition each winter on the reservation.[27] (The Kiowas believed that Texans were not Americans and were puzzled by the outrage expressed by U.S. officials concerning their raids.) In general, the U.S. Indian policy and its implementation united and concentrated potential enemies, multiplied their grievances, and even supplied them with arms and ammunition. It is hard to imagine a better recipe for frontier war.

By and large, Canadian justice was evenhanded; both white and Indian malefactors were caught and punished. The Indians of western Canada seemed to get along as well with the Mounties as any people would with those who policed them. These reasonable relations applied even to refugee warriors from south of the border—for example, the bitterly antiwhite Chief Sitting Bull. The Mounties were and behaved as policemen, not soldiers, in their dealings with Indians and with others. As historian Robert Utley puts it, the paramilitary Mounted Police "could deal with individuals as well as tribes. It did not have to go to war with a whole people to enforce order."[28] Since Mountie officers also served as magistrates, the legal system on the Canadian frontier resembled a mild form of martial law. Typically, the Canadian government ensured the benefits of peace and raised the costs of all crime—especially homicide—for both newcomers and natives. As well, the restraint exercised by the Indians of western Canada as they were subjugated and dispossessed is evidence of how much injustice people will tolerate for the sake of peace if they are assured of receiving the means to survive, certain punishment for breaking the peace, and impartial protection of their persons and property if they keep it. Peace, like war, has its price, and some parties pay more for it than others.

In the U.S. and Mexican realms, crimes committed against Indians went unpunished or were punished less severely than similar offenses against whites. Similarly, the tribes were averse to punishing fellow tribesmen for crimes committed against settlers. White law officers lacked legal jurisdiction over independent Indians, who in any case refused to surrender tribesmen to a foreign and obviously unfair legal system. Because of these legal deficiencies, a state of primitive war often arose between the Indians and the settlers, as these groups' war parties and "militias" exchanged murders, raids, and massacres in cycles of retaliation. When the U.S. and Mexican governments did intervene in these feuds, it was invariably on the side of the colonists. Even on those occasions when the U.S. government or its representatives tried to secure more equitable legal treatment for the Indians, their efforts were usually sabotaged by local legislatures, politicians, and juries.[29] The frequent resort to vigilantism by American settlers indicates that their own legal systems often failed to provide them with adequate redress for crimes committed among themselves. It is, then, hardly surprising that these weak and highly localized frontier legal systems were incapable of redressing crimes committed by Indians or those committed against them. In the nineteenth century, the American West was hardly lawless—on the contrary, it suffered from a plethora of insular, mutually unco-operative systems of law and legal enforcement: customary tribal (various); Spanish and Mexican colonial; American federal, state/territorial, and local (or vigilante).

The primary difference between the Canadian and the American western frontiers has been succinctly summarized by a Canadian historian: "the Cana-dian government got to the West first"—that is, before the settlers. In the American West, effective federal control of land allotments, treaty negotiations, and law enforcement lagged far behind the expansion of settlement. The pri-mary role played by the U.S. government on the western frontier involved supplying a regular army to extinguish the numerous brushfire wars ignited between the equally independent, aggressive, and weakly policed settlers and tribes. Even decades after the first Euro-American colonization, the American West remained in a virtually stateless (or tribal) condition.

Comparing the examples of the Xingu and of nineteenth-century western Canada, it is difficult to isolate common features that might represent general-izable preconditions for peace. Like Xingu society, early-nineteenth-century Canadian society was founded by three abjectly defeated groups: resident French-Canadians and refugee American Loyalists and Highland Scots. But the term "defeated refugees" hardly applies to Canada's later immigrants or to the native tribes of the Canadian West. The trade in specialities linking Indians and Europeans in Canada was hardly arbitrary in the fashion of the Xingu exchanges. The Canadian peace was predominantly the product of the media-tion and police powers of the central state and the use made of them, but the Xinguanos lacked such Hobbesian institutions entirely. Geographic isolation may have played a role in limiting external wars in the Xingu, but this situation did not apply to Canada in relation to its western Indians. Looking at these peaces from the point of view of Xinguanos accused of witchcraft (who had to fear for their lives) or Canadian Indians living in diminished (and sometimes destitute) circumstances on reserves in the late nineteenth century, one could hardly call them attractive. Nevertheless, these peaces do share one enticing feature: they worked.

The only thing both cases clearly demonstrate is that interethnic harmony and intercultural appreciation are *not* preconditions for peace. Victorian Canada and the Xingu provide evidence that a workable peace can be forged and maintained between highly ethnocentric, mutually suspicious, and factious groups. What interethnic peace appears to require is a minimal and practical tolerance by the different parties for the harmless differences between them: one's own group lives the right way and lets others live their own irrational, erroneous way. By and large, the attitude of the allied Xingu tribes was to let their fellow Xinguanos speak a brutish language, wear shocking or ridiculous fashions, eat disgusting foods, worship in the wrong way, and call noise "music"—as long as they honored debts and commitments, did not break the general peace, and refrained from unduly interfering with one's own "proper" mode of life. These allied tribes treated one another with what Gregor describes a "false good manners." Although various forms of covert and overt intolerance among its various ethnic groups have engendered many of Canada's major political quarrels, the only organized violence these have generated since 1820 has been a handful of interethnic killings and two minimally bloody, comic-opera uprisings. That peace may flourish in the face of mildly biased attitudes is heartening, since a condescending tolerance seems less difficult to inculcate than eliminating the universal feeling that one's own ways are best or training people to cherish uncritically precisely those behaviors and beliefs most different from their own. Peace may require minding one's own business and sustaining coolly correct manners, but not wholesale brainwashing.

The Xingu, Canadian, and other cases previously mentioned suggest a few factors that seem to help peace endure. As noted, geographic isolation limits the number of provocations that can lead to war. The bitter aftertaste of a catastrophic defeat and dispossession can foster an aversion to war among the losers that can last for generations. The existence of a powerful third party that effectively and impartially punishes violence and theft can prevent war. A degree of mutual sufferance for the customs and beliefs of others is obviously helpful, but it is not necessary to banish all ethnocentrism or eliminate all economic and social injustice. Allowing allies to specialize in the production of items that a society could produce itself also seems to help maintain peace. On the other hand, neither trade nor intermarriage encourages peace, but often helps to rupture it. The cases discussed here are evidence that peace is as demanding a state as war, requiring for its maintenance effort, economic sacrifice, and even occasional violence. Peace is not an effortless inertial or "natural" state to which people and societies revert in the absence of perturbation.

THE IRRELEVANCE OF BIOLOGY

One persistent claim made regarding the scarcity of peace is that humans (especially men) are driven by their "biology" or "nature" to war on one another. Obviously, nothing in humans' nature inhibits them from making war, but this lack hardly creates an automatic compulsion to fight. Almost all higher animals are capable of violence against their own kind. Humans seem no more predisposed to aggressive behavior than any other species that commonly fights and occasionally kills its own kind over territory, sexual access, or social dominance. Even some species of plants may be considered as "homicidal," since they kill other individuals of their own species in slow motion by shading or other forms of crowding. Humans are such social animals that almost any activity, however basic to individual existence or reproductive success, involves the cooperation of a group. It is hardly surprising that violence, whether against other species or against other humans, often involves group cooperation. Other highly social creatures, from ants to rhesus monkeys, also display forms of group violence that have been called warfare. Warfare is ultimately not a denial of the human capacity for social cooperation, but merely the most destructive expression of it.

One difficulty for a sociobiological explanation is precisely humans' inborn aptitude for social cooperation, the most obvious and unique expression of which is language. Our capacity for and use of violence is neither remarkable nor excessive compared with that of many other animal species, whereas our sociability and cooperativeness are unique. The Hobbesian "war of all against all" might be used to describe some solitary species of nonhuman animals, but it cannot be applied to any known human society. All societies, however bellicose or violent, use social and cultural devices to preserve havens of peace and cooperation within a group—even if only within a small band or village. If humans can occasionally construct huge societies involving hundreds of millions of individuals *within* which homicide is nearly eliminated, there is no biological reason why such social units could not include all of humanity. Regarding humans' inborn capacities, it is far easier to explain peace than war.

But the greatest problem for a biological explanation of warfare—or of almost any aspect of our behavior—is the incredible plasticity of human conduct. Human behavior is shaped by learning and decision making to an extraordinary and overwhelming degree. Several examples have already been given of people regarded as especially peaceable or warlike changing within a few generations and even within a single lifetime to the opposite extreme. In many societies, members are extremely unaggressive and nonviolent toward one another and yet are very aggressive and violent toward outsiders.[30] Most groups treat certain outsiders with friendship and kindness, others with cool suspicion and reserve, and yet others with hostility and cruelty. Human history is replete with examples in which such relationships change from familiar friendship to bitter enmity and back again with remarkable rapidity. To anthropologists, who have spent over a century exploring the huge variety of human behavior and its mutability, human biology looks less like destiny and more like its absence.

To use a modern analogy, if we look at the identical microchips in two computers, there is nothing intrinsic to explain why one is playing a war game while the other is doing accounts, or why the same computer can at one moment be targeting a missile and in the next designing a toy factory. Modern computers of exactly the same architecture are *capable* of directing aerial battles, conning ships, performing music, formulating genealogies, and simulating thousands of other warlike and peaceable activities, but in no sense does their hardware (that is, their "nature") *require* them to perform these activities. They can and will perform such tasks only if they have "learned" how to do them by being programmed and then receive the proper "social and environmental stimuli" in the form of commands and other inputs. Like computers, their far simpler and entirely passive reflections, human individuals and societies possess the "hardware" to conduct wars and create peace but will not unless they have the proper programs and stimulating circumstances.

WHY WAR AND WHY NOT PEACE?

One social reason for the existence of war is that peace is sometimes too costly. When the effects of peace are the same as those of war—loss of members to homicide and kidnapping, impoverishment by theft and vandalism, and diminished access to critical resources—people have little to lose by going to war and potentially much to gain. Like those referred to in the famous signs of the Paris zoo, humans are dangerous animals because when attacked they will defend themselves. There are situations when it is better to send men to die on their feet than have everyone live on their knees.

Many people (and some anthropologists) deny that any gains are attainable through warfare, although they do concede that, in a Hobbesian world of war, declaring unilateral peace amounts to committing social suicide. The positive benefits of war as a rule come only with success. The loot and captives commonly obtained by a victor or successful raider may amply compensate for the risks and penalties of combat. Warfare offers one way to increase supplies of food and essential materials, expand territory, and enlarge the pool of labor and sexual partners. With its hazards and hardships, warfare may be (in the Western phrase) "a hard dollar," but it yields gains nonetheless. To encourage warfare, these benefits need not be the goal, motivation, or cause of warfare; nevertheless, they often enough reward those who decide for whatever reasons to make war.

One explanation for why young men (especially young bachelors) are usually the most aggressive in initiating and conducting warfare is that they have the least to lose and the most to gain from successful combat.[31] They are (often) unmarried, possess little or no property, and have far less status or influence than do older men. If they are killed, their deaths leave behind no widows or orphans who might become a burden to fellow tribesmen or suffer the degradations of captivity in defeat. If only wounded, they recover from their injuries more readily than do older men. If they succeed, war can gain them wealth, renown, and even a wife. No wonder, then, that young bachelors must be restrained by older men and women who have more to lose from defeat and less to gain from victory.

The circumstances under which regional pacification developed is another arena in which relative costs and benefits played a role in determining the incidence of war and peace. As we have seen, in many tribal areas, peace was imposed by an external power that punished fighting with superior force. Some areas pacified themselves when repeating rifles became readily available and trade with the wider world increased—like in many areas of Melanesia and among the Kalinga of the Philippines.[32] In all these cases, changes made either warfare significantly more costly or peace substantially more profitable (or both).

But the costs of peace and the benefits of war are not completely sufficient explanations for aggressive behavior. First, we have seen instances where peace has been kept even though the price borne by some of the parties to it was disproportionately high, as in the case of the Indians of western Canada during the latter half of the nineteenth century. Second, although people tend to be overly optimistic about their chances of success in war, combat is a very risky business. Peace may have its risks too—droughts, diseases, pests, and countless human errors—but these are mostly unpredictable, whereas the risks of war are expected and obvious. Third, since these costs and risks are relatively higher for tribal societies (because of their smaller populations and thinner subsistence surpluses), war should be less common among such groups than among states and empires. But, as we have seen, the opposite appears to be true. Its high frequency at all levels of social organization implies that war may be many times more profitable or less risky than peace. This implication of the cost–benefit explanation for war conflicts not only with most scholars' expectations, but also with the opinions of all tribal peoples polled by ethnographers. The universal preference for peace is not just the product of arbitrary moral choice or deep psychology; it is practical and rational. War is frankly parasitic—absorbing the profits of peaceful endeavors while imposing additional costs. Clearly some factor beyond costs and gains must be included in explanations of war.

This additional element surely involves the difficulty that societies experience in establishing and maintaining peace with equals. When no third party exists to adjudicate disputes over marriage arrangements, personal injuries, trade, territory, and other economic concerns, or when the mediators that do exist cannot enforce their decisions on the recalcitrant, disputants regularly resort to violent self-help. Peace is unavoidably rare in settings where no institutions have the moral authority and physical power to maintain it by compelling restitution or retribution for injuries, imposing resolutions to disputes, and ensuring the survival of component social units. Any peace lacking powerful institutions to uphold it usually amounts to little more than a prolonged truce. As anthropologist Marvin Harris put it: "Primitive peoples go to war because they lack alternative solutions to certain problems—alternative solutions that would involve less suffering and fewer premature deaths."[33]

But to have peace, it is not enough to establish Hobbes's Leviathan. Institutions of mediation and enforcement merely guarantee that the costs of violence or war will be high and that the enjoyment of any gains so obtained will be limited. To ensure a peace, a society must provide rewards—or at least no penalties—for keeping it. If people are confident that their labor will provide at least the necessities of life and some access to comforts and luxuries, violence will generally attract only the pathological. At the same time, even when peace is institutionalized in the form of courts and police it will be broken by violence, sabotage, or rebellion if it becomes more costly and risky than war. To put it simply, people must be given more inducement than just fear of punishment if peace is to endure.

Why war and why not peace? War represents a method, derived directly from hunting, for getting from one group what another one lacks and cannot peacefully obtain. It also serves as a means of preserving a group's persons and possessions from the predatory or desperate and as a way of enforcing the harsh reciprocity of the *lex talionis* when no other mode of satisfaction is available. However, such simple answers are of little practical use in the complex and highly various social situations in which human beings strive to prevent wars and sustain peace. The proceeds of war vary tremendously with time, place, and culture: here cattle, there petroleum reserves, elsewhere slaves or salt cakes. The price of peace can be raised by belligerent neighbors, rapid population rises, trade imbalances, climatic changes, and a host of other difficulties peculiar to a time and place. Which methods and institutions are most effective in preserving peace is a question that has exercised the minds of leaders, rulers, councils, philosophers, and visionaries for millennia, without producing any enduring or generally applicable answers.

ELEVEN

Beating Swords
into Metaphors

The Roots of the Pacified Past

s the preceding chapters have demonstrated, the
anthropological concepts of primitive war and prehis
toric peace are extremely contrary to ethnographic
and archaeological fact. But how and why did such delusions
develop, especially among academics? Why were they maintained in the face of contrary facts? Why did Quincy Wright
ignore the implications of his casualty figures for primitive
societies? Why did Harry Turney-High never consider the
actual effects and effectiveness of primitive compared with
civilized warfare? Why have Brian Ferguson and others
never mentioned the archaeological data that was so obviously relevant to their theory of prehistoric peace? Why have
archaeologists glibly interpreted remains that testify unam-
biguously to violent conflict in symbolic or ritualistic terms?
Each of these questions points to a prevailing studied silence
about prestate warfare; the causes of this silence are to be
found in events and intellectual currents outside academic
anthropology.

SEEING THE ELEPHANT

The concepts that provide the framework for the pacified past originated in the period immediately following World War II. Several features of that particular war and its aftermath encouraged a pervasive and profound odium for everything connected with warfare. Since the hearth and wellspring of modern Western culture remains western Europe, the events in and the attitudes of that region are of key concern because they soon radiate to the New World and beyond.[1]

World War II was an especially traumatic experience for western Europe, which had not seen combat across its whole territory since the days of Napoleon. During World War I, the fighting in the West had been confined to a narrow strip of territory along the trench lines. But almost every populous region of France, Spain, Italy, Germany, England, and the Low Countries was an arena of combat and devastation during World War II or the preceding Spanish Civil War. Guerrilla warfare spread the horror even to remote rural areas. For the previous 125 years, for most western Europeans, war had always taken place elsewhere, and it had therefore been viewed with a degree of detachment.

Unlike previous European wars, World War II left most western Europeans (and North Americans) with plentiful scars from direct injuries and stains of innocent blood on their hands. The devastation, disease, displacement of populations, and near famine of the war's aftermath encouraged self-pity among the nations that started the war and charity from the United States—the war's only unequivocal victor. After the passions of the war had cooled, the widespread slaughter of noncombatants by bombing became distasteful even to those who had inflicted it. Even in our revisionist age, it is difficult to deny that the Allied victory delivered the world from evil, but the total war necessary to achieve this deliverance entailed economic, human, and moral costs that still seem staggering.[2] And the almost immediate development of the Cold War revealed that all this suffering had merely eliminated one rivalry only to expose another even more dangerous. Europe remained an armed camp. Historian John Keegan notes that World War I persuaded only the victors that "the costs of war exceeded its rewards," whereas World War II convinced the "victors and vanquished alike of the same thing."[3] After generations of seeing war masked by a degree of comfortable distance, western European society was brought face to face with its true visage, and it conceived a most profound aversion for it.

This general change in the Western appreciation of war can be seen in two areas of popular and academic culture. The war stories, novels, and poems of the nineteenth century celebrated the adventure, heroism, and glory of war.[4] Those produced between the world wars treated war and soldiers' experience of it as an epic tragedy that, if lacking in any pretense to glory, nevertheless provided the stage for stoic heroism and comradely self-sacrifice.[5] The literature of the past fifty years, by contrast, has tended to treat war as a brutal bedlam in which humans merely struggle, usually unsuccessfully, to preserve their lives and sanity. Postwar American war novels, for example, portray men as the dazed neurotic victims of psychotic officers, the petty tyrannies and stupefying boredom of military life, and the mindless cruelty of war itself.[6] War had changed in literature from an uplifting melodrama, to a elegiac tragedy, to a surrealist black comedy.

The great American academic historians of the nineteenth century often dealt with military subjects—for instance, Parkman's *France and England in North America*, Prescott's *History of the Conquest of Mexico*, and Mahan's very influential naval histories. But by the middle of the twentieth century, history professors at prestigious universities were concerned almost exclusively with social and economic matters.[7] A recent acknowledgment of this tendency occurs in the preface to Princeton historian James McPherson's magnificent *Battle Cry of Freedom*, in which the author feels compelled to justify the space (about 40 percent of the book) devoted to military campaigns, in a book about the American Civil War! Military history has been relegated to a few professors at provincial institutions and the military academies, to nonacademics, and to amateurs. As war has come to be represented in literature as an absurd nightmare, academic interest in military history has waned.

The newly discovered madness of war is symbolized by the mushroom cloud. Not only did atomic weapons immediately exterminate and devastate on a gigantic scale, but their radiation continued to kill and maim for generations after hostilities had ceased. These Old Testament qualities of nuclear weapons had such a special resonance for the Western mind that people began to speak not of another world war but of Armageddon. As the Cold War developed and nuclear weapons proliferated, "atomic fear" gripped the civilized world. Even before it was a practical proposition, visions of an atomic apocalypse appeared in the popular literature and films of the 1950s and 1960s. Typically, these productions asked not whether humanity could survive a nuclear war, but whether such a war was worth surviving. They depicted a world returned to the Stone Age, populated by nightmarish mutant species and tiny tribes of impoverished survivors. Once "mutually assured destruction" (with its perfect acronym, MAD) became technologically possible in the 1960s, the concepts of victory and defeat, "good guys" and "bad guys" lost their significance. War was seen as more than just stupid or cruel; in its atomic form, it was suicidal lunacy—a lunacy that Western civilization had induced and could not cure. Western Europe had "seen the elephant" (as American soldiers called seeing combat during the Civil War), and the very thought of it became an anathema.

THE END OF IMPERIALISM

By the dawn of the nineteenth century, Hobbes's view of primitive life had gained the upper hand because it was, of course, superbly convenient to European colonial and imperial ambitions. What political or territorial rights could be granted to heathens whose lives were one long criminal spree, who (because of their violent anarchy) could neither produce nor enjoy any of the fruits of civilized industry, whose very proximity radiated disorder and anxiety into the frontier zones of civilized settlement? With such a view, colonists and colonial administrators could no more tolerate "unpacified" Hobbesian primitives nearby than they could leave pirates or brigands unmolested. The consequences of these applications of Hobbes's arguments were transformed, by the end of the nineteenth century, into the sanctimonious "white-man's burden" of bringing the peace and bounty of civilization to "lesser breeds without the Law." Few Westerners paused to consider that the "law" they brought often meant slavery and penury to the natives or that these "lesser breeds" might legitimately view the greedy colonials as pirates and brigands whom the natives could ill-afford to leave unmolested.

In the second half of the nineteenth century, however, sociologists and anthropologists united the neo-Hobbesian perspective with something quite foreign to Hobbes's careful arguments for human equality: Social Darwinism and racism. Imperialists had long been troubled by the common and often violent refusal of native peoples to acknowledge the superiority of European culture and religion or adopt them willingly. The new doctrines of the struggle for existence and survival of the fittest provided a cornucopia of explanations and justifications. The spread of Western civilization and Europeans at the expense of other cultures and races became a splendid illustration of Spencer's survival of the fittest. Inherited mental inferiority thus "explained" the intractable resistance to European civilization by "primitive races." The lives of savages were "nasty, brutish and short" because the humans who lived them were both culturally and genetically limited. Late-nineteenth-century imperialists thus discovered a moral duty and a biological right to wrest dominion of the earth from such less-favored peoples.[8]

If prewar European imperialism encouraged a view of war and conquest as normal and right, World War II and its aftermath severely challenged it. One especially shocking aspect of World War II was that the Nazis attempted to do to fellow Europeans what the latter had long been doing (less efficiently and less brutally) to non-Europeans. The Nazis justified genocidal "clearances," the grossest forms of labor exploitation, and tyrannical government over conquered peoples by an uncomfortably familiar reference to a self-proclaimed superiority of race, technology, and culture. After the Nazis, warfare and conquest looked less like noble crusades or direct expressions of a law of nature and more like the basest of crimes. After four centuries of western European imperialism, the sauce for the goose had finally been applied to the gander.

However bitterly contested and involuntary it may have been, postwar decolonization also lifted a considerable burden from the backs of western European intelligentsia. The demise of their nations' empires virtually eliminated any need for apology or self-reproach. Indeed, in the postwar period, European nations became quasi-colonies themselves—their empires liquidated, their economies dependent on those of the United States and the Soviet Union, and they themselves reduced to second-rate client-states of "the Great Powers" (which no longer included them). Postwar western European intellectuals, both right and left, began seeing themselves and their societies as *victims* of imperialism and neocolonialism, even if they felt the peas of their victimization through increasing mattresses of prosperity.[9] A generation after the end of World War II, it became intellectually fashionable in western Europe to identify with the many non-Western peoples that once were colonial subjects.

THE DISAPPEARING PRIMITIVE

As cynics often observed in the United States during the nineteenth century, the nobility of "savages" was directly proportional to one's geographic distance from them.[10] During the late nineteenth century, Easterners were thus very sympathetic to the plight of the western Indians, doted on James Fennimore Cooper's sentimental portrayals of eastern Indians, and put the fine speeches of Indian orators in their children's schoolbooks. Yet the grandparents of these same sympathetic Easterners had offered bounties on Indian scalps and had ruthlessly expelled the natives from their states. One such rapid shift in white attitudes was responsible for the irony that the general who presided over the final defeats of the western tribes, Ohio-born Tecumseh Sherman, was named for a great Shawnee chief (William was added only when he was nine). Of course, it had been a generation before Sherman's birth that Chief Tecumseh had pursued his vain quest for a great tribal coalition to drive the Americans out of the old Northwest, including Ohio. Most Westerners still in direct contact with "wild" Indians, on the other hand, regarded them as dangerous vermin, turbulent brigands, or useless beggars to be expelled or exterminated at any opportunity. Once the natives were safely reduced to living on reservations, however, Westerners were just as inclined to become sentimental about them and their traditional ways of life as Easterners were.

This change from fearful hatred to nostalgia as distance in time or space increases is not peculiar to the United States. The difference in attitude toward the German tribes evidenced by Julius Caesar and Tacitus, the increasing admiration of neo-Australians for Aborigines (actually, "traditional" Aborigines), the Boer fascination with the Bushmen, and the softening of Japanese attitudes toward the Ainu are examples of similar phenomena. It is much easier to admire tribal life once it has been destroyed and little chance remains, except in fantasy, of its returning. In Western popular culture, Rousseau triumphs over Hobbes only when "man in a state of nature" is no longer a viable competitor and has faded from direct sight.

The disappearance of uncivilized ways of life began with the evolution of the first urban societies 6,000 years ago, but the incorporation of tribal peoples into civilized economies definitely accelerated after World War II. Before the war, "primitives" could still be found living traditional lives in some isolated areas of the world, such as highland New Guinea, west-central Australia, and parts of tropical South America, the Phillipines, and Africa. But the rapid postwar growth in Third World populations, dramatic improvements in transportation and communications technology, and the voracious appetite of industrial economies for ever-scarcer raw materials have carried modern civilization to every corner of the inhabited world. As anthropologists are acutely aware, the primitive world of traditional prestate economies and cultures had completely vanished by the late 1960s. Thus tribal societies can no longer impede civilized enterprises, and direct observations can no longer contradict sentimental views of them. Any unpleasant behavior on the part of the subjugated remnants of such societies can be dismissed as being due to their corruption and degradation by Western civilization. The increasing bowdlerization of precivilized life in popular culture over the past few decades is just a broader and more final version of the changing attitudes toward traditional Indian lifeways observed in the United States during the nineteenth century.

THE FADING HOPE OF PROGRESS

The great shock of World War II savagery, atomic fear, the ex post facto awakening to the evils and indignities of imperial conquest, and the later spread of ecological sensitivity eroded all that remained of the Western myths of progress and civilized superiority. Attacks on these moribund notions have reached frenzied proportions in the past few decades. Industrial expansion and technological advance are now regarded merely as harbingers of ecological disaster and more destructive wars, while advances in medicine have only encouraged overpopulation and further misery. Mass communications and cheap transportation are regarded as having eroded human linguistic and cultural diversity while bringing the commercial corruptions of the West to every doorstep. These accusations imply some rather drastic cures—technological regression, depopulation, deindustrialization, decreasing human mobility, and censorship or suppression of global communications. Ironically, these prescriptions, taken simultaneously, resemble less Rousseau's golden age and more the post-apocalyse world envisioned in science fiction. These neo-Rousseauian arguments curiously imply that we are only a nuclear winter away from a springtime of human equality and harmony.

Cynics have observed that those who have benefited the most from "progress"—the citizens of the First World—are the people most inclined to disdain it. The privileged few who eat better, lead longer and more stimulating lives because of modern agriculture, medicine, education, mass communications, and travel, and are most cushioned from physical discomfort and inconvenience by industrial technology are the most nostalgic about the primitive world. This attitude is more difficult to find among the real "victims of progress" in the Third World except among members of these nations' Western-educated elites. Despite the odds against them, the inhabitants of these countries flow in dense streams toward those shabby islands of modernity, the cities, attracted by the slim hope of material progress they offer. For many of these migrants, the primitive world they are fleeing is not a legend but a living memory. Perhaps the most bizarre expression of this impulse was the elevation of the notion of material progress to a religion by the Cargo Cults of the tribesmen of New Guinea.[11] The concept behind these cults was to obtain the material plenty and comforts of civilization (Cargo) by magical means. The current Western distaste for progress may be just another luxury Westerners enjoy. But a less cynical gloss is that civilization inevitably looks grimmer to those intimately familiar with its thousand discontents, whereas its streets seem paved with gold in the eyes of those farthest from its citadel.

Most of the evils attributed to civilization and progress—such as social inequality and subordination, murder, theft, rape, vandalism, and conquest—are found concentrated in the conduct and effects of war. Therefore, in a neo-Rousseauian world view, war itself constitutes one of the principal products of Western progress, and the precivilized condition and the non-Western world before European expansion must have been idyllic and peaceful. As ever, when faith in the myth of progress declines, the myth of the golden age finds new adherents.

THE CREATION OF MYTH

In the postwar atmosphere of anxiety, malaise, and dissatisfaction with Western civilization, anthropologists have introduced doctrines concerning precivilized violence consistent with this mood. But the concepts of primitive war and prehistoric peace were *not* the products of pure imagination or conscious falsehood. They relied on available evidence, but often the data cited were quite irrelevant to their key ideas. Thus the proponents of safe and ineffective primitive war have focused on stylized and low-casualty battles in preference to the rarer massacres and much more frequent raids that killed most people. These proponents have evaluated the effectiveness of tribal war entirely on the ethnocentric grounds of how similar its conduct was to modern warfare rather than on the basis of its actual effects. They have devoted special attention to the murky question of motives. Similarly, the advocates of prehistoric peace ignore the very archaeological evidence that disproves their case. Archaeologists, relying on the time-honored method of "ethnographic analogy," have contributed to the pacification of the past by blithely ignoring the problem of prehistoric violence. The resulting fashionable ideas concerning precivilized warfare are the products of discrimination, then, not ignorance or prevarication.

The anthropologists whose interpretations have helped artifically to pacify the past were in a sense merely possessed by the spirit of their times. As is true of all ideas everywhere, scientific understanding is usually rooted in the values and attitudes of a particular era or culture. What saves scientific propositions from being mere intellectual fashions is their ability to withstand testing against critical evidence. The concepts of the pacified past are wrong not because they are fashionable or biased, but because they are incompatible with the most relevant ethnographic and archaeological evidence.

Yet there is something to be criticized in the fashions themselves, whether those of the neo-Hobbesian past or those of the neo-Rousseauian present. Both deny tribal peoples their complete humanity. A previous era refused to acknowledge the intelligence, sociability, and generosity of uncivilized people and the richness, effectiveness, and rationality of their ways of life. Today, popular opinion finds it difficult to attribute to tribal peoples a capacity for rapaciousness, cruelty, ecological heedlessness, and Machiavellian guile equal to our own. (For example, when ecological accusations fly, who recalls the ten marvellous and unique species of flightless birds [Moas] hunted to extinction by the ancient Polynesians who first settled New Zealand?) Both laypersons and academics now prefer a vision of tribal peoples as lambs in Eden, spouting ecological mysticism and disdain for the material conditions of life. In short, we *wish* them to be more righteous and spiritual (in our terms, not theirs), happier and less emotionally complicated, and less prone to rational calculations of self-interest than ourselves.[12] With only rare exceptions, Westerners of the past few centuries have found it difficult to accept that primitive and prehistoric people were ever as clever, as morally equivocal, and as emotionally complex as themselves. When we attribute to primitive and prehistoric people only our virtues and none of our vices, we dehumanize them as much as ourselves.

A wise writer once noted that "he who makes a beast of himself gets rid of the pain of being a man."[13] By believing that primitive and prehistoric peoples were far more humane and peaceful than their modern civilized counterparts, we metaphorically make beasts of ourselves. Our capacity for organized violence, the universal ugliness of war, and the intricate difficulties of keeping a peace are part of the "pain" of being human. Accepting the despairing myth of the pacified past encourages us to neglect solving these universal problems in the only place we can—in the present, among ourselves.

TWELVE

A Trout in the Milk

Discussion and Conclusions

What the dead had no speech for, when living
They can tell you, being dead; the communication
Of the dead is tongued with fire beyond the
      language of the living.

        • • •

We shall not cease from exploration
And the end of all our exploring
Will be to arrive where we started
And know the place for the first time.

        T. S. Eliot, "Little Gidding"

These favorite lines from an unfavorite poet sum up what this book has been about. The "communications" recorded here from the dead world of prehistory and the recently deceased "primitive" one are indeed eloquent on the subject of war. The burned villages, the arrowheads embedded in bones, the death tolls, and the mutilated corpses speak more truthfully, more passionately on this dismal subject than all the recorded verbiage of the living, which is riddled with cant, sophistry, and flights of fancy. The dead voices heard here tell us that war has an ugly sameness; it is always a compound of crimes no matter what kind of society is involved or when in time it occurs. After exploring war before civilization in search of something less terrible than the wars we know, we merely arrive where we started with an all-too-familiar catalog of deaths, rapes, pillage, destruction, and terror.

This is a brutal reality that modern Westerners seem very loathe to accept. They seem always tempted to flee it by imagining that our world is the best of all possible ones or that life was better when the human world was far simpler. During this century, anthropologists have struggled with such complacent and nostalgic impulses, even in themselves. Their ambition was and is to explore the human condition at all times and in all places, to enlarge the narrow view of it that the written records of civilized life provide and to, in every sense, "arrive where we started and know the place for the first time." But these goals and the raw subject matter of anthropology—the origins of humans and their various cultures, social life before cities, states, and historical records—are in every culture but our own the province of mythology. Myths are a consequence of many impulses and serve many purposes, but chief among these are didactic and moralizing ones. Anthropologists would be less than human themselves if they were immune to such impulses, and it is difficult to deny that on the subject of war before civilization they have shown a special susceptibility. After the depressing shocks of two world wars, anthropologists compromised between complacency and nostalgia, Hobbes and Rousseau, by conceiving of primitive war as a sometimes common but unserious and ineffectual activity. A few now seem poised to abandon even this compromise by quietly assuming or boldly declaring that life before civilization was remarkably peaceful. Yet whatever their tendency to mythologize, anthropologists have steadily accumulated observations and physical evidence through their ethnographic and archaeological fieldwork. It is precisely these painfully accumulated facts that prevent anthropology from lapsing into mythology.

The facts recovered by ethnographers and archaeologists indicate unequivocally that primitive and prehistoric warfare was just as terrible and effective as the historic and civilized version. War is hell whether it is fought with wooden spears or napalm. Peaceful prestate societies were very rare; warfare between them was very frequent, and most adult men in such groups saw combat repeatedly in a lifetime. As we have seen, the very deadly raids, ambushes, and surprise attacks on settlements were the forms of combat preferred by tribal warriors to the less deadly but much more complicated battles so important in civilized warfare. In fact, primitive warfare was much more deadly than that conducted between civilized states because of the greater frequency of combat and the more merciless way it was conducted. Primitive war was very efficient at inflicting damage through the destruction of property, especially means of production and shelter, and inducing terror by frequently visiting sudden death and mutilating its victims. The plunder of valuable commodities was common, and primitive warfare was very effective in acquiring additional territory, even if this was a seldom professed goal.

Primitive war was not a puerile or deficient form of warfare, but war reduced to its essentials: killing enemies with a minimum of risk, denying them the means of life via vandalism and theft (even the means of reproduction by the kidnapping of their women and children), terrorizing them into either yielding territory or desisting from their encroachments and aggressions. At the tactical level, primitive warfare and its cousin, guerrilla warfare, have also been superior to the civilized variety. It is civilized warfare that is stylized, ritualized, and relatively less dangerous. When soldiers clash with warriors (or guerrillas), it is precisely these "decorative" civilized tactics and paraphernalia that must be abandoned by the former if they are to defeat the latter. Even such a change may be insufficient, and co-opted native warriors must be substituted for the inadequate soldiers before victory belongs to the latter.

The real weakness of precivilized war making has been at the highest strategic level, rooted in the weaker logistic capacities imposed by small populations, slim economic surpluses, and limited transportation capacities. These true deficiencies, all determined by the social and economic features inherent in tribal life itself, have made it almost impossible for tribal warriors to conduct planned campaigns and prolonged sieges. It was the concentration of resources and power in hierarchical political organizations, the millions of cannon-fodder citizens subject to their disposal, the galleon, compass and sextant, the ox-wagon, steam engine, railroads, and factory production, as well as smallpox, measles, and weeds, that allowed the nations of western Europe to gain ascendancy over the uncivilized world during the past half-millennium. It was *not* the much discussed and theatrical weaponry, discipline, and tactical techniques that gave soldiers their eventual triumphs, but their mastery of the rather pedestrian arcana of logistics. In modern guerrilla warfare, when superior primitive tactics are wedded to even very limited civilized logistics, more completely civilized adversaries are very commonly discomfited. Guerrilla warfare merely incorporates manpower and supply capacities on a civilized scale and uses more up-to-date weaponry. Primitive warfare is simply total war conducted with very limited means.

The discovery that war is total—that is, between peoples or whole societies, not just the armed forces who represent them—is credited by historians to recent times. Some point to the French Revolution's "nation in arms" or Napoleon's aggressive use of it. Against this claim can be posed the doctrines of Jomini, Clausewitz, and (in naval warfare) Mahan, who analyzed the Napoleonic Wars and concluded that the primary objective in warfare should be the destruction of an enemy's "main force" military units by formal battles, ideally a single decisive trial of strength. Other military historians claim with better justification that the realization of war's total nature belongs to those peculiarly American military geniuses, Grant and Sherman, who are credited individually or jointly with the awful invention of modern total war. It should be clear from this book that this Western "discovery" is comparable to the European discovery of the Far East, Africa, or the Americas. The East Asians, sub-Saharan Africans, and Native Americans always knew where they were; it was the Europeans who were confused or ignorant. So it is with total war. For millennia, tribal warriors have been conducting smaller-scale and more ruthless versions of Sherman's march and Grant's war of attrition by ringing fruit trees, stealing or destroying herds and crops, burning houses and canoes, stealthily slaughtering individuals and small groups, and gradually abrading a foe's manpower in very frequent but low-casualty battles. Primitive war is "war to the knife," *guerre à l'outrance*. War has always been a struggle between peoples, their societies, and their economies, not just warriors, war parties, armies, and navies.

Western nations gradually lost sight of this simple truth over many centuries after the decline of Rome. They more and more preferred to conduct war purely between proportionally smaller forces of specialists—first armored nobility, then mercenaries, and, later, professionals or regulars. They took what had been a nasty free-for-all, often literally a struggle for existence (like that between Rome and Carthage), and turned it into a chess game with highly specialized units, stylized movements, and constrained rules. This chess analogy may be trite, but it is a revealing one for civilized war. For example, the celebrated military historian John Keegan notes that for commanders warfare had changed very little over the 200 years before Waterloo. He employs the chess analogy in noting that despite many changes in technology and the social context of military leadership, the nature of civilized combat was very similar over several centuries. He approves of Wellington's description of the Battle of Waterloo as "Napoleon just moved forward in the old style and was driven off in the old style." Yet in his choice of examplars of military leadership, he skips from Alexander the Great (ca. 300 B.C.) to Wellington (ca. A.D. 1800), a "jump" of more than 2,000 years, implying that the rate of evolution in Western military methods was very slow during these two millennia.[1] The results of this prolonged stultification or recoil from primitive realism in Western military culture were indecisiveness or stasis in a host of chess-like wars.[2] Our modern names for several of these conflicts reflect their indecisiveness: for example, the Crusades, the Hundred Years' War, and the Thirty Years' War. It was only in the outposts, where the victors' manpower consisted primarily of native levies naturally versed in *real* war and colonial militias who had relearned it from the natives, that the results were conclusive. While the fighting in the European heartland continued indecisively between A.D. 1500 and 1830, France, Spain, Portugal, and (to a lesser degree) the Netherlands lost great domains beyond Europe in the New World and in parts of Asia.

But does this chess analogy apply to Grant's repeated tactical defeats by Lee—which culminated in Lee's, not Grant's, surrender—or Sherman's March *away* from the main Rebel force opposing him? No, Grant and Sherman defied the rules and doctrines of Western civilized warfare. It was not until World War II that the rest of the civilized world followed suit. Indeed, what is submarine warfare at sea or strategic bombing in the air but guerrilla (read "primitive") warfare by new technological means in new mediums?

When we turn to those old questions of what causes wars and helps maintain peace, we find that primitive societies are essentially similar to civilized ones. As with civilized wars, the motives of primitive participants and the causes of their violent confrontations have often been murky and complex. It seems universal that it is usually an act of violence by one side that precipitates a war and behind such acts are usually disputes of an economic character. The only difference that can be seen in this area between states and nonstates is that the latter never claim or appear to be fighting to subjugate another society—to subordinate an independent population to one group's central political institutions. Since tribal and band societies lack institutional subordination and have decentralized political systems, their "ignorance" of this motive is hardly surprising.

Leaving the muddy waters of immediate motives and causes, a broader consideration of contexts that encourage war leads to several interesting conclusions. Contrary to common sense, neither the intensity nor the frequency of war or other violent behavior is correlated with human population density. Another surprise is that trade and intermarriage between societies increase, rather than decrease, the likelihood of war between them. On the other hand, some common expectations are correct. For example, regions and periods of frequent bitter warfare are often centered on especially aggressive societies that "spoil their neighborhood." In several ethnographic and historical cases, these "bad apples" were experiencing rapid population increases. Consistent with Hollywood folklore, frontiers between cultures are prone to violence, especially when moving. And, as we might think, wars are very frequent during the hard times created by natural and man-made disasters.

Despite a universal preference for peace and revulsion for homicide, even that of enemies, making peace between equals is fraught with pitfalls. Maintaining a peace between independent societies over several generations is even more difficult and thus even rarer. The rarity in both the primitive and civilized worlds of sustained peaces makes it hard to isolate the favorable factors. However, two have long appeared to be useful: employing strong institutions to resolve disputes and punish peace breaking and ensuring that those who keep the peace are rewarded, or at least not punished. If these prescriptions seem vague and too simplistic, the reason is that one cannot describe the form of institutions or the kinds of rewards that might be universally and eternally applicable. If it were not so difficult to design social systems that delivered these desiderata, peace would be a far less scarce commodity.

But before developing too militant a view of human existence, let us put war in its place. However frequent, dramatic, and eye-catching, war remains a lesser part of social life. Whether one takes a purely behavioral view of human life or imagines that one can divine mental events, there can be no dispute that peaceful activities, arts, and ideas are by far more crucial and more common even in the most bellicose societies. Even when the most violent scenes are unfolding on some battlefield or raided village, all around the arena of combat, often at no great distance, children are being conceived and born, crops and herds attended, fish caught, animals hunted, meals prepared, tools made or mended, and thousands of other prosaic, peaceful activities pursued that are necessary to sustain life or serve other human needs. No society can sustain itself purely on the proceeds of war; even pirates and brigands must trade their booty with more peaceful folk or subordinate some of the latter as tributaries to survive. War is impossible without the food, clothing, weapons, or other devices, and, of course, combatants produced by peaceful activities. If warfare did actually absorb most of the energies and time of human beings, wars would truly, in the words of the Forty-sixth Psalm, "cease in all the world" with the rapid extinction of our species. Humans cannot photosynthesize or passively absorb nutrients from the elements; we lack the broad grinding teeth of herbivores or the sharp claws and teeth of a predator; we are relatively slow-footed and weakly muscled; we cannot gestate and nurse more than a single child each year and must continue to care for those we do birth over the many years they take to reach self-sufficiency. To be distracted for a sustained period by warfare (or the tense expectation of it) from the intricate labors and countless mental exertions required to feed, shelter, and reproduce ourselves would soon be fatal to individuals and populations. If Rousseau's primitive golden age is imaginary, Hobbes's perpetual donnybrook is impossible.

While peace (that is, the absence of combat or any immediate prospect of it) may be essential to human existence, warfare is far from insignificant or absent except under civilized conditions. In a few hours, warfare can expend or destroy resources and constructions that are the products of months of labor, and it kills persons who represent years of care by their families (in Kipling's phrase, "two thousand pounds of education drops to a ten rupee jezail" [Afghan musket]). The attrition caused by raids and battles undertaken a few days a month but sustained over time, or just a single climactic massacre, can displace, disperse, or even exterminate whole social units. As we have seen, these dire effects of war affect all levels of social organization and were having an impact long before civilization appeared. War may not be necessary to human existence, but it is a very important aspect of that existence because its effects are so momentous and its occurrence is so frequent.

The myth making about primitive warfare resulting from the current Western attitude of self-reproach is, of course, censurable on scholarly and scientific grounds. But it also deplorable on practical and moral grounds. The ever-immediate problem of how all of humanity can, in Lincoln's immortal words, "achieve and cherish a lasting peace among ourselves and with all nations" is not likely to be solved while we are in the thrall of nostalgic delusions. The doctrines of the pacified past unequivocally imply that the only answer to the "mighty scourge of war" is a return to tribal conditions and the destruction of all civilization. But since the primitive and prehistoric worlds were, in fact, quite violent, it seems that the only practical prospect for universal peace must be more civilization, not less. Adherence to the doctrines of the pacified past absolve us from considering the difficult question of what a truly global civilization should consist of and, more importantly, what its political structure should be.

Depictions of precivilized humans as saints and civilized folks as demons are as hypocritical as they are erroneous. Rousseau never left his very civilized circumstances to join tribesmen living in his ideal state—for example, the hunting-gathering bands of Tasmania. Similarly, the modern-day primitive nostalgist listens to tribal music celebrating the sacredness of nature on a stereo composed of completely artificial materials ultimately extracted from strip mines and oil wells on territories seized or extorted from tribal societies. If Westerners have belatedly recognized that they are not the crown of creation and rightful lords of the earth, their now common view of themselves as humanity's nadir is equally absurd. What is morally wrong with longer life; lower infant mortality; wider knowledge of the universe (including a *science* of ecology); water and food cleansed of parasites and pathogens; photography; Western literature, art, and music; or larger numbers of humans living on less land with fewer premature deaths, including violent ones? But the converse also applies. Can we morally or practically disdain the "social welfare" system of the Plains Indians, the sculpture and winter clothing of the Eskimos, the music and art of tribal Africans, the navigation skills of the Polynesians, the survival techniques of the Australian Aboriginals, the medical botany of countless tribal peoples, or the many "primitive" methods for resolving disputes without recourse to violence or lawyers? The myths of either primitive or civilized superiority deny the intellectual, psychological, and physiological equality of humankind. In fact, the proponents of the pacified past disclaim the idea that all peoples share a common human nature by denying that all societies are capable of using violence to advance their interests.

Anthropologists in this century have long argued for the "psychic unity" of humankind; in other words, all members of our species have within rather narrow limits of variation the same basic physiology, psychology, and intellect. This concept does not exclude *individual* variations in temperament or even the various components of intellect, but finds that such variations have no value in explaining *social or cultural* differences between groups. It is *not* accidental that the descendents of illiterate villagers from various "backward" parts of the world, and of a variety of racial backgrounds, have become Nobel Prize–winning scientists, mathematicians, and fiction writers using languages very different from those spoken by their ancestors. Anthropologists have long recognized that the many and profound differences in technology, behavior, political organization, and values found among societies and cultures can be best explained by reference to ecology, history, and other material and social factors. Thus, with a few rare exceptions, anthropologists argue with one another only about the relative importance of these nongenetic factors in explaining cultural variety and cultural evolution. This attitude reflects not just the antiracist tenor of the twentieth century, but also the accumulated facts and especially the experiences of ethnographers. Human psychic unity is not just a theory but a fact, one that can be demonstrated even in a survey of so dark a topic as war. The fact that despite our universal distaste we do "arrive where we started"—that is, at the blunt ugliness of war—unfortunately represents one of the clearest expressions of our shared psychology. Our common humanity, viewed realistically, can be as much a source of despair as hope.

If war has always been horrible and seldom rare, what lessons, if any, can anthropology offer us in our pursuit of a more peaceful future? Some of the points raised in this work could be very useful, even if they do not suggest easy or comfortable prescriptions.

First, we should consider trade as an especially productive source of violent conflicts and treat our closest trading partners with special care. Allowing other societies arbitrarily to monopolize the production of some goods that we could produce ourselves may be a good way to foster and maintain peace; attacking such monopolies by self-production is likely to lead to trouble. In the absence of international trade tribunals with the power to enforce their decisions, a compromising approach to trade disputes seems highly recommended. The attitude that "business is war," often attributed to the Japanese, is exceptionally ignorant, encourages ruthlessness, and makes a habit of tickling the dragon's tail by inciting and exacerbating trade grievances. The consequences of business, trade, and exchange may include penury and unemployment; but the consequences of war, even for the victors, are death, wounds, and destruction and, for the losers, the very depths of human misery. Mistaking trade for war seems an excellent way of learning firsthand the awful differences between them.

Second, in our vain pursuit of military security, we should concentrate on economic and peaceful technological development rather than strictly military techniques and weapons. The former advantages can be rapidly transformed, via logistic superiority, into military advantages, whereas superior weapons and military techniques cannot make up for deficient logistics and economic infrastructures. The role played by Detroit in World War II, when all the Allied armies (including the Soviet one) rode to victory on American trucks, and the importance of Silicon Valley to the Allied victory in the Gulf War are just two modern examples. We have repeated observed in this study that military techniques and technology are heavily dependent on peaceful technology and social and economic organization. To feed the parasite at the expense of the host only weakens both.

Third, we should strive to create the largest social, economic, and political units possible, ideally one encompassing the whole world, rather than allowing those we do have to fragment into mutually hostile ethnic or tribal enclaves. The degree of mutual interdependence created by modern transportation and communications long ago rendered the concepts of national and ethnic self-sufficiency and self-determination absurd and dangerous delusions. The inter-ethnic violence and general suffering unleashed by the breakup of the central political institutions in the former Soviet Union, Yugoslavia, and Somalia are almost perfect illustrations of this point. As with imperialism, the mere mainte-nance of domestic peace cannot be an excuse for totalitarian tyranny, disastrous economic policies, or state imposition of cultural or religious uniformity, since many states of more equitable, prosperous, and tolerant character are just as internally peaceful. It is very instructive to compare Spain's peaceful conversion from totalitarian tyranny to federal democracy, despite regional and ethnic an-tagonisms as virulent as any in Europe, with the violent lunacy unleashed a few years later in Yugoslavia and Somalia. In Spain, the institution of a central state and many of its basic components were preserved through the transition; in Yugoslavia and Somalia, they disintegrated. The antidote to war is an effective political organization with legislative, judicial, and police powers, whether its scale comprises a family band, a village, a tribe, a chiefdom, a city-state, a nation, or the whole earth. Obviously, the larger the scale and the longer the life span of any such political organization, the more general and enduring is the extent of peace. However, prehistory, history, and ethnography also indicate that there are many possible political organizations and that the decision about which is the best is on extremely complicated one to make.

The final lesson of this survey is the crucial importance of the physical circumstantial evidence produced and interpreted by archaeologists. In our legal system, circumstantial evidence is treated with a statutory reserve, although all law-enforcement and legal professionals know that it is actually eyewitness testimony that is notoriously unreliable and contradictory. In real life, the eye-witness accounts of untrained observers, like verbal contracts, aren't "worth the paper [they're] written on." As all scientists know, all of the most fundamental and useful truths science has uncovered about the universe and its mechanisms have been inferred from and confirmed by purely circumstantial evidence. For example, many people have seen ghosts, but no one has ever seen an electron or a gravitational field. Yet most of us are very dubious about the existence of the former, and we are certain enough of electrons and gravitational fields to stake our lives on technology premised on their existence. Until humans traveled into the upper atmosphere and outer space, there were no eyewitnesses to attest to the reality of such long-accepted but only circumstantially evidenced phe-nomena as the Gulf Stream, limited atmosphere, cyclonic tropical storms, the shape of the continents, and even the sphericity of the earth and moon. Contrary to legal statute, as evidence of "what really happens," physical circumstance is far superior to standard eyewitnesses (who could, for example, honestly pro-claim the earth flat) and expert *opinion* (invariably contradictory). The very physicality of circumstantial evidence, while it may be and often is misin-terpreted, makes it immune to dismissal and resistant to distortion.

It is certainly difficult to bowdlerize or dismiss an arrow point embedded in a victim's spine, although anyone can glibly argue that any witnesses to the homi-cide are liars or deluded. The circumstantial evidence of archaeology is, after written records exist, an essential corrective and complement to history. Using a modern historical example, military historians have been arguing for over a century about what happened to Custer's annihilated third of the Seventh Cavalry at the Little Bighorn. Since 1876, it has been fashionable for Euro-American historians to discount or dismiss the testimony of Native American eyewitnesses to Custer's destruction. Most historians have been content to ignore the accounts of Sioux and Cheyenne warriors who fought against Custer and the few Crow Scouts who saw the Last Stand from a distance after being released by Custer (apparently because they advised him against attacking). The contentious historians have preferred their own reconstructions of how Custer *should have* behaved based on their assessments of his personality and military skill, as well as their own inferences based on such assumptions and the second- or third-hand accounts of survivors from the Reno–Benteen unit. But recently archaeologists, using only circumstantial evidence, have resolved several of the key issues concerning the Last Stand. These resolutions include determining that although the army had no repeating rifles, the Indians had many and used them decisively in repulsing Custer's initial thrust; that Custer's command was not suddenly overwhelmed by superior numbers, but had time to organize a defensive formation; and that the Seventh Cavalry's dead were horribly muti-lated.[3] While the long-despised Native American eyewitness accounts appeared typically distorted and fragmentary, most of them, whether from hostile or allied Indians, generally conformed to the events reconstructed by the archaeologists.

The moral of this story is that historical records are usually biased and then subject to every whim and rhetorical device of historians. In the end, it was only the pedestrian empiricism of some archaeologists, analyzing the rifle shells and reconstructing the shattered skulls left behind on that fateful June 25, that restored to the Native American participants respect for their veracity. Only archaeology compels us to regard the Sioux, Cheyenne, Crow, and Arikawa men and women who left behind personal accounts of that terrible event as the equals of America's most celebrated writers of diaries and memoirs of the Civil, Second World, and Vietnam wars—that is, as human beings like ourselves caught up in traumatic events.

It will always be easy to claim that historical accounts are essentially false—for instance, that Celtic hill-forts were only status symbols that Julius Caesar portrayed as real fortifications to enhance his military reputation, that historical first-contact or ethnographers' reports are merely biased records of disturbed situations, that the red color of watermelon flesh was created by the knife. Fortunately, archaeology is able to look inside the watermelon before it was cut and give the lie to such sophistries. Before civilization and the written records it produces, archaeologists' circumstantial evidence is all that we can ever know of the deeper human past. It is a shame that archaeologists have given so little thought to prehistoric violence and warfare while quietly recording its effects. What is even more disappointing is that this inattentiveness has obscured the fact that some prehistoric regions and periods were remarkably peaceful over many generations. Any lessons that these ancient peaces might hold for us still await the analysis of contrasting them with more violent places and periods. In the present intellectual climate, such comparisons depend first on a recognition by anthropologists that warfare both was common and had important effects in prehistory.

Whatever their personal biases and favored theories, archaeologists basically and ultimately want to know what happened in the past. The physical circumstantial evidence already available repeatedly attests that what transpired before the evolution of civilized states was often unpleasantly bellicose. It also demonstrates that, as with the Native American accounts of the Battle of the Little Bighorn, we cannot summarily dismiss the ethnographic reports that give the same message. As Thoreau said, when he suspected his milkman of watering the milk, "Some circumstantial evidence is very strong, as when you find a trout in the milk." This book has been an extended exercise in finding the trout in the milk.

APPENDIX

Tables

Table 2.1 *Political Organization Versus Frequency of Wars*

Political Organization	Warfare Frequency							
	Continuous		Frequent		Rare/Never		Total	
State	4		6		0		10	
		40.0%		60.0%		—		100%
Chiefdom	3		2		1		6	
		50.0%		33.3%		16.7%		100%
Tribe	20		2		3		25	
		80.0%		8.0%		12.0%		100%
Band	3		5		1		9	
		33.3%		55.6%		11.1%		100%
Total	30		15		5		50	
		60.0%		30.0%		10.0%		100%

Source: Otterbein 1989.

Table 2.2 *Subsistence Economy Versus Frequency of Warfare*

	Warfare Frequency				
Economy	Continuous		Frequent		Rare/Never		Totals

Economy	Continuous		Frequent		Rare/Never		Totals	
Intensive agriculture	8	47.1%	8	47.1%	1	5.8%	17	100%
Shifting cultivation	12	85.7%	2	14.3%	0	—	14	100%
Animal husbandry	8	88.9%	0	—	1	11.1%	9	100%
Hunting-gathering	2	20.0%	5	50.0%	3	30.0%	10	100%
Total	30	60.0%	15	30.0%	5	10.0%	50	100%

Source: Otterbein 1989.

Table 2.3 *Political Integration Versus Frequency of Warfare*

Political Integration	Warfare Frequency								Totals	
	Once per year		Once per 5 years		Once per generation		Rarely or never			
Household-village (0–1)	20	51.3%	7	17.9%	6	15.4%	6	15.4%	39	100%
Tribe-chiefdom (2)	16	61.6%	7	26.9%	0		3	11.5%	26	100%
State (3–4)	17	77.3%	2	9.1%	0		3	13.6%	22	100%
Total	53	60.9%	16	18.4%	6	6.9%	12	13.8%	87	100%

Source: Murdock and Provost 1973; Ross 1983.

Table 2.4 *Frequency of Offensive Raids and of Defense Against Raids Among Western Indians*

Type of Warfare	Raid Frequency			Totals	
	More than 4 per year	2–4 per year	None or 1 per year		
Offensive raid	44	50	63	157	
	28.0%	31.9%	40.1%		100%
Defense against raid	52	77	26	155	
	33.5%	49.7%	16.8%		100%
Offensive or defensive warfare	68	68	21	157	
	43.3%	43.3%	13.4%		100%

Source: Jorgensen 1980.

Table 2.5 *Frequency and Duration of Warfare by Nation-States, 1800–1945*

Nation	Number of Wars	Wars/Generation (25 yrs)	Years of War (per century)
Russia (USSR)	21	3.6	49.3
Great Britain	34	5.9	48.3
Spain	16	2.8	42.4
China	11	1.9	38.6
Turkey	15	2.6	34.1
France	29	5.0	32.8
Argentina	6	1.0	25.5
Uruguay	4	0.7	24.8
Guatemala	7	1.2	24.5
Mexico	6	1.0	24.1
Salvador	9	1.6	23.8
Portugal	6	1.0	20.7
Bolivia	5	0.9	20.3
Costa Rica	8	1.4	19.6
Italy[a]	13	2.2	19.3
Germany (Prussia)	10	1.7	19.3
Nicaragua	10	1.7	18.3
Chile	5	0.9	17.9
Japan	9	1.6	17.2
Honduras	9	1.6	17.2
Austria	12	2.1	16.9
Poland[b]	6	1.0	16.5

(continued)

Table 2.5 *Frequency and Duration of Warfare by Nation-States, 1800–1945 (continued)*

Nation	Number of Wars	Wars/Generation (25 yrs)	Years of War (per century)
Greece	9	1.6	16.2
Belgium[c]	5	0.9	15.9
United States	11	1.9	15.5
Denmark	5	0.9	13.8
Peru	5	0.9	13.8
Netherlands	4	0.7	13.4
Paraguay	3	0.5	13.1
Ecuador	4	0.7	12.1
Brazil	5	0.9	11.7
Venezuela	2	0.3	10.3
Iran (Persia)	3	0.5	9.3
Colombia	2	0.3	8.6
Montenegro[d]	5	0.9	7.6
Haiti	5	0.9	6.2
Afghanistan	3	0.5	5.2
Sweden	2	0.3	4.5
Dominican Republic	3	0.5	4.1
Thailand (Siam)	2	0.3	4.1
Switzerland	0	0.0	0.0
World averages		1.4	18.5
World medians		0.9	16.9

[a] Includes wars fought by Sardinia, Naples, and Venice.
[b] Includes wars fought as an independent nation and insurrections.
[c] Includes Napoleonic Wars as part of Netherlands.
[d] Includes World War II as part of Yugoslavia.
Source: Wright 1942: Tables 37–41, 44, 46.

Table 2.6 *Combat Unit Sizes and Social Unit Populations*

Group[a]	Maximum Unit Size[b]	Male Population[c]	% Males Mobilized
Rome (A.D. 100–200)	400,000	25,000,000	2
W. Abenaki	100	2,500	4
Huron	600	9,000–11,000	5–7
Mohave	100	1,500	7
Egypt (1250–1300 B.C.)	100,000+	1,300,000	8+
Iroquois	600	6,000	10
Caribs (Venezuela)	600(?)	5,000	12
Cahuilla	400	3,000	13
Parantintin	20	125	16
Timacua	1,500	9,000–17,500	9–17
U.S. World War II	11,490,000	66,000,000	17
Modoc	100	500	20
USSR World War II	20,000,000	91,000,000	22
Maori	350+	1,250–3,750	9–28+
Germany World War II	10,800,000	34,250,000	32
Nandi	4,710	14,140	33
Mae Enga (one clan)	70	175	40
Zulu State (1879)	50,000	125,000	40
Huli (minor war)	100	250	40
Miyanmin (1938)	200	<500	40+
France World War I	8,410,000	19,500,000	43
Tahiti	7,760	17,683	44

[a] States are italicized.
[b] Offensive war parties, standing armies, total number who served in armed forces during war, etc.
[c] Estimated by dividing total population in half.
Sources: Ferrill 1986: 26; Dobson 1989: 198; Edgerton 1988: 21, 28; Wright 1942: 664; Ray 1963: 135; *HNAI* vol. 15, 1978: 153, 157; Bean 1972: 77, 131; Glasse 1968: 29, 97; Oliver 1974: 30, 34; Gabriel and Metz 1991: 221; Romer 1982: 23; Meggitt 1977: 101–102; Stewart 1965: 377; *HNAI* vol. 10, 1983: 57; Morren 1986: 274–75; Huntingford 1953: 80; *HSAI* vol. 3, 1948: 285, 290.

Table 3.1 *Association Between Weapons and Armor*

Weapon Type	Protection Armor used	Shield only	None
Shock only or shock and missile	10 / 91%	12 / 75%	5 / 45%
Missile only	1 / 9%	4 / 25%	6 / 55%
Totals	11 / 100%	16 / 100%	11 / 100%

Source: Otterbein 1989: Appendix D.

Table 3.2 *Prestate Fortifications*

Group Name	Fort Description	Location	Political Organization
Timacua	Palisade, moat, baffle gates, gate houses	Principal towns with chief in residence	High chiefdom
Natchez	Palisade, towers, baffle gates	?	High chiefdom
Creek	Palisade (sometimes multiple), towers, battlements	Border with Cherokee; border with Mobile	Tribal confederacy, council of hereditary chiefs
Mobile	Palisade (daub wall), towers	Principal town and few others in its vicinity	High chiefdom/petty state
Choctaw	Palisade	Border villages	?
N. Carolina Algonquians	Palisade, baffle gate	"Only some villages"	High chiefdom with council of nobles
Virginia Algonkians	Palisade	Border with Iroquoians	High chiefdom
Nanticoke	Palisade	Borders only	Petty chiefdoms
Delaware	Palisade	"Few" villages	Petty chiefdom with council
Mahican	Palisade, baffle gates	"Common"	Petty chiefdom; semi-independent clans
Pequot	Palisade, baffle gate (enclosed 2 acres)	Principal town and at least one other	Petty chiefdom, one head, and 26 subordinate chiefs
Western Abenaki	Palisades	"Borders of territory"	Tribe; separate war and civil chiefs; tribal council
Maliseet	Palisade	"Some villages" but not principal village	Petty chiefdom; head chief resides at principal village

Micmac	Palisade	Only two border villages	Tribe; council of chiefs
Huron	Multiple palisades, baffle gates	Largest towns and borders villages	Confederacy of chiefs
Iroquois	Multiple palisades, bastions	Largest towns	Confederacy of hereditary chiefs
Southwestern Chippewa	Fortified settlements	Villages on border with Sioux	Tribe; village bands
Mandan	Palisade, ditch, bastions	All 9 villages (lineal territory along Missouri R.)	Tribe; council of elders
Pueblos (Tiwa, Towa, and Zuni)	Adobe walls, baffle gates	Border Pueblos of Taos, Pecos, and Hawikuh	Tribe; council of elders
Quinault	Palisade	Few villages for brief period of internecine war	Tribe (richest man leader)
Tlingit	Palisade, drawbridge gates	Some houses and villages	Petty chiefdom
Kwakiutl	Palisade	Refuges separate from village?	Chiefdom
Snohomish-Skagit	Palisade, ditch with sharpened stakes	Few villages	Petty chiefdom
Tsimshian	Palisade	Certain border villages on trade routes	Chiefdom
North Straits Salish	Palisade, ditch with stakes, "doors with protective devices"	?	Petty chiefdoms
Eyak	Palisades	"Each village"	Petty chiefdom
Lilloet	Palisades	"Particularly common"	Tribe
Atsegewi	Stone walls	Places of refuge	Bands

(continued)

Table 3.2 *Prestate Fortifications (continued)*

Group Name	Fort Description	Location	Political Organization
SW Panama	Multiple palisades	Towns "often fortified"	Chiefdoms
Ancerma, Pozo (Cauca Valley)	Palisade	"Villages usually defended"; also fortified refuges	High chiefdoms
Turbaco, etc. (N. Columbia)	Multiple palisades	All villages?	High chiefdoms
Pantagoro and Amani	Multiple palisades, ditch, traps at gates	All villages?	Petty chiefdoms
Achagua	Palisade, berm	All villages	Chiefdom
Caribs (Venezuela)	Multiple palisades	"Villages in interior" (frontier settlements?)	Chiefdoms
Guarani	Multiple palisades, moat	?	Chiefdoms
Tupinamba (Brazil)	Multiple palisades	"Villages exposed to enemy attack" (frontier?)	Tribe? council ruled in peace
Bauré and Mojo	Multiple palisades, ditch	All villages?	Chiefdoms
Omagua	"Fortified settlements"	Border villages	Tribe
Canichana	Palisades	All villages?	?
Chiriguano	Single or double palisade	"Some villages"	Chiefdom; Chane tribe subjected to serfdom
Canelo	"Palisaded villages with secret entrances"	All villages?	Village bands

Jivaro	"Barricades," pitfalls ditches with stakes	All villages?	Village bands
Witotoans	"Shallow trenches with poisoned stakes"	"Some villages"	Village bands
Maori	Ditch, rampart, palisade	Larger towns (seats of tribal chiefs)	Petty chiefdoms
Marquesans	Multiple palisades	Places of refuge	Chiefdoms
Tahitians	Stone wall and platforms	Places of refuge	High chiefdoms
Fijians	Stone walls	Refuges and some villages	High chiefdoms
Mae Enga	Stout fences and ditches	All villages	Tribe; Big Men
Kalinga	"Stockades"	All villages?	Tribe; Big Men; elders
Pokomo	"Fortified village"	"In times of severe raids" lineal territory along river	Tribe; council of elders
Mijikenda	Hilltops with high palisades and "special" gates	All villages (surrounded by enemies on isolated hills)	Tribe; wealthy elders rule
Kikuyu	"Fortified settlements" on ridge tops	Especially on frontier with Masai	Tribe; council of elders
Cuka	14-mile-long wall with tunnel-like gates	Frontier with Meru	Tribe; council of elders

Sources: Cannon 1992; Carneiro 1990; Codere 1950; Dobyns 1983; Dozier 1967; Driver and Massey 1957; Drucker 1965; Fadiman 1982; Fox 1976; Haeberlin and Gunther 1930; Handy 1923; *HNAI* vol. 7, 1990; *HNAI* vol. 8, 1978; *HNAI* vol. 9, 1979; *HNAI* vol. 15, 1978; Hemming 1978; Hickerson 1962; *HSAI* vol. 3, 1948; *HSAI* vol. 4, 1948; Hudson 1976; Krause 1956; Meggitt 1977; Oliver 1974; Olson 1967; Schwimmer 1966; Spears 1981; Spencer and Jennings 1977; Swanton 1979; Will and Spinden 1906.

Table 4.1 *Casualties from Formal Battles*

Date	Group[a]	Number Engaged	% Killed	% Wounded	% Casualties
Winners					
1810	Mtetwa–Zulu	1,800	1.1	?	?
490 B.C.	*Athens* (Marathon)	10,000	1.9	?	?
1863	*Union* (Gettysburg)	85,000	3.7	17.1	20.8
202 B.C.	*Rome* (Zama)	50,000	4.0	?	?
1813	Mtetwa–Zulu	1,800	8.3	?	?
1771	Maori	60	16.7	?	?
Inconclusive or indeterminate					
1930s	Mae Enga "Great Fight"	2,000	0.5	?	?
1840s	Cahto vs. Yuki	700	1.3	?	?
1971	Mae Enga (one clan)	70	1.4	38.6	40.0
1850s	Modoc (average)	60	7.5	?	?
1850s	Mohave (average)	50	12.0	18.0	30.0
1916	*Britain* (Somme)	156,000	13.5	25.0	38.5
1959	Masatfak Dani	130[b]	26.2	?	?
Losers					
1863	*Confederates* (Gettysburg)	65,000	4.0	19.6	23.6
1810	Butelezi	600	8.3	?	?
1956	Manamba Maring	180[b]	11.1[c]	?	?
1700s?	Tejon Chumash	400	17.5	?	?
1813	Ndnandwe	2,500	20.0	?	?
490 B.C.	*Persia* (Marathon)	20,000	32.0	?	?
1807	Nga Pahi Maori	500	34.0	?	?
202 B.C.	*Carthage* (Zama)	50,000	40.0	20.0	60.0
1857	Mohave–Yuma	282	49.6	?	?
1478	*Aztecs* (Michoacan)	24,000	87.1	0.0	87.1
1849	Assiniboin[d]	52	100.0	0.0	100.0

[a] States are italicized.
[b] Assuming males engaged = 30% of population.
[c] Battle deaths only; in the rout that followed, 4.4% more died.
[d] Raiding party caught by larger Blackfoot war party.
Sources: Otterbein 1967: 356; Vayda 1976: 25; Vayda 1960: 86, 89; Meggitt 1977: 17, 101, 192; Gabriel and Metz 1991: 85–87; Isaac 1983: 125; Stewart 1965: 377–79; Kroeber 1925: 753; Kroeber 1965: 400; Chandler 1966: 1,065–66, 1,093; Ewers 1967: 339; Heider 1970: 129; *HNAI* vol. 8, 1978: 534; Ferrill 1985: 109–10; Keegan 1976: 215, 255.

Table 6.1 *Annual Warfare Death Rates*

Society[a]	Region	Annual % Rate	Source
Kato (Cahto) 1840s	California	1.45	Kroeber 1965: 397–403
Dani-S. Grand V.	New Guinea	1.00	Heider 1970: 129
Piegan	N. Plains	1.00	Livingstone 1968: 9
Dinka 1928	N.E. Africa	.97	Kelly 1985: 55
Fiji 1860s	Melanesia	.87[b]	Carniero 1990: 199
Chippewa 1825–1832	Minnesota	.75	Hickerson 1962: 28
Telefolmin 1939–1950	New Guinea	.74	Morren 1984: 188
Buin	Solomon Is.	.71	Wright 1942: 569
Kalinga (headhunts)	Phillippines	.60[c]	Dozier 1967: 71
Mtetwa 1806–1814	S. Africa	.59[d]	Otterbein 1967: 356–57
Dugum Dani 1961	New Guinea	.48[e]	Heider 1970: 128
Manga 1949–1956	New Guinea	.46	Pflanz-Cook and Cook 1983: 188; Vayda 1976: 109
Modoc	California	.45[f]	Ray 1963: 134–35, 143
Auyana 1924–1949	New Guinea	.42	Robbins 1982: 211
Murngin 20 years	Australia	.33	Wright 1942: 569
Tauade 1900–1946	New Guinea	.32[g]	Hallpike 1977: 120, 202
Mae Enga 1900–1950	New Guinea	.32[h]	Meggitt 1977: 12–13, 109
Yanomama 1938–1958	Brazil	.29[i]	Early and Peters 1990: 18
C. Mexico 1419–1519	Mesoamerica	.25	Thieme 1968: 17
Yurok	California	.24	Wright 1942: 570
Mohave 1840s	Calif.-Ariz.	.23	Stewart 1965: 377, 379
Gebusi 1940–1982	New Guinea	.20[j]	Knauft 1985: 119, 376–77
Tiwi 1893–1903	Australia	.16	Pilling 1968: 158
Germany 1900–1990	Europe	.16	various[k]
Russia 1900–1990	Europe-Asia	.15	various[k]
Boko Dani 1937–1962	New Guinea	.14	Ploeg 1983: 164
France 1800–1899	Europe	.07	Wright 1942: 570
Japan 1900–1990	Asia	.03	various[k]
Andamanese 30 years	Indian Ocean	.02	Wright 1942: 569
Sweden 1900–1990	Europe	.00	various[k]
Semai	S.E. Asia	.00	Dentan 1979

[a] States are italicized.

[b] 1,500–2,000 deaths each year (average = 1,750), population in 1860 = 200,000.

[c] For a regional population of 1,000, if it was 500, then rate doubles; "battle" not included only raid deaths.

[d] 85 deaths/battle; 5 battles 1806–1814; population of 9,000.

[e] Does not include deaths from "secular" war occurring once every 10–20 years; were these included, the rate would be .85–1.23.

[f] Average of one raid per year; average loss 7.5% of average war party of 60; population of 1,000 estimated from various sources including Ray 1963: 204–11.

[g] Intertribal killings only; including intratribal ones raises the rate to .53.

[h] 200 wars in 50 years, averaging 4 deaths/war, for an average population of 5,000.

[i] Contact population of 121, 7 war deaths ca. 1938, and no warfare because of isolation until 1958.

[j] Raid and battle deaths only; internal homicides excluded.

[k] Populations averaged from Kennedy 1987: 199, 436; war deaths from Wright 1942: 664; Wilmott 1989: 477; Winter 1989: 206 and other sources. If these rates were calculated for only the bloodier period from 1900 to 1950, they would more or less double.

Table 6.2 *Percentage of Deaths Due to Warfare*

Society[a]	Male Deaths	Female Deaths	All Deaths[b]	Source
Jivaro	59.0	27.0	32.7[c]	Ross 1984: 96
Yanomamo-Shamatari	37.4	4.4	20.9	Chagnon 1974: 160
Mae Enga	34.8	2.3[d]	18.6	Meggitt 1977: 110–12
Dugum Dani	28.5	2.4	15.5	Heider 1970: 128
Murngin	28.0	—	—	Harris 1975: 262
Yanomamo-Namowei	23.7	6.9	15.3	Chagnon 1974: 160
Huli	19.6	6.1	13.2	Glasse 1968: 98
Anggor	—	—	11.9	Huber 1973: 639
Gebusi	8.3	8.2	8.3	Knauft 1985: 117–19
Ancient Mexico	—	—	5.0	Thieme 1968: 17
France 19th century	—	—	3.0	Wright 1942: 665
Western Europe 17th C.	—	—	2.0	Wright 1942: 212
U.S. and Europe 20th C.	<1.0	—	—	Harris 1975: 262

Prehistoric Examples

Nubia: Site 117 10,000 B.C.	47.7	45.0	40.7	Wendorf 1968: 993
N. British Columbia 1500 B.C.–A.D. 500	—	—	32.4	Cybulski n.d.: 25
British Columbia A.D. 500–1774	—	—	27.6	Cybulski n.d.: 25
Nubia: Qadan burials 10,000 B.C.	—	—	21.4	Wendorf 1968: 869–74, 993
Illinois A.D. 1300	35.0	29.0	16.3	Milner et al. 1991
Ukraine: Vasylivka (Mesolithic)	—	—	15.9	Vencl 1991: 220
Northeast Plains 1325–1650	—	—	15.0[e]	Willey 1990: xxiv
Denmark: Vedbaek 4100 B.C.	—	—	13.6	Price 1985: 351
S. California: Ven-110 A.D. 100–1100	—	—	10.0	Walker and Lambert 1989: 210
Brittany 6000 B.C.	—	—	8.0	Vencl 1991: 220
Kentucky: 2500–3000 B.C.	—	—	5.6	Webb 1974: 236
Central California 1500 B.C.–A.D. 500	—	—	>5.0	Moratto 1984: 183
Sweden: Skateholm ca. 4300 B.C.	—	—	3.8	Price 1985: 352
Algeria: Columnata ca. 6000 B.C.	—	—	1.7	Vencl 1991: 220

[a] States are italicized.
[b] Where necessary estimated by averaging male and female figures, thus assuming sex ratio is equal.
[c] Firearms used; male and female % of adult deaths, "all deaths" includes 12% of children's deaths.
[d] Estimated from the ratio of 6 female combat deaths to 91 male.
[e] Percentage of all burials with evidence of scalping.

Table 7.1 *Territorial Gains and Losses from Warfare per Generation*

Group (Location)	% Loss/Gain per 25 Years
Hunter-gatherers	
Walbiri (Australia)	+3
Ingalik (Alaska)	−6
Wappo (California)	+10
Kutchin (Yukon)	−11
Comox (British Columbia)	−50
Pastoralists and horticulturalists	
Mohave (California)	+5
Cuka Meru (Kenya)	−20
Telefolmin (New Guinea)	+33
Tyenda Maring (New Guinea)	−35
Nuer (Sudan)	+62
Civilized states	
European hegemony, 1800–1914	+22
United States, 1800–1900	+29
Roman hegemony, 250 B.C.–A.D. 100	+36

Sources: Calculated from maps and other information in the following sources: (Walbiri) Meggitt 1962: 42; (Wappo) Kroeber 1925: 219–21, Plate 27; *HNAI* vol. 8, 1978: 258, 260; (Comox) *HNAI* vol. 7, 1990: 359–60, 442; (Kutchin, Kolchan, and Ingalik) *HNAI* vol. 6, 1981: 516, 602–603, 618; (Mohave) *HNAI* vol. 10, 1983: 1, 8, 55, 93; (Meru) Fadiman 1982: 35; (Telefolmin) Morren 1984: 181–86; (Maring) Vayda 1976: 32; (Nuer) Kelly 1985: 1; (civilized states) Rand-McNally 1988: 90, 173; Dudley 1975: 35, 262; Parker 1988: 5.

Table 7.2 *Population Density and Width of Buffer Zones*

Group(s)	Population Density (per square mile)	Zone Width (in miles)
Dani (New Guinea)	414.0	0.6
Nandi-Masai (Kenya)	35.0	5.0
Wappo-Pomo (California)	10.0	10.0
Mahican (New York)	1.2	20–25.0
Shamatari Yanomamo (Venezuela)	0.9	30.0
Namoweiteri Yanomamo	0.4	50.0
Chippewa-Sioux (Minnesota)	0.1	50–100.0

Sources: Heider 1970; Huntingford 1953: 85–88; Kroeber 1925; *HNAI* vol. 15, 1978: 198, 200; Chagnon 1974: 127, 129; Hickerson 1962: 17, 32; Hickerson 1970: 74.

Table 8.1 *Motives and Causes of Wars in Nonstate Societies*

	Western North American Indians*	
Purpose of Raids	*Percent Affirmative[a]*	*Number of Groups Coded*
Revenge for killing	93.5	169
Retaliation for poaching	60.1	143
Capture of women (for wives)	58.0	162
Economic booty (including food)	46.4	151
Prestige	32.9	164
Capture of slaves	26.8	168
Visions or dreams	12.2	115

	Sample of Ethnographic Societies†	
Motive or Aim	*States (N = 10) % Affirmative*	*Nonstates (N = 36) % Affirmative*
Subjugation and tribute	70.0	5.6
Plunder	70.0	75.0
Trophies and honors	40.0	44.0
Land	30.0	19.4
Revenge and defense	20.0	75.0

(continued)

Table 8.1 *Motives and Causes of Wars in Nonstate Societies (continued)*

	Comparison		
	Indians	Nonstates	
		World	States
Grouped Motives for Warfare	% affirmative	% affirmative	% affirmative
Revenge, retaliation, and defense	94	75	20 [a]
Economic (booty, land, poaching, slaves)	70	86 [b]	90 [b]
Capture of women	58	nc	nc
Personal (prestige, trophies, visions)	36	44	40
Political (subjugation, tribute)	nc	6	70

[a] These percentages are the proportion of all societies that were recorded as making war for these motives.
[b] Includes captives.
nc Not coded.
Sources: *Jorgensen 1980: 509–15.
†Otterbein 1989: 146, 148–49.

Table 8.2 *Causes of Warfare in New Guinea*

Causes	Wars[a]
Auyana (1924–1949)*	
Homicides (including sorcery)	13 (31.0%)
Pigs (thefts and garden depredations)	13 (31.0%)
Women (adultery and marriage arrangements)	12 (28.6%)
Other	4 (9.5%)
Mae Enga (1900–1950)[†]	
Land	41 (57.7%)
Mobile Property (including pigs)	17 (23.9%)
Homicides	11 (15.5%)
Women (rape and marriage arrangements)	2 (2.8%)
Huli[‡]	
Revenge	14 (32.6%)
Unpaid homicide indemnities	13 (30.2%)
Pig theft	7 (16.3%)
Adultery and rape	6 (14.0%)
Land disputes	3 (7.0%)

[a] Auyana, $N = 42$; Mae Enga, $N = 71$; Huli, $N = 43$.
Sources: *Robbins 1982: 215.
[†] Meggitt 1977: 13.
[‡] Glasse 1968: 91.

Table 8.3 *Population Density versus Frequency of Warfare*

Population Density (per square mile)	Warfare Frequency (Internal and External)					
	Once Per Year	Once Per 5 Years	Once Per Generation	Rarely or Never	Total	
<0.2	7	4	2	3	16	
	44%	25%	12%	19%		100%
0.2–1.0	10	1	2	1	14	
	72%	7%	14%	7%		100%
1.1–5.0	6	2	1	3	12	
	50%	17%	8%	25%		100%
5.1–25.0	6	3	1	1	11	
	55%	27%	9%	9%		100%
26–100	11	4	0	1	16	
	69%	25%	—	6%		100%
>100	13	2	0	3	18	
	72%	11%	—	17%		100%
Total	53	16	6	12	87	
	61%	18%	7%	14%		100%

Sources: Murdock and Wilson 1972; Ross 1983.

Table 9.1 *Distribution of Arrow Wounds at Jebel Sahaba*

Sex of Skeleton	Wound Location				
	Left Side	Right Side	Central or Indeterminate	Totals	
Adult male	17	13	9	39	
	44%	33%	23%		100%
Adult female	5	12	11	28	
	18%	43%	39%		100%

Sources: From descriptions in Wendorf 1968; Anderson 1968.

NOTES

Chapter 1

In order not to clutter the text with footnotes, the references for each paragraph have been consolidated into the footnotes attached to the first or the final sentence of each paragraph.

1. See Divale 1973: 3–9; Ferguson 1988: 114–21.

2. This original spelling is used by several anthropologists as a shorthand reference to Hobbes's vision of small-scale societies and to characterize some ethnographic situations in which violence of all kinds was extremely common.

3. This is, of course, a libel, since Hobbes "concluded" no such thing. It is interesting that the neo-Rousseauian, Brian Ferguson, repeated this misrepresentation in 1990 but neglected to acknowledge Rousseau's precedence or even to mention his existence!

4. Ryan 1981: 49–57.

5. Sumner 1911 versus Malinowski 1941.

6. Divale 1973: xvii.

7. Herdt 1987: 47–48.

8. Keegan 1976: 36–46.

9. Divale 1973: xxii.

10. For example, the anthropology graduate student whose master's thesis was part of the project, Harry Hoijer, later co-authored the most widely used anthropology textbook of the 1950s and 1960s (Beals and Hoijer 1965). Thus anthropologists did not need to consult Wright's massive book to be influenced by it.

11. Wright 1942 [1964]: 7.

12. I can find nothing in his writings or in anything written about him to indicate that

he ever experienced combat. He certainly would have seen much of its ugly aftermath in liberated Belgium. In any case, *Primitive War* was written before World War II, which was his only chance to see combat.

13. Wright 1942: 62, 69, 74–76; Turney-High 1949: 141–68; 1981: 26, 36–40. Regarding the sportive or entertainment motive among primitives, Wright offers no documentation for his statements. Turney-High's arguments and examples on this point are rather strange: war stories are "the most entertaining stories, and in order to spin yarns there must be wars"; California Indians knew they were "athletic humbugs" but would not admit it (!); and so on. No one reading his works can doubt that Turney-High thought war was fun—an easier attitude for a rear-echelon M.P. to maintain than for a front-line "grunt."

14. Wright 1942: 80–85; Turney-High 1949: 21–137.

15. Turney-High 1949: 85, 87.

16. Turney-High 1981: 34.

17. Turney-High 1981: 34.

18. Various places in Turney-High 1949: 25–137; summary in 1981: 35–44, 56, 58.

19. Keegan 1976: 22–23.

20. Turney-High 1981: 69.

21. Wright 1942: 85–88; Turney-High 1981: 38.

22. Wright 1942: Appendix XII, 569–70. In this appendix, Wright listed annual war death rates for four tribal societies, three of which were from three to ten times higher than nineteenth-century France's war death rate (the highest civilized rate known to him in 1941).

23. Wright 1942: 242–48; 1964: 59–62. Ennumeration indicated that civilized battles have been becoming *less* deadly over the last four centuries. Thus to save his hypothesis, Wright had to include all deaths "indirectly related" to war, dismiss the figures from seventeenth-century Britain and Germany, and include some highly estimated "indices" created by sociologists.

24. Turney-High 1949: xiv–xv, 25.

25. Ferguson 1984a: 6.

26. For example, Harris 1979.

27. For example, Harris 1975; Ferguson 1984a. However, it was never claimed that casualties alone could be a method of population control.

28. For example, Harris 1984: 129; Ferguson 1990: 29.

29. Chagnon 1983 (first edition 1968).

30. For example, Chagnon 1983; Koch 1974; Hallpike 1973, 1977.

31. Hallpike 1973: 454. Another neo-Hobbesian, K.-F. Koch (1974: 159–75), accepts four of five possible explanations for warfare in highland New Guinea—every possibility *except* the economic one.

32. For example, Fagan 1989; Wenke 1988; Sharer and Ashmore 1987; Thomas 1988. A recent exception is Hayden 1993.

33. For example, Green and Perlman 1985; Rouse 1986; Gregg 1988; Bogucki 1988.

34. Fagan 1989: 311; Whittle 1985: 219–20. Whittle does mention that at least one camp appeared to have been attacked by archers.

35. Dixon 1988; Mercer 1988.

36. For example, palisades around Mississippian villages to keep out deer (?); the "peaceful Pueblos" of the American Southwest (see Wilcox and Haas 1991); the "peaceful" Maya.

37. This example is not completely hypothetical example since the extensive Ancient Mayan road systems now being documented in the Yucatán are being interpreted by many scholars as "ritual roads" (B. Hayden, personal communication).

38. Ferguson 1992a, 1992b. His colleague, Neil Whitehead (1990: 160), blames Hobbes directly, claiming that intruding Westerners brought with them Hobbes's "ideology of war" (what that ideology is remains unclear since Hobbes never praised war or suggested how it should be conducted). Another proponent of prehistoric peace is Blick (1988).

39. Ferguson 1992a: 113. Except for a single clause in one sentence, Hobbes did not mention any "wild violence" by natives to support his case.

40. Gabriel and Metz 1991: 3, 19. In his latest book, the justly celebrated military historian John Keegan (1993) "buys" Turney-High "lock, stock and barrel," probably because the latter's book remains the only general anthropological synthesis on prestate warfare available to nonanthropologists.

41. Rochberg-Halton 1991: B6–B7.

42. Manchester 1980: 102.

Chapter 2

1. Otterbein 1989: 21, 143–44, 148.

2. Ross 1983: 179, 182–83.

3. The Cayapa were indeed peaceful since they had no traditional memory of warfare since mythological times (*HSAI* vol. 4, 1948: 282).

4. Jorgensen 1980: 503–6, 509–15, 613–14.

5. The Panamint, Battle Mountain, and Hukundika Shoshone; the Gosiute and the Kaibab Paiute of the Great Basin; the Wenatchi and Columbia Salish of central Washington.

6. Harris 1989: 288–89; Meggitt 1962: 38, 42, 246.

7. Knauft 1987; Lee 1979: 387–400; Harris 1989: 288; *HNAI* vol. 5, 1984: 340–41, 401–402, 409, 429, 440–41, 455; J. G. Taylor 1974: 92–92; *HSAI* vol. 1, 1946: 94–95. Knauft's (1987) paper on violence in "simple societies" is extremely useful, and most of the homicide rates referred to here were taken from his Table 2. He also calculates that the Semai, the archetype of a nonviolent society, had a homicide rate three times that of the modern United States.

8. *HSAI* vol. 1, 1946: 94–95.

9. Lee 1979: 399; Harris 1989: 288.

10. To equal the Gebusi annual homicide rate of 683 homicides per 100,000 (Knauft 1987: 464), the armed forces of the United States (with an average population of 200 million and homicide rate of 10) would have had to kill 1,350,000 people each year. In

nine years, this would amount to 12 million deaths; the population of South Vietnam in 1965 was less than 14 million.

11. Knauft 1987: 463. My conservative calculation (i.e., excluding deaths from disease and starvation) of the annual homicide rate of Nazi Germany (1933 to 1945) yields a figure of approximately 2,000 per 100,000 (over three times that of the Gebusi), indicating that it qualifies as the most homicidal society ever recorded.

12. *HNAI* vol. 5, 1984: 577–79, 585.

13. Even if only one homicide occurred every fifty years in such a small population, their homicide rate would equal that of the United States.

14. For example, Tonkinson 1978: 32, 118, 123–28; Steward 1938: 83, 91, 140, 176, 179.

15. See also Ember 1978.

16. See Ember and Ember 1992: 248–49.

17. Dentan 1979:58–59. See Knauft (1987: 458) for the Semai homicide rate.

18. Dentan (1979: 2) suggests that the Semai (and, presumably, the related Semang) tradition of flight from violence is a consequence of countless defeats and slave raiding at the hands of the more numerous and aggressive Malays. In other words, the Semai can be characterized as defeated refugees.

19. Appendix, Tables 2.1–2.4; see also Ember and Ember 1990: 255.

20. Heider 1970: 107; Chagnon 1968: 141.

21. Hackett (ed.) 1989: 140, 170, 193.

22. Appendix, Table 2.5.

23. Pospisil 1963: 59–60; Edgerton 1988: 39,107; Steward and Faron 1959: 190, 209, 223, 245; Grinnell 1923 (II): 44–47; *HNAI* vol. 8, 1978: 219, 260, 380, 547; *HSAI* vol. 3, 1948: 480; Vayda 1960: 41; Meggitt 1977: 98–99.

24. Chandler 1966: 1,102, 1,106, 1,113–14; Perret 1989: 553; Gabriel and Metz 1991: 89.

25. For example, Dart 1957; Roper 1969.

26. (Australopithicines) Brain 1981; (Neanderthals) Klein 1989: 333–34; Vencl 1991.

27. Vencl 1991; Klein 1989: 387; Jelinek 1991; Gambier and Sacchi 1991; Svoboda and Vlcek 1991; Wendorf and Schild 1986; Wendorf 1968; Greene and Armelagos 1972.

28. Wendorf 1968.

29. Vencl 1991; Frayer, in press; Price 1985. See also Appendix, Table 6.2.

30. For example, Courtin 1984; Keeley 1990.

31. Wahl and König's (1987) exceptionally intelligent and thorough analysis of the Talheim mass grave deserves far greater notice from archaeologists than it has received.

32. O. Bar-Yosef, personal communication. (Incidentally, Bar-Yosef interprets the Early Neolithic "fortifications" at Jericho as being flood protection and a temple tower.)

33. For example, Milner et al. 1991 (eastern United States); Jurmain 1988 (California); Chatters 1989 (Columbia Plateau); Wilcox and Haas 1991; Turner and Turner 1992 (American Southwest). For additional references, see Appendix, Table 6.2.

34. For example, Milner et al. 1991; Rohn 1975; Wilcox 1989; *HNAI* vol. 7, 1990: 348; MacDonald 1989.

Chapter 3

1. Ferguson 1984a: 26 (referring to Otterbein 1989).

2. Rogers 1970: 14; Oliver 1974: 382; Vayda 1960: 38–40; Carniero 1990: 194–95.

3. Meggitt 1977: 67–69.

4. Turney-High 1981: 34.

5. Koch 1974: 214.

6. Warner 1931; Utley 1984: 105; Robbins 1982: 187; Meggitt 1977: 86–91; Glasse 1968: 92; Heider 1970; Ferrill 1985: 22.

7. Utley 1984: 99–118.

8. Malone 1991: 22.

9. Meggitt 1977: 57.

10. Turney-High 1949: 26.

11. Turney-High 1981: 69. Despite the importance Turney-High accorded to this "law" of warfare, it has not been taught to officer trainees by the modern armed forces of the United States, Britain, or the former Soviet Union since World War II.

12. Political system versus military sophistication, $r = .64$; but military success versus military sophistication, $r = .44$ (Otterbein 1989: 74, 95).

13. Otterbein's "primary mode of subsistence" and "sociopolitical complexity" codes combined explain 52 percent of the variability ($r^2 = .52$) in his "military sophistication index," whereas the frequency of war (the lowest number in columns 4–6) and the "military success" codes together explain only 17 percent ($r^2 = .17$).

14. Gabriel and Metz 1991: 56–75.

15. Driver and Massey 1957: 357.

16. See Appendix, Table 3.9.

17. Meggitt 1977: 57–58.

18. The elaborate, finely finished prehistoric axes commonly found at sites in the Southwest and Great Plains of North America—regions where both wood and woodworking were rare—may represent similar cases, especially on the Plains, where warfare victims have tomahawk traumas on their skulls (Willey 1990: 118).

19. Gabriel and Metz 1991: 72; Malone 1991: 15–18.

20. Tonkinson 1978: 32.

21. Meggitt 1977: 57; Connolly 1989: 162.

22. Gabriel and Metz 1991: 75; Handy 1923: 133.

23. DuBois 1935: 125; *HSAI* vol. 1, 1946: 295, 297, 425, 428; Handy 1923; Heider 1970: 285; Bohannon and Bohannon 1953; L. Bohannon, personal communication; Fadiman 1982: 116; Steward and Faron 1959: 190, 244, 249, 321, 323, 357; Spier 1930: 193–94; Gibbon n.d.; Steward 1941: 338; Aginsky 1943: 456; Stewart 1941: 385; Stewart 1942: 268; *HSAI* vol. 4, 1948: 4; Mercer 1980: 142; *HNAI* vol. 15, 1978: 112.

24. Underhill 1989: 221.

25. Gabriel and Metz 1991: 89–91.

26. Weber 1992: 229.

27. Webb 1974: 254–55; Keeley 1993; Wahl and König 1987: 178–79; D. Frayer, personal communication.

28. For exceptions, see Steward and Faron 1959: 190, 221, 358; *HSAI* vol.3, 1948: 35; *HSAI* vol. 4, 1948: 489; Morren 1984: 195.

29. Marshall 1987: 248–49. A similar calculation from Keegan's (1976: 234, 255) figures for the British bombardment at the Somme in 1916 gives a ratio of 250 shells fired for each German casualty inflicted (from all causes).

30. Connell 1984: 259.

31. Turney-High 1981: 42.

32. The basic information and references for this section can be found in the Appendix, Table 3.2.

33. Keeley 1992; Bamforth 1994; Champion et al. 1984: 213–15, 283; *HNAI* vol. 9, 1979: 65–66, 136, 433.

34. *HNAI* vol. 8, 1978: 238; Chatters 1989: 241.

35. See Haas and Creamer's (1993) fine study of this phenomenon in northeastern Arizona.

Chapter 4

1. Heider 1970: 107; Vayda 1976: 18; Dozier 1967: 68; Otterbein 1967: 352; *HNAI* vol. 8, 1978: 130, 198, 251, 344, 454, 488, 513, 697.

2. Glasse 1968: 92.

3. Keegan 1976: 296, 309.

4. Grinnell 1923 (II): 28–38; Hoebel 1978: 75–77.

5. Mae Enga warriors who killed or seriously wounded several enemies in a single formal battle, thus determining the successful outcome of the combat, were permitted to assume a knotted cord as a mark of honor. Additional knots could be added if the feat was repeated (Meggitt 1977: 66–67).

6. Hanson 1989: 190. No one can read Hanson's descriptions of a Greek hoplite battle and imagine it a game.

7. The Allies did parole the Sicilians among the Italian prisoners taken during the invasion of Sicily in World War II.

8. Keegan 1989: 390.

9. Edgerton 1988: 178–79; Morris 1965: 449.

10. For example, Manchester 1980: 225–26.

11. *HNAI* vol. 8, 1978: 698.

12. For example, Grinnel 1923 (II): 45–47; Hoebel 1978: 79.

13. Of course, the frequency of battle dramatically increased under Grant and Sherman in the summer of 1864. It is interesting to note that in the fierce battles for Atlanta in July and August 1864 the proportion of Sherman's army that was killed in action (usually half of those counted as "killed and missing") never exceeded 2 percent (Sherman 1886: 608–11).

14. Oliver 1974: 398; Vayda 1976: 25; Carneiro 1990: 199.

15. For example, Herdt 1987: 48–55; Morren 1984: 186.

16. Vayda 1976: 22–23; Turney-High 1949: 124; Robbins 1982: 185, 188; Meggitt 1977: 75–76, 110; *HNAI* vol. 6, 1981: 408; *HNAI* vol. 5, 1984: 477; Morren 1984: 188.

17. Chagnon 1968: 141; *HNAI* vol. 6, 1981: 287; Chagnon 1983: 170; Hogbin 1964: 59.

18. Cannon 1992; Kent 1980.

19. (Plateau) Chatters 1989; (Illinois) Milner et al. 1991; (British Columbia) *HNAI* vol. 7, 1990: 58; (California) Walker and Lambert 1989; Lambert and Walker 1991; Jurmain 1988; Hohol 1982; (Egypt) compiled from Wendorf 1968 and Anderson 1968.

20. Milner et al. (1991: 583) estimate that the Norris Farms no. 36 cemetery was used only "for a few decades" (thus, let us say thirty years). Prorating the 43 homicides over 30 years gives 1.43 homicides per annum. If the base population of the group using this cemetary was 100, then the homicide rate was 1,430 per 100,000, or 140 times the U.S. rate of 10 per 100,000. If the population was 200, a more reasonable village size (R. Hall, personal communication), then the rate was 717. This latter homicide rate is seventy times that of the United States in 1980, 150 times that of the United States in 1953, and 1,400 times that of Britain in 1959 (Knauft 1987: 464).

21. Vayda 1976: 23; Heider 1970: 78, 119; *HNAI* vol. 8, 1978: 506, 510, 513, 674, 687; *HNAI* vol. 6, 1981: 286–87, 494; Slobodin 1960: 83; Chagnon 1968: 141; Herdt 1987: 54–55.

22. Heider 1970: 105; Herdt 1987: 54; *HNAI* vol. 6, 1981: 287; Cannon 1992: 509–10.

23. (Middle Missouri) Zimmerman 1980; Willey 1990; Bamforth 1994; (Southwest) Haas 1990: 187, and personal communication.

24. Milner et al. 1991: 595. Milner and his colleagues also provide a long list of references to evidence of warfare deaths among prehistoric Native Americans in the eastern prairies and woodlands. A popular account of the Crow Creek site is given in Zimmerman and Whitten (1980); a detailed analysis of the bones appears in Willey (1990).

25. Wahl and König 1987; Courtin 1984: 448.

Chapter 5

1. Regarding the identity of the Skraelings, archaeology indicates that they were Indians ancestral to the historic Beothuk, since the Dorset Eskimo had disappeared from Newfoundland and adjacent parts of Labrador several centuries before the Norse appeared (*HNAI* vol. 15, 1978: 69; Fitzhugh 1985: 25–29). Given that their technology and diet were the same as the historic Beothuk, the population density (no more than one person per 25 square miles) and settlement pattern (small-band encampments scattered along the coast) of the proto-Beothuk Skraelings were probably comparable. That being the case, there would have been no more than 100 potential Skraeling warriors within a 200-mile radius of the Viking settlements. Since the Viking colony consisted of 250 men and women (Morison 1971: 54), the Vikings could never have been outnumbered or attacked by a "multitude" of Skraelings as the sagas claim.

2. Morison 1971: 32–62; see also Roesdahl 1991: 274–75; Fitzhugh 1985: 28.

3. Parker 1988: 120.

4. For examples, see Allred et al. 1960; Utley and Washburn 1977; Utley 1984; *HNAI* vol. 4, 1988: 128–63; *HNAI* vol. 10, 1983: 496.

5. For example, Utley 1984; *HNAI* vol. 15, 1978: 625.

6. The Narragansett fort successfully stormed by Massachusetts militia in 1675 was incomplete.

7. One would think that the repeated thrashing of better-disciplined European and fanatically disciplined Asian armies by American "rabble" (and the nasty treatment dealt the French by highly "irregular" Mexican Juaristas) would eventually disabuse these Colonel Blimps of their condescension. But it shows no signs of abating; see, for example, the works of Max Hastings and Dan van der Vat.

8. Morris 1965; Edgerton 1988 (this work, written by an anthropologist, is especially recommended). The Zulu polity was a true state, and Zulu regiments were disciplined units that fought in massed formations and thus were easier for a civilized army to defeat than hit-and-run skimishers like the Apaches.

9. Porch 1986: 120–23, 140, 165–72, 227–30.

10. Edgerton 1988: 119–213.

11. Bodley 1990: 46.

12. Utley and Washburn 1977: 53, 134, 210; *HNAI* vol. 4, 1988: 130, 159, 162, 164, 170–72; *HNAI* vol. 15, 1978: 99–100; Utley 1984: 95–96; Porch 1986: 209–10; Parker 1988: 119–20, 207 n. 49; Eid 1985.

13. Eid 1985: 139; *HNAI* vol. 15, 1978: 99–100. Malone (1991) also makes this point in greater detail, marred only by his unsupported belief that the precontact warfare of the New England tribes did not inflict many casualties.

14. Malone 1991: 6. Apologies to Patrick Malone for appropriating the title of his fine book *The Skulking Way of War* to head this chapter.

15. Utley 1984: 95–96.

16. This is abstracted from accounts in Utley 1984; Utley and Washburn 1977; and *HNAI* vol. 4, 1988: 168, 174–76.

17. Dudley 1975: 90–91, 98, 157–70; Connolly 1989: 165–67; Dobson 1989: 205–12.

18. McGovern 1985: 311–14; *HNAI* vol. 5, 1984: 551–55; Fitzhugh 1985: 27–31. Some academics dismiss these Inuit and Norse accounts because they contain certain fantastic or stylized elements. This dismissal is analogous to doubting that Magellan's expedition sailed around the world, simply because Pigafetta's account of the voyage mentions fabulous animals and minor miracles. In any case, scholarly scepticism has not discouraged the Greenlanders (a term now used only for those of Inuit descent) from mischievously celebrating this ancestral genocide of Scandinavians in every conceivable form of art.

19. Mercer 1980: 157–58, 184–93; Crosby 1986: 79–89.

20. For example, *HSAI* vol. 3, 1948: 218, 467, 505, 509, 563, 618, 729.

21. (Pawnee) Weber 1992: 171; (Seminoles and Red Cloud) Utley and Washburn 1977: 128, 131–35, 211–15.

22. Crosby 1972, 1986.

23. Aztec casualties from Thomas (1993: 528–29) do not include the 170,000 esti-

mated to have died from starvation and disease during the siege of Tenochtitlán. Disease mortality is calculated from various estimates of the decline in central Mexico's population cited by Thomas (1993: 609–13); Crosby (1972: 53); and Fagan (1984: 286).

24. Crosby 1986: 133–47 and 1972: 35.

25. Williams 1970: 198–99.

26. Malone 1991.

27. Schiefenhövel 1993: 327; P. Weissner, personal communication.

28. One popular folly in the antebellum American South was that the United States could "annex" Mexico proper, specifically in order to expand the slave economy. Similar southern ambitions were entertained regarding Cuba and Central America. Any such southern-supported "filibuster" would undoubtedly have been a bloody failure, as was the only actual attempt in Nicaragua from 1855 to 1857 (McPherson 1988: 47–116).

29. Updating Laqueur's (1984: 441–42) list, my count is as follows. Guerrilla wins: Mexico (1911–1919), Ireland (1919–1922), Arabia (Ibn Saud), Nicaragua (Sandino 1927–1933), Yugoslavia (World War II), Albania (World War II), Palestine (Israelis 1944–1948), Indochina (1945–1954), Indonesia, Algeria, Cyprus (independence), Cuba (Castro), Vietnam, Laos, Cambodia, Angola, Mozambique, Guinea-Bissau, Rhodesia (Zimbabwe), Aden-Yemen, Namibia, Afghanistan, Nicaragua (Sandinista).

Guerrilla victories correlated with conventional military victories: Arabia (World War I), China (1927–1945), USSR (World War II), Greece (World War II), France (World War II), Italy (World War II).

Guerrilla losses: Boers (1899–1902), Philippines (1899–1902), Soviet Union (Basmatchi 1919–1930), Morocco (1921–1927), Brazil (Prestes), Palestine (Arab 1936–1939), Poland (1944), Iraqi Kurds (1945–1975), Philippines (Huk 1946–1956), Greece (communists 1947–1949), Malaya (communist), Kenya (Mau-Mau), Venezuela (1962–1965), Peru (1962–1965), Oman (1962–1976), Guatemala (1964–1967), Bolivia (Guevara).

Ties: German East Africa (1914–1918, surrendered only at general armistice), southern Sudan (1955–1972), Syria (1925–1936), and Yemen Civil War (1962–1970) (in the three latter cases, the guerrillas were granted considerable concessions, as were the defeated Boer commandos, the Filipino Huks, and the Kenyan Mau-Mau).

Although a number of guerrilla wars are currently unresolved, by my count, guerrilla wins outnumber losses by almost two to one. Also note that many of these "losses" amd "ties" have engendered several new and continuing guerrilla wars, such as in the Philippines (Huk) and in the Sudan.

It is difficult to classify urban terrorists as guerrillas, since their actions never intend or accomplish the slightest harm to the military strength or basic economy of their enemies, they never clear or control any territory, and they have an unbroken losing record for at least the last two centuries. Since they rely on the mass media for their theatrical effects, they seem better classified as dramatic performers (Laqueur 1984: xi).

It is fair to note that some military analysts find little to appreciate in guerrilla techniques (for example, Laqueur 1984 and Van Creveld 1989). They note the dependence of modern guerrillas on external logistic support and suitable geography. But they also denigrate guerrilla victories by attributing them primarily to the political or "moral" failings of their conventional opponents rather than the military effectiveness of the guerrillas. Thus they argue that the Dutch in Indonesia, the British and the Portuguese in countless wars of decolonization, the French in Indochina and Algeria, and the Americans in Vietnam lost because of a lack of will at home, a liberal squeamishness about human rights and the brutalities required to win, or an inability to commit their full military resources to the struggle. These arguments are merely special pleadings. In *all* wars, the defeated side loses its will to continue, either because it has suffered intolerable human and economic losses or because it judges continuing warfare would be more costly than making a disadvantageous peace. Guerrilla wars have been won and lost for the same reasons as conventional wars. The totalitarian, unsqueamish Soviet Union was neither hindered by a free press nor domestic political dissent in its war in Afghanistan; yet it was defeated. The division of military resources also affected the victors in some notable conventional wars: the United States in World War II and Korea (the Pacific/Asia versus Europe/NATO), Israel in 1967 and 1973 (Syria versus Egypt), and Britain in the Falklands War (Northern Ireland/NATO versus Argentina).

30. Weigley (1991) details the futility of 200-year quest by European armies for "decisive" battles.

31. For example, McNeill 1982; Parker 1988.

32. One defense analyst (Friedman 1991: 251) attributes all of Iraq's military deficiencies to general social and economic factors and concludes: "It is difficult to escape the conclusion that military superiority is a function of social organization."

Chapter 6

1. *HNAI* vol. 5, 1984: 177, 218, 333, 477; *HNAI* vol. 6, 1981: 408, 455; *HNAI* vol. 7, 1990: 215, 336, 465, 495; *HNAI* vol. 8, 1978: 199, 380, 393, 488, 547; *HNAI* vol. 10, 1983: 329; *HNAI* vol. 15, 1978: 262, 278, 316, 386, 676; *HSAI* vol. 1, 1946: 195, 314, 391, 498; *HSAI* vol. 3, 1948: 88, 112–26, 188, 278, 291, 528, 647, 701, 756; Matthews 1877: 61; Slobodin 1960: 83; Stewart 1965: 381–82; Ray 1963: 143; Meggitt 1977: 89–91; Handy 1923: 133–34; Evans-Pritchard 1940: 128; Brown 1922: 85.

2. Meggitt 1977: 102–103.

3. Edgerton 1988: 130. Actually, other Nguni tribes and the Mtetwa (Zulu) a hundred years before the Zulu War sometimes took male prisoners who were later ransomed for cattle; the custom of killing prisoners was an innovation of King Shaka (Otterbein 1967: 352).

4. Oliver 1974: 395–98; *HNAI* vol. 8, 1978: 380, 393, 547; *HNAI* vol. 10, 1983: 329; *HNAI* vol. 15, 1978: 220, 316, 386, 628, 676; Hudson 1976: 253–57; *HSAI* vol. 3, 1948: 119–26, 291, 339.

5. *HNAI* vol. 15, 1978: 316, 386.

6. Vayda 1960: 70; Handy 1923: 138; Carneiro 1990: 199; Balee 1984: 246–47; Whitehead 1990: 155; Steward and Faron 1959: 209, 236, 244, 305, 323–27, 331, 335; *HNAI* vol. 8, 1978: 330, 380; Morren 1984: 175, 179, 193; *HNAI* vol. 15, 1978: 386, 676; *HSAI* vol. 3, 1948: 291, 339, 701.

7. For example, Glasse 1968: 93; Pospisil 1958: 93.

8. Of the 230 or so tribal groups (worldwide but the majority in the Americas and Oceania) for which I have notes on this issue, I have found only 8 that sometimes spared adult male captives for any reason: the Shawnee and Fox of the midwestern United States, the Mojo and Baure of central South America, the Macushi Carib of Guiana, the Nandi and Meru of East Africa, and the Nguni of southeastern Africa (*HNAI* vol. 15, 1978: 628, 642; *HSAI* vol. 3, 1948: 418, 852; Huntingford 1953: 77–78; Fadiman 1982: 46; Otterbein 1967: 352). In all these cases, the ethnographic accounts indicate that such acts of mercy were at least unusual, if not exceptional.

9. Evans-Pritchard 1940: 128–29; Kelly 1985: 55–57.

10. *HNAI* vol. 5, 1984: 177; *HNAI* vol. 6, 1981: 455; *HNAI* vol. 7, 1990: 215, 336, 465; *HNAI* vol. 8, 1978: 219, 547. *HNAI* v ol. 15, 1978: 676; Ray 1963: 143; *HSAI* vol. 3, 1948: 262, 710, 786; Steward and Faron 1959: 188.

11. For example, Hogbin 1964: 59; Meggitt 1977; Pospisil 1963: 59; Robbins 1982: 188.

12. Porch 1986: 80.

13. Jorgensen 1980: 514.

14. Fadiman 1982: 46; Meggitt 1962: 38; *HNAI* vol. 7, 1990: 465; *HNAI* vol. 8, 1978: 380, 547; *HNAI* vol. 10, 1983: 329; *HNAI* vol. 15, 1978: 157.

15. *HSAI* vol. 4, 1948: 549; Steward and Faron 1959: 322; Rouse 1986: 188. Whitehead (1990) dismisses both the Island Carib traditions and the complementary reconstructions of linguists as being the result of early confusion between the Caribs of the mainland and the linguistically complex islanders. He also attributes this confusion to exclusive reliance on Spanish sources. Since the only sources on the early contact period islanders are Spanish, it is difficult to locate an alternative. He claims that the Island Carib "pidgin" was just a "trade language" shared with their friends the mainlanders. The idea that Island Carib men would use a mere trade lingo when speaking with their wives and among themselves seems far more improbable than the traditional explanation.

16. For example, Early and Peters 1990: 20, 67–70; see also Kelly 1985 on the demographic effects of the capture of Dinka women by the Nuer.

17. *HNAI* vol. 11, 1986: 382; *HNAI* vol. 10, 1983: 476; *HNAI* vol. 8, 1978: 199, 329, 440, 547, 694–700; *HNAI* vol. 6, 1981: 408, 494; *HNAI* vol. 5, 1984: 218, 333, 477; *HSAI* vol.1, 1946: 498; *HSAI* vol. 3, 1948: 721; Steward and Faron 1959: 358; Slobodin 1960: 83; Oliver 1974: 398; Handy 1923: 133–34; Vayda 1960: 92; Brown 1922: 85.

18. Zegwaard 1968: 443; Morren 1984: 176. Among an Asmat population of about 5,000 people, eighty-three such raids were recorded in just one year. If each raid killed only one person (a very conservative estimate), the annual war death rate would be 1.66 percent, or higher than any group listed in Figure 6.1.

19. Pakenham 1991: 609–15; Edgerton 1988: 210–12.

20. Utley and Washburn 1977: 42, 206–7, 217–18; *HNAI* vol. 15, 1978: 106–7; *HNAI* vol. 7, 1990: 586, 592; *HNAI* vol. 8, 1978: 107–108, 178, 195, 205, 249, 362–63. In the United States, public condemnation of such slaughters came primarily from representatives of the federal government: Indian agents and officers of the regular army.

Similarly infamous genocides of native Tasmanians and South African "Bushmen" were committed by colonial militias, commandos, and allied native tribes.

21. Some readers may be unconvinced by percentage comparisons between populations of hundreds or thousands of people and populations of millions and tens of millions—that is, they are more impressed by absolute numbers than ratios. However, consistent with such views, such skeptical readers must also disdain any calculations of death *rates* per patient or passenger-mile and therefore always chose to undergo critical surgery at small, rural, Third World clinics and fly on small airlines. At such medical facilities and on such airlines, the *total* number of passenger or patient deaths are always far fewer than those occurring on major airlines or at large university and urban hospitals. These innumerate readers should also prefer residence on one of the United States's small Indian reservations to life in any of its metropolitan areas since the annual *absolute* number of deaths from homicide, drug abuse, alcoholism, cancer, heart disease, and automobile accidents will always be far fewer on the reservations than in major cities and their suburbs.

22. Lindeman 1987: 115.

23. Keegan 1976: 313.

24. Meggitt 1977: 112.

25. See Appendix, Table 6.2, for references for Figure 6.2. Several of these prehistoric war death percentages are comparable (and actually higher than) that of the Jivaro, whose high figure is claimed to be the result of the introduction of firearms.

26. Cybulski, n.d. in press.

27. Keegan 1989: 592.

28. Recent figures indicate that nearly 25 million Soviet citizens died during World War II, of whom less than once-third were military (Weinberg 1994: 894). Almost all these military casualties (about 8 million) would have been male and, given that almost 25 percent of all Soviet males were in the military, a conservative estimate of female casualties is 60 to 65 percent of the civilian deaths. By this crude estimate, the Germans killed almost 15 million Soviet males and over 10 million civilian females, giving a female:male death ratio of less than 1:2. A more complete estimate must include the millions of non-Soviets of both sexes killed by Nazi death squads and camps. In modern history, Nazi Germany is unique in both the scale and the indiscriminateness of its homicides.

29. See Appendix, Table 6.2.

30. (New Guinea) Robbins 1982: 212–13; the Auyana cited this as a high, but not extraordinary, casualty rate; (Papuans) Pospisil 1963: 45, 57; (Blackfoot) Livingstone 1968: 9.

31. The Soviet Union was 25 percent deficient in males (sex ratio 133:100) at the end of World War II, and West Germany's population still showed a 22 percent deficiency in males (sex ratio 128:100) in 1960. Poland's losses, amounting to 20 percent of its prewar population, were proportionally the most severe of any nation during World War II (Keegan 1989: 591–92). In its 1865 to 1871 war against Brazil, Argentina, and Uruguay, Paraguay lost 65 percent of its population and 80 percent of its adult males (McPherson 1988: 856).

32. Vayda 1976: 23; Meggitt 1977: 174; *HNAI* vol. 6, 1981: 329, 454–56; *HNAI*

vol. 9, 1979: 392; *HNAI* vol. 11, 1986: 370, 381; Ferguson 1984b: 277, 281, 285; Bean 1972: 130–31; Chagnon 1968: 129. See Kelly 1985: 19–20 for a possible African case.

33. Rhodes 1986: 779 (citing Gil Eliot).

34. This scenario is not ecologically impossible. Many horticultural tribes in New Guinea and Africa sustained population densities ranging from 100 to over 200 persons per square mile (see Brown 1978: 106; Murdock and Wilson 1972: 257–58, 266–72). In 1988, the continental population densities of Europe and Asia had still not exceeded 180 persons per square mile and those of North America, South America and Africa were approximately 60 persons per square mile. The Huron tribe of Canada (lacking plows and domestic animals) supported a precontact population density of 60 per square mile (*HNAI* vol. 15, 1978: 369). The 1990 *Times Atlas* (Plate 5) shows this same area today having a population density between 50 and 100 persons per square mile.

35. (Mae Enga) Meggitt 1977: 101; (Mohave) Stewart 1965: 377–79.

36. Hattaway and Jones 1991: 409, 725.

37. Keegan 1976: 215, 255.

38. (Gettysburg and the Somme) Appendix, Table 4.1; (Waterloo) Keegan 1976: 305; (Atlanta) Sherman 1886: 566, 607.

39. Meggitt 1977: 100, 103–104.

40. Gabriel and Metz 1991: 87. Most of these casualties, especially the deaths, were inflicted during the routs that were the common aftermath of ancient battles. The close contact involved in ancient warfare meant that those fleeing defeat had almost no head start over their pursuers.

41. For example, of the 1.3 million Frenchmen killed in World War I, 640,000 (nearly half) of them died during the first four months of fighting (McNeill 1982: 318 n. 24).

42. For example, Heider 1970: 233; Meggitt 1977: 104; Spier 1930: 128; Grinnell 1923 (II): 159, 173; Gunther 1973; Robbins 1982: 37; Warner 1937: 220–21; Stewart 1965: 378; (antibiotic plants) Gabriel and Metz 1991: 121.

43. Handy 1923: 269; Steward and Faron 1959: 100; Gabriel and Metz 1991: 113–14.

44. McPherson 1988: 486–87.

45. Grinnell 1923 (II): 147–48.

46. (New Guinea) Meggitt 1977: 104; Robbins 1982: 188; Morren 1984: 196 notes that a shaman accompanied Miyanmin war parties; (North America) Spier 1930: 128; Gifford and Kroeber 1937: 156; Drucker 1941: 134; Voegelin 1942: 109; Stewart 1942: 301; Essene 1942: 40; Grinnell 1923 (II): 141; Stewart 1965: 378.

47. After reading McPherson (1988: 477–89) on medical care during the American Civil War, I am convinced that one of the most effective innovations in nineteenth-century military medicine was the begrudging acceptance of women nurses. Victorian sexism focused women's intelligence and practical curiosity on precisely those subjects that were eventually recognized as primary medical concerns—cleanliness (antisepsis), nutrition, convalescent care, and patient morale. The respect and gratitude that Union soldiers, from privates to generals, accorded Clara Barton, Dorothea Dix, "Mother Mary" Bickerdyke, and their less famous counterparts was as rational as it was sentimental.

Chapter 7

1. Oliver 1974: 395.

2. *HNAI* vol. 7, 1990: 215, 359, 465; *HNAI* vol. 8, 1978: 454, 488; *HNAI* vol. 15, 1978: 316; Zelenietz 1983: 91–92; Steward and Faron 1959: 267, 305, 321, 338, 339; Pakenham 1991: 439; Chadwick 1971: 49–50.

3. Vayda 1960: 95.

4. For example, Frayer 1993; Drusini and Barayan 1990; Milner et al. 1991; Snarkis 1987: 111; Quilter 1991: 414; Bouville 1987.

5. *HNAI* vol. 5, 1984: 477, 499; *HNAI* vol. 6, 1981: 408; *HNAI* vol. 7, 1990: 215; *HNAI* vol. 8, 1978: 199, 219, 239, 245, 251, 330, 344, 380, 440, 547, 596; *HNAI* vol. 9, 1979: 360, 396, 401, 414; *HNAI* vol. 10, 1983: 64, 107, 320, 336, 375, 437; *HNAI* vol. 15, 1978: 316, 696, 744; Hudson 1976: 251.

6. See Milner et al. 1991: 585 for references.

7. *HNAI* vol. 8, 1978: 534; Steward and Faron 1959: 209, 321, 357; *HSAI* vol. 4, 1948: 23; Baxter 1979: 69.

8. Steward and Faron 1959: 217–18, 281, 305; *HSAI* vol. 4, 1948: 306–7.

9. For example, Edgerton 1988: 44; Meggitt 1977: 24, 76, 102; Connell 1984: 160–61, 284–88; Hudson 1976: 251; (overkill with arrows) Editors of Time-Life Books 1974: 37, 117; Koch 1974: 78 (Plate 18).

10. Willey 1990; Owsley et al. 1977; Scott et al. 1989: 85–86; Bamforth, in press.

11. (Sand Creek) Utley and Washburn 1977: 206–207; (World War II) Sledge 1981: 120, 148; (Vietnam) Maclear 1981: 278; Caputo 1977: 64.

12. Arens 1979.

13. For example, Villa et al. 1986; White 1992.

14. For an excellent critical review of this evidence and a model study of one instance from the American Southwest, see White 1992. Because the subject is such an emotional (indeed mythological) one, White's study and a few others he cites provide spectacular demonstrations that the circumstantial evidence produced by archaeology and physical anthropology can cut the Gordian knots that the verbiage and subjectivity of other social scientists have created.

15. Steward and Faron 1959: 190, 209, 219, 236, 305, 323–24, 358; Carneiro 1990: 205.

16. Carneiro 1990: 205; Vayda 1960: 70; Morren 1986: 55, 281–82; Zegwaard 1968: 430, 443–44. For archaeological evidence, see White 1992: 19–22.

17. Pakenham 1991: 447.

18. For reviews and bibliographies, see White 1992; Turner and Turner 1992.

19. Villa et al. 1986; (Fontébregoua) Villa et al. 1988; Jelinek 1957, cited in White 1992: 23.

20. Harner 1977; Harris 1979, 1989.

21. Fagan 1984: 233–35.

22. Isaac 1983.

23. For example, Edgerton 1988: 45; White 1983: 116; Handy 1923: 218–21;

Steward and Faron 1959: 244, 326–27, 357–58; *HNAI* vol. 6, 1981: 377; *HNAI* vol. 15, 1978: 386.

24. (Ethnography) Handy 1923: 218–21; (Archaeology) Kirch 1984: 159; White 1992: 20.

25. For example, Handy 1923: 133; Vayda 1960: 97–100; Oliver 1974: 398; Meggitt 1977: 90, 207; Brown 1978: 208; Herdt 1987: 55; Kelly 1985: 48–49; *HNAI* vol. 7, 1990: 495; Kroeber 1925: 51, 220; Steward and Faron 1959: 326; Ray 1963: 137; Spier 1930: 27; Carneiro 1990: 200.

26. Adams 1989: 104; Haas 1990: 187; *HNAI* vol. 9, 1979: 98, 136, 143; Turner 1989; Wilcox and Haas 1991. Fish and Fish (1989: 121) note that, in the Tucson Basin between A.D. 1000 and 1300, burned houses "often exceed 60 percent" of those recorded, but they attribute these to a "mortuary practice."

27. For example, Courtin 1984; Mellaart 1965: 112–13.

28. The Air Minister was Sir Kingsley Wood, whose attitudes concerning the economic aspects of warfare were probably colored by his former profession of insurance consultant (Deighton 1977: 56).

29. Ember and Ember 1990: 255; Otterbein 1989: 148 (col. 7, codes 1, 3, and 4).

30. Meggitt 1977: 14.

31. Kroeber 1925: 219–21.

32. For example, Kirch 1984; Handy 1923: 123; Vayda 1960: 109–16; Carneiro 1990: 201; Balee 1984: 248–49; *HNAI* vol. 11, 1986: 370, 381; Cannon 1992: 514.

33. Vencl 1984: 124.

34. For example, Keeley 1992 (on the Early Neolithic in northwestern Europe); *HNAI* vol. 9, 1979: 136 (on Anasazi abandonment of Navajo Reservoir and Gobernador regions). See also Haas and Creamer 1993: 138.

35. See references in Appendix, Table 7.2; *HNAI* vol. 15, 1978: 198; Ross 1984: 97; Brown 1978: 127–28, 209; Wilson 1983: 85; Morren 1984: 194–97; Pakenham 1991: 352.

36. See Appendix, Table 7.2.

37. Vayda 1976: 83.

Chapter 8

1. Ferguson 1984a and 1990 provide excellent reviews of these controversies.

2. Koch 1974: 213–16.

3. Otterbein 1989: 63–64; Jorgensen 1980: 509–15, 613.

4. See Appendix, Table 8.1.

5. Heider 1970: 100; Koch 1974: 154–55: Hallpike 1977: 230; *HNAI* vol. 8, 1978: 694–700; Biolsi 1984; Ferguson 1984b; *HNAI* vol. 15, 1978: 744–45: Fukai and Turton 1979: 9; Fadiman 1982: 42; Meggitt 1962: 42.

6. Otterbein 1989: 66.

7. *HSAI* vol. 1, 1946: 306–7; *HNAI* vol. 10, 1983: 722.

8. For example, Koch 1974: 179–224; Hallpike 1977: 211–29; Chagnon 1983: 189.

9. For example, Cohen 1985.

10. See Appendix, Table 8.3. A similar result is obtained by adding population density figures to Otterbein's 1989 data. Recent research indicates that there is also no correlation between density and violence in rhesus monkeys (*Discover*, February 1994, p. 14).

11. Britain's population in 1300 was less than 5 million, but it had risen to 50 million by 1982; see for homicide rates, Knauft 1987.

12. Chagnon 1974: 127, 160.

13. For example, Steward 1938: 254–55 (especially Owens Valley Paiute); Jorgensen 1980: compare pp. 407–409 to p. 447.

14. Henry 1985: 374–376; O. Bar Yosef, personal communication; Frayer 1993.

15. For hunter-gatherers, see Hayden 1981; Price and Brown 1985; Keeley 1988.

16. Ferguson 1984a: 17–18.

17. Ember and Ember 1990: 256.

18. *HNAI* vol. 5, 1984: 306, 341, 348; *HNAI* vol. 6, 1981: 469, 494, 582; *HNAI* vol. 8, 1978: 168–69, 205, 213, 238, 245, 329–31, 344–45, 352–53, 363, 379–80; *HNAI* vol. 10, 1983: 40, 719–22; Balee 1984: 257–59; MacDonald and Cove 1987: xx; Meggitt 1962: 42; Meggitt 1977: 42, 80–81; Morren 1984: 171, 183; *HSAI* vol. 3, 1948: 367, 850; Matthews 1877: 27; Spears 1981: 100.

19. Tefft 1973.

20. For example, *HSAI* vol. 3, 1948: 309, 318; Kroeber 1965: 399.

21. In aboriginal North America, the practice of salting food was highly correlated with a predominantly plant diet because a diet rich in plants, unless supplemented with mineral salt, could cause physiological problems (Driver and Massey 1957: 249).

22. *HNAI* vol. 8, 1978: 286; Kroeber 1925: 236.

23. For example, Ferguson and Whitehead 1992; Abler 1992: Ross 1984; Ferguson 1984b.

24. For example, MacDonald and Cove 1987: 17, 19, 187–90; *HNAI* vol. 10, 1983: 40, 717; *HSAI* vol. 3, 1948: 850.

25. *HNAI* vol. 10, 1983: 719–22; Spencer and Jennings 1977: 331.

26. An old Apache, with pawky wit, told one of my colleagues that his forefathers had regarded Pueblo villages as "an early kind of welfare office" to which the Apaches regularly repaired to receive free food.

27. For example, *HNAI* vol. 10, 1983: 721; Porch 1986: 65–82.

28. Hart and Pilling 1979: 83–84; Meggitt 1977: 13; *HSAI* vol. 4, 1948: 532; Pospisil 1963: 58, 61, 68–69; MacDonald and Cove 1987: 34–35; Tefft 1973.

29. Fitzhugh 1985: 31; *HNAI* vol. 5, 1984: 553; see also McGovern 1985. It remains a possibility that the Inuit scavenged some of these items from already-abandoned Norse settlements; radiocarbon dates indicating contemporaneity between Norse and Thule Inuit in southwestern Greenland, however, imply that some items were obtained directly from the Norse.

30. For example, Secoy 1953; Biolsi 1984; Spears 1981: 100–101; Fadiman 1982: 45.

Chapter 9

1. Jorgensen 1980: 240–47.

2. *HNAI* vol. 9, 1979: 189.

3. For example, between 1890 and 1913, Germany's population increased by 35 percent, whereas Britain's and France's increased by 22 percent and 3 percent respectively. Between the wars, Germany's growth rate was higher than those of the Soviet Union, the United States, France, and Britain (Kennedy 1987: 199).

4. Kelly 1985; for an alternative view, see de Wolf 1990. The Oromo and Masai expansions in East Africa also may have been fueled by population growth (Spears 1981: 63–67).

5. For example, Mohave versus Maricopa, *HNAI* vol. 10, 1983: 57, 75; Mackenzie Eskimo versus Kutchin, *HNAI* vol. 5, 1984: 349; *HNAI* vol. 6, 1981: 530; Sioux versus Arikara, Secoy 1953: 74–75; Khoikhoi versus San, Elphick 1977 and Spears 1981: 52–53; Oromo and Masai versus Pokomo, Mijikenda, and Kikuyu, Spears 1981: 63, 66–67; Telefolmin expansion, Morren 1984: 183–84.

6. Spears 1981: 63–67.

7. Otterbein 1967; Edgerton 1988: 10.

8. See especially Green and Perlman's (1985) anthology devoted to frontiers and boundaries in which warfare, conflict, and raiding are hardly mentioned. Other examples: Gregg 1988; Bogucki 1988.

9. Sioux for Bannock; Eskimo for Ingalik; Comanche for Mescalero Apache; Inuit for Hare; Hopi for Navaho; Mbya for Guayaki; ("enemies") Yavapai for Pima; Pima–Papago for Navaho–Apache; Wintu for Yuki; Takelma for Shasta.

10. For example, Thompson and Lamar 1981; Bodley 1990; Ferguson and Whitehead 1992.

11. Spears 1981: 64–67, 99–100.

12. Colin Turnbull (1962, 1965) has emphasized the independence of the Mbuti Pygmies from their Bantu patrons. His arguments, however, are mostly special pleadings—Bantu crops are staples of the Pygmy diet only because the Mbuti have acquired "a taste for plantation foods"; Pygmies only rely on the metal weapons and utensils obtained from the villagers because this is "convenient"; Pygmy boys are initiated into manhood and Pygmy marriages arranged and sanctified under Bantu supervision and according to Bantu custom, but the Mbuti do not take these rituals very seriously; in the presence of even a single Bantu, the Pygmies behave in a "submissive, almost servile" fashion but are a "different people" when their "masters" are absent; in the presence of Bantu, Pygmy music and dances are less complex and creative than those performed among themselves; the Mbuti have an underground social, political, and religious life that they hide from their Negro "masters." All of Turnbull's arguments for Pygmy "independence" would apply equally well to African slaves in the Americas (except those regarding agriculture and metallurgy because native West Africans were accomplished farmers and metallurgists).

13. Bailey et al. 1989: 62–63.

14. For the general argument, see Bailey et al. 1989. Also, the Masai and Oromo pastoralists of Kenya considered the local foragers to be nothing more than an untouchable "low caste" (Spears 1981: 51).

15. Saunders 1981: 151–55; Giliomec 1981: 80, 83, 86, 113; Thompson and Lamar 1981: 18–19; Phillipson 1985: 210–11; Lee 1979: 31–32; Wilson and Thompson 1983: fig. 4 (compare San headdresses in fig. 6), 63–64, 70–71, 105–7, 165; Silberbauer 1972: 272–73; Thompson 1990: 14, 28–29; Spears 1981: 52–53.

16. Oliver 1991: 195. This statement was recorded in 1926 when Bechuanaland (now Botswana) was still autonomous in internal affairs. Only later, in the 1930s, did Britain take a more direct and active role in the administration of this isolated protectorate.

17. Lee 1979: 77.

18. Steward and Faron 1959: 432, 438; *HSAI* vol. 1, 1946: 250, 532; *HNAI* vol. 10, 1983: 14, 237, 361, 476, 497: *HNAI* vol. 11, 1986: 340, 354.

19. For example, Crosby 1986: 79–100; Langer 1972: 150, 375; Bodley 1990.

20. Hudson 1976: 82–84; Milner et al. 1991: 582; Bamforth 1994; *HNAI* vol. 9, 1979: 86–88, 136, 142–43; Wilcox 1989; Fish and Fish 1989.

21. Evans 1987; Bouville 1987; Roudil 1990; Keeley 1992, 1993.

22. Ember and Ember 1990: 255; Ember and Ember 1992. Another fascinating result of this study is that disaster- and war-prone societies also commonly socialize children to be mistrustful of both nature and other people.

23. *HNAI* vol. 9, 1979: 185; *HNAI* vol. 10, 1983: 73; Aldred 1984: 117, 121–22, 151; Editors of Readers Digest 1988: 82; Morren 1984: 185.

24. Haas 1990.

25. White 1992; Wilson and Thompson 1983: 391, 395, 399.

26. Bamforth 1994; Walker and Lambert 1989; Lambert and Walker 1991; Greene and Armelagos 1972; Anderson 1968.

Chapter 10

1. Gregor 1990: 106–107.

2. Glasse 1968: 93; Whitehead 1990: 153; Fadiman 1982: 16; Harndy 1923: 135; *HNAI* vol. 6, 1981: 406; Hudson 1976: 252; *HNAI* vol. 10, 1983: 107; *HNAI* vol. 7, 1990: 495; *HNAI* vol. 8, 1978: 160, 239, 596; see Turney-High 1971: 223–26 for further examples.

3. *HNAI* vol. 10, 1983: 411, 428–29, 443, 475–76; *HNAI* vol. 7, 1990: 213, 251–52, 276–77, 329, 401; Meggitt 1977: 8, 66–70; Brown 1978: 194–97; Moore 1990.

4. Meggitt 1977: 99.

5. (Jalemo) Koch 1983: 201; (Kapauku) Pospisil 1963: 57; (Jivaro) Karsten 1967: 307; (Apache) *HNAI* vol. 10, 1983: 373–76, 475–76.

6. See various papers in Rodman and Cooper 1983; Fadiman 1982: 135; Robbins 1982: 189.

7. (Auyana) Robbins 1982: 189; (Tauade) Hallpike 1977: 261.

8. Dr. J. Costigan, personal communication.

9. Oliver 1974: 390–91, 395.

10. Turney-High 1949: 226.

11. Hudson 1976: 257; see also notes 12 and 13.

12. For example, Pospisil 1963: 61; Turton 1979: 194; Glasse 1968: 98. Where paying blood money is customary, each side must pay for every death it inflicted since compensation is owed to the relatives of each victim. In other words, equal deaths on both sides do not cancel out the necessity to pay blood money.

13. Meggitt 1977: 116–20, 126.

14. See Appendix, Table 8.2c.

15. Pospisil 1963: 61; Meggitt 1977: 105, 110, 199–200; Brown 1978: 209; Herdt 1987: 47.

16. Warner 1937: 174–75.

17. Heider 1970.

18. Gregor 1990.

19. Gregor 1990: 111–112.

20. Chagnon 1983: 149–50. For some reason, Ferguson (1992b: 211) finds this story unbelievable, even though he heard Gregor's paper describing the same kind of artificial monopolies (albeit more stable ones) among the Xingu just three years earlier.

21. Keeley and Cahen 1989, 1990; Sliva and Keeley 1994; Keeley 1993.

22. For example, *HNAI* vol. 7, 1990: 159–60; *HNAI* vol. 4, 1988: 81–95.

23. *HNAI* vol. 6, 1981: 411; *HNAI* vol. 7, 1991: 159–68; McInnis 1969: 397; Brown 1991: 352–56.

24. Utley (1984: 270–71) claims that the Second Northwest Rebellion was a real Indian war, comparable to those in the United States and arising from the same grievances and antagonisms. This view ignores several important facts: (1) the revolt was entirely a Métis initiative; (2) Métis grievances were quite different from those of the local Indians, a majority of whom remained neutral; and (3) the Cree did little fighting and inflicted only a handful of casualties. This half-hearted uprising of two small bands, by being a unique occurrence in the history of the Canadian West, represents the exception that highlights the rule.

25. *HNAI* vol. 4, 1988: 335–90.

26. *HNAI* vol. 4, 1988: 91–92, 202–10; Brown 1991: 347–50.

27. Utley 1984: 112–14, 142–48; Connell 1984: 147.

28. Utley 1984: 271; see also Brown 1991: 350–51.

29. For example, Utley 1984: 52, 138; Utley and Washburn 1977: 179–83.

30. For example, the Cheyenne (Hoebel 1978) or the Japanese before World War II.

31. For example, Baxter 1979: 83–84; Meggitt 1977: 110, 116; Warner 1958: 176.

32. Rodman and Cooper 1983; Dozier 1967.

33. Harris 1974: 62.

Chapter 11

1. For example, no American academic can ignore the strong influence exerted in the humanities and social sciences by the European doctrines of existentialism, struc-

turalism, structural Marxism, poststructuralism, and postmodernism. These successive enthusiasms have left American universities a "burned-over district" like those areas of nineteenth-century New England exhausted by a succession of religious evangelisms.

2. In his excellent one-volume history of World War II, British historian H. P. Willmott (1989: 477) concludes that even 57 million dead might be "a small price to pay for ridding the world of depraved wickedness."

3. Keegan 1989: 594.

4. For example, Kipling, Scott, Tennyson, and Hugo.

5. For example, Graves, Remarque, Owen, and Hemingway.

6. For example, Vidal, Mailer, Vonnegut, and Heller.

7. For example, in contrast to Parkman, Bancroft, and Prescott, Frederick Merk (1978) (the late Gurney Professor of History at Harvard), hardly mentions warfare with the Indians induced by this movement, concerning himself instead with land allocation, economic development, and frontier politics.

8. These doctrines provided Europeans and later some Asians with such an agreeable boost to their already Olympian self-admiration that many remain reluctant to abandon them even now, despite massive evidence to the contrary. Of course, the blunt racism of the late nineteenth and early twentieth centuries has become a minority opinion in modern North America and western Europe. However, the anti-Semitism resurfacing in eastern Europe and certain statements by some Asian leaders concerning the "mongrel" society of the United States indicate that crude racism is hardly extinct.

Nonracist Social Darwinism universally remains a theme in conservative political thinking (including, ironically enough, "conservative" Marxism). The core idea is that whoever or whatever is currently "successful" (whether individuals, social groups, techniques, institutions, or values) is "more fit" and worthy of emulation than any less-successful or displaced competitors.

Indeed, throughout my career, many American and European university professors of varying political persuasions have asked me why anthropologists bothered to study societies and cultures that had clearly failed to survive or were surely doomed to extinction (i.e., preindustrial non-Western cultures).

9. During my student years in western Europe in the 1970s, in Britain, France, Spain, and Belgium, I was often haragued by both rightists and leftists concerning "U.S. imperialism" in their respective countries.

10. For example, *HNAI* vol. 4, 1988: 545 (and references).

11. A fine popular account of these can be found in Harris 1974: 97–111.

12. Currently, the popular media prefer to portray the mentality of primitive peoples as childlike (in the romantic sense)—trusting, guileless, prerational, and intuitive. Such portrayals can also be read to imply that precivilized folks were rather dim-witted. It is tragicomic that such portraits are intended to be, and are widely accepted as, sympathetic and complimentary to those so portrayed.

13. Alas, I cannot attribute this line recalled from my school days.

Chapter 12

1. Keegan 1987.

2. For a very acute analysis of the crisis years of the European focus on *the* decisive battle, see Weigley 1991. Unfortunately, this author, while delineating the foolishness of the Clausewitzian concept of a decisive formal battle, goes on to underestimate the decisiveness of modern total war. He fails to note that as military powers those modern nations who have suffered total defeats (i.e., revolutionary–Napoleonic France, the American South, Austro-Hungary, Germany, and Japan), either disappeared completely or have never again, despite the passage of generations, reached first-rank status as military powers.

3. See the very interesting report of Scott et al. 1989.

BIBLIOGRAPHY

ABBREVIATIONS

HNAI	*Handbook of North American Indians*
HSAI	*Handbook of South American Indians*
UCAR	*University of California Anthropological Records*
UCPAAE	*University of California Publications in American Archaeology and Ethnology*

Abler, T. 1992. "Beavers and Muskets: Iroquois Military Fortunes in the Face of European Colonization." In *War in the Tribal Zone*, ed. R. Ferguson and N. Whitehead, pp. 151–74. Santa Fe, N.M.: School of American Research Press.

Adams, E. C. 1989. "The Case for Conflict During the Late Prehistoric and Proto-historic Period in the Western Pueblo Area of the American Southwest." In *Cultures in Conflict*, ed. D. Tkaczuk and B. Vivian, pp. 103–14. Calgary: University of Calgary.

Aginsky, B. 1943. "Culture Element Distributions: XXIV Central Sierra." *UCAR* 8, no. 4.

Aldred, C. 1984. *The Egyptians.* London: Thames and Hudson.

Allred, B., J. Dykes, F. Goodwyn, and D. Simms. 1960. *Great Western Indian Fights.* Lincoln: University of Nebraska Press.

Anderson, J. 1968. "Late Paleolithic Skeletal Remains from Nubia." In *The Prehistory of*

Nubia, vol. 2, ed. F. Wendorf, pp. 996–1,040. Dallas: Southern Methodist University Press.

Arens, W. 1979. *The Man-Eating Myth.* Oxford: Oxford University Press.

Bailey, R., G. Head, M. Jenike, B. Owen, R. Rechtman, and E. Zechenter. 1989. "Hunting and Gathering in Tropical Rain Forest: Is it Possible?" *American Anthropologist* 91: 59–82.

Balee, W. 1984. "The Ecology of Ancient Tupi Warfare." In *Warfare, Culture, and Environment,* ed. R. Ferguson, pp. 241–67. Orlando, Fla.: Academic Press.

Bamforth, D. 1994. "Indigenous People, Indigenous Violence: Precontact Warfare on the North American Great Plains." *Man* 29: 95–115.

Baxter, P. 1979. "Boran Age-sets and Warfare." In *Warfare Among East African Herders,* ed. K. Fukai and D. Turton, pp. 69–95. Osaka, Japan: National Museum of Ethnology.

Bean, L. 1972. *Mukat's People: The Cahuilla Indians of Southern California.* Berkeley: University of California Press.

Biolsi, T. 1984. "Ecological and Cultural Factors in Plains Indian Warfare." In *Warfare, Culture, and Environment,* ed. R. Ferguson, pp. 141–68. Orlando, Fla.: Academic Press.

Blick, J. 1988. "Genocidal Warfare in Tribal Societies as a Result of European-Induced Culture Conflict." *Man,* n.s., 23: 654–70.

Bodley, J. 1990. *Victims of Progress* 3d ed. Mountain View, Calif.: Mayfield.

Bogucki, P. 1988. *Forest Farmers and Stockherders.* Cambridge: Cambridge University Press.

Bohannon, L., and P. Bohannon. 1953. *The Tiv of Central Nigeria.* London: International African Institute.

Bouville, C. 1987. "Les Restes Humaines de la Baume Font Bregoua à Salenes (Var)." In *Première Communautés Paysannes en Méditerranée Occidentale,* ed. J. Guilaine, J. Courtin, J.- L. Roudil, and J.- L. Vernet, pp. 69–75. Paris: Éditions du CNRS.

Brain, C. 1981. *The Hunters or the Hunted.* Chicago: University of Chicago Press.

Brown, C. 1991. *The Illustrated History of Canada.* Toronto: Lester.

Brown, P. 1978. *Highland Peoples of New Guinea.* Cambridge: Cambridge University Press.

Brown, R. 1922. *The Andaman Islanders.* Cambridge: Cambridge University Press. Reprint. New York: Free Press, 1964.

Burch, E., and T. Correll. 1972. "Alliance and Conflict: Inter-Regional Relations in North Alaska." In *Alliance in Eskimo Society,* ed. L. Guemple, pp. 17–39. Seattle: University of Washington Press.

Campillo, D., O. Mercadal, and R.-M. Blanch. 1993. "A Mortal Wound Caused by a Flint Arrowhead in Individual MF-18 of the Neolithic Period Exhumed at Sant Quirze del Valles." *International Journal of Osteoarchaeology* 3: 145–50.

Cannon, A. 1992. "Conflict and Salmon on the Interior Plateau of British Columbia." In *A Complex Culture of the British Columbia Plateau,* ed. B. Hayden, pp. 506–24. Vancouver: University of British Columbia Press.

Caputo, P. 1977. *A Rumor of War.* New York: Ballantine Books.

Carneiro, R. 1990. "Chiefdom-Level Warfare as Exemplified in Fiji and the Cauca Valley." In *The Anthropology of War*, ed. J. Haas, pp. 190–211. New York: Cambridge University Press.

Chadwick, N. 1971. *The Celts*. Harmondsworth: Penguin Books.

Chagnon, N. 1968. "Yanomamo Social Organization and Warfare." In *War*, ed. M. Fried, M. Harris, and R. Murphy, pp. 109–59. Garden City, N.Y.: Natural History Press.

———. 1974. *Studying the Yanomamo*. New York: Holt, Rinehart and Winston.

———. 1983. *Yanomamo: The Fierce People* 3d ed. New York: Holt, Rinehart and Winston.

Champion, T., C. Gamble, C. Shennan, and A. Whittle. 1984. *Prehistoric Europe*. New York: Academic Press.

Chandler, D. 1966. *The Campaigns of Napoleon*. New York: Macmillan.

Chatters, J. 1989. "Pacifism and the Organization of Conflict of the Plateau of Northwestern America." In *Cultures in Conflict*, ed. D. Tkaczuk and B. Vivian, pp. 241–52. Calgary: University of Calgary.

Codere, H. 1950. *Fighting with Property*. Seattle: University of Washington Press.

Cohen, M. 1985. "Prehistoric Hunter-Gatherers: The Meaning of Social Complexity." In *Prehistoric Hunter-Gatherers*, ed. T. Price and J. Brown, pp. 99–119. Orlando, Fla.: Academic Press.

Connell, E. 1984. *Son of the Morning Star*. San Francisco: North Point Press.

Connolly, P. 1989. "The Early Roman Army; The Roman Army in the Age of Polybius." In *Warfare in the Ancient World*, ed. Sir J. Hackett, pp. 136–68. New York: Facts on File.

Courtin, J. 1984. "La Guerre au Néolithique." *La Recherche* 15: 448–58.

Crosby, A. 1972. *The Columbian Exchange*. Westport, Conn.: Greenwood Press.

———. 1986. *Ecological Imperialism*. New York: Cambridge University Press.

Cybulski, J. In press. "Culture Change, Demographic History, and Health and Disease on the Northwest Coast." In *In the Wake of Contact*, ed. G. Milner and C. Larsen. New York: Wiley-Liss.

Dart, R. 1957. "The Ostoedontokeratic Culture of the Australopithecus Africanus." *Memoirs of the Transvaal Museum* 10: 1–105.

Deighton, L. 1977. *Fighter*. New York: Ballantine Books.

Dentan, R. 1979. *The Semai: A Nonviolent People of Malaya*. New York: Holt, Rinehart and Winston.

de Wolf, J. 1990. "Ecology and Conquest: Critical Notes on Kelly's Model of Nuer Expansion." *Ethnology* 29: 341–63.

Divale, W. 1973. *Warfare in Primitive Societies: A Bibliography*. Santa Barbara, Calif.: ABC-Clio Press.

Dixon, P. 1988. "The Neolithic Settlements on Crickley Hill." In *Enclosures and Defenses in the Neolithic of Western Europe*, ed. C. Burgess, P. Topping, C. Mordant, and M. Maddison, pp. 75–87. BAR I.S. no. 403(i). Oxford: British Archaeological Reports.

Dobson, B. 1989. "The Empire." In *Warfare in the Ancient World,* ed. Sir J. Hackett, pp. 192–221. New York: Facts on File.

Dobyns, H. 1983. *Their Number Became Thinned.* Knoxville: University of Tennessee.

Dobyns, H., P. Ezell, and G. Ezell. 1963. "Death of a Society." *Ethnohistory* 10: 105–61.

Dozier, E. 1967. *The Kalinga of Northern Luzon, Philippines.* New York: Holt, Rinehart and Winston.

Driver, H., and W. Massey. 1957. "Comparative Studies of North American Indians." *Transactions of the American Philosophical Society,* n.s., 47: 165–456.

Drucker, P. 1941. "Culture Element Distributions V: Southern California." *UCAR* 1, no. 1.

———. 1965. *Cultures of the North Pacific Coast.* Scranton, Penn.: Chandler.

Drusini, A., and J. Barayan. 1990. "Anthropological Study of Nasca Trophy Heads." *Homo* 41: 251–65.

DuBois, C. 1935. "Wintu Ethnography." *UCPAAE* 36, no. 1.

Dudley, D. 1975. *Roman Society.* New York: Penguin Books.

Early, J., and J. Peters. 1990. *The Population Dynamics of the Mucajai Yanomama.* San Diego, Calif.: Academic Press.

Edgerton, R. 1988. *Like Lions They Fought.* New York: Ballantine Books.

Editors of Reader's Digest. 1988. *Illustrated History of South Africa.* Pleasantville, N.Y.: Reader's Digest Association.

Editors of Time-Life Books. 1974. *The Soldiers.* Old West Series. New York: Time-Life Books.

Eid, L. 1985. "'National' War Among Indians of Northeastern North America." *Canadian Review of American Studies* 16: 125–54.

Elphick, R. 1977. *Kraal and Castle.* New Haven, Conn.: Yale University Press.

Ember, C. 1978. "Myths About Hunter-Gatherers." *Ethnology* 17: 439–48.

Ember, C., and M. Ember. 1990. *Cultural Anthropology* 6th ed. Englewood Cliffs, N.J.: Prentice-Hall.

———. 1992. "Resource Unpredictability, Mistrust, and War: A Cross-Cultural Study." *Journal of Conflict Resolution* 36: 242–62.

Essene, F. 1942. "Culture Element Distributions: XXI Round Valley." *UCAR* 8, no. 1.

Evans, J. 1987. "The Development of Neolithic Communities in the Central Mediterranean." In *Premières Communautés Paysannes en Méditerranée Occidentale,* ed. J. Guilaine, J. Courtin, J.-L. Roudil, and J.-L. Vernet, pp. 126–37. Paris: Éditions du CNRS.

Evans-Pritchard, E. 1940. *The Nuer.* Oxford: Oxford University Press.

Ewers, J. 1967. "Blackfoot Raiding for Horses and Scalps." In *Law and Warfare,* ed. P. Bohannon, pp. 351–57. Garden City, N.Y.: Natural History Press.

Fadiman, J. 1982. *An Oral History of Tribal Warfare: The Meru of Mt. Kenya.* Athens: Ohio University Press.

Fagan, B. 1984. *The Aztecs.* New York: Freeman.

———. 1989. *People of the Earth.* 6th ed. New York: Scott, Foresman.

Ferguson, R. 1984a. "Introduction: Studying War." In *Warfare, Culture, and Environment,* ed. R. Ferguson, pp. 1–82. Orlando, Fla.: Academic Press.

————. 1984b. "A Reexamination of the Causes of Northwest Coast Warfare." In *Warfare, Culture, and Environment*, ed. R. Ferguson, pp. 267–328. Orlando, Fla.: Academic Press.

————. 1988. *The Anthropology of War: A Bibliography*. New York: Harry Frank Guggenheim Foundation.

————. 1990. "Explaining War." In *The Anthropology of War*, ed. J. Haas, pp. 26–55. New York: Cambridge University Press.

————. 1992a. "A Savage Encounter: Western Contact and the Yanomami War Complex." In *War in the Tribal Zone*, ed. R. Ferguson and N. Whitehead, pp. 199–227. Santa Fe, N.M.: School of American Research Press.

————. 1992b. "Tribal Warfare." *Scientific American* 266: 108–16.

Ferguson, R., and N. Whitehead, eds. 1992. *War in the Tribal Zone*. Santa Fe, N.M.: School of American Research Press.

Ferrill, A. 1985. *The Origins of War*. London: Thames and Hudson.

————. 1986. *The Fall of the Roman Empire: The Military Explanation*. London: Thames and Hudson.

Fish, P., and S. Fish. 1989. "Hohokam Warfare from a Regional Perspective." In *Cultures in Conflict*, ed. D. Tkaczuk and B. Vivian, pp. 112–29. Calgary: University of Calgary.

Fitzhugh, W. 1985. "Early Contacts North of Newfoundland before A.D. 1600: A Review." In *Cultures in Contact*, ed. W. Fitzhugh, pp. 23–43. Washington, D.C.: Smithsonian Institution Press.

Fox, A. 1976. *Prehistoric Maori Fortifications on the North Island of New Zealand*. Auckland, N.Z.: Longman Paul.

Frayer, D. 1993. "Violence in the Central European Mesolithic." Paper given at American Anthropological Association Annual Meeting, Washington, D.C.

————. In press. "Offnet: Evidence for Violence in the Central European Mesolithic." Symposium on Upper Paleolithic, Mesolithic, and Neolithic Populations of Europe and the Mediterranean Basin, Budapest.

Friedman, N. 1991. *Desert Victory*. Annapolis, Md.: Naval Institute Press.

Fukai, K., and D. Turton. 1979. *Warfare Among East African Herders*. Osaka, Japan: National Museum of Ethnology.

Gabriel, R., and A. Metz. 1991. *From Sumer to Rome: The Military Capabilities of Ancient Armies*. New York: Greenwood Press.

Gambier, D., and D. Sacchi. 1991. "Sur quelque restes humains leptolithiques de la Grotte de La Crouzade, Aude." *L'Anthropologie* 95: 155–80.

Gibbon, E. n.d. *The Decline and Fall of the Roman Empire*. vol. 1. New York: Modern Library.

Gifford, E., and A. Kroeber. 1937. "Culture Element Distributions IV: Pomo." *UCPAAE* 37, no. 4.

Giliomec, H. 1981. "Processes in the Development of the Southern African Frontier." In *The Frontier in History*, ed. H. Lamar and L. Thompson, pp. 76–119. New Haven, Conn.: Yale University Press.

Glasse, R. 1968. *Huli of Papua: A Cognathic Descent System*. The Hague: Mouton.

Green, S., and S. Perlman, eds. 1985. *The Archaeology of Frontiers and Boundaries.* Orlando, Fla.: Academic Press.

Greene, D., and G. Armelagos. 1972. *The Wadi Halfa Mesolithic Population.* Department of Anthropology Research Reports, no. 11, University of Massachusetts, Amherst.

Gregg, S. 1988. *Foragers and Farmers.* Chicago: University of Chicago Press.

Gregor, T. 1990. "Uneasy Peace: Intertribal Relations in Brazil's Upper Xingu." In *The Anthropology of War,* ed. J. Haas, pp. 105–24. New York: Cambridge University Press.

Grinnell, G. 1923. *The Cheyenne Indians.* 2 vols., Lincoln: University of Nebraska Press.

Gunther, E. 1973. *The Ethnobotany of Western Washington.* Seattle: University of Washington Press.

Haas, J. 1990. "Warfare and the Evolution of Tribal Polities in the Prehistoric Southwest." In *The Anthropology of War,* ed. J. Haas, pp. 171–89. New York: Cambridge University Press.

Haas, J., and W. Creamer. 1993. *Stress and Warfare Among the Kayenta Anasazi of the Thirteenth Century* A.D. Fieldiana: Anthropology, n.s., 21. Chicago: Field Museum of Natural History.

Hackett, Sir J. ed. 1989. *Warfare in the Ancient World.* New York: Facts on File.

Haeberlin, H., and E. Gunther. 1930. *The Indians of Puget Sound.* Seattle: University of Washington Press.

Hallpike, C. 1973. "Functionalist Interpretations of Warfare." *Man,* n.s., 8: 451–70.

Hallpike, C. 1977. *Bloodshed and Vengeance in the Papuan Mountains.* Oxford: Oxford University Press.

Handbook of North American Indians (HNAI). 1978–1990. Washington, D.C.: Smithsonian Institution.

       1978. Vol. 8, *California.*

       1978. Vol. 15, *Northeast.*

       1979. Vol. 9, *Southwest.*

       1981. Vol. 6, *Subarctic.*

       1983. Vol. 10, *Southwest.*

       1984. Vol. 5, *Arctic.*

       1986. Vol. 11, *Great Basin.*

       1988. Vol. 4, *History of Indian–White Relations.*

       1990. Vol. 7, *Northwest Coast.*

Handbook of South American Indians. (HSAI). 1946–1948. Washington, D.C.: Government Printing Office.

       1946. Vol. 1, *Marginal Tribes.*

       1948. Vol. 3, *Tropical Forest Tribes.*

       1948. Vol. 4, *Circum-Caribbean Tribes.*

Handy, E. 1923. *The Native Culture in the Marquesas.* B. Bishop Museum Bulletin, no. 9.

Hanson, V. 1989. *The Western Way of War.* New York: Oxford University Press.

Harner, M. 1977. "The Ecological Basis for Aztec Sacrifice." *American Ethnologist* 4: 117–35.

Harris, M. 1974. *Cows, Pigs, Wars, and Witches.* Glasgow: Fontana/Collins.

———. 1975. *Culture, People, Nature.* 2d ed. New York: Crowell.

———. 1979. *Cultural Materialism.* New York: Random House.

———. 1984. "A Cultural Materialist Theory of Band and Village Warfare: The Yanomamo Test." In *Warfare, Culture, and Environment,* ed. R. Ferguson, pp. 111–40. New York: Academic Press.

———. 1989. *Our Kind.* New York: Harper & Row.

Hart, C., and A. Pilling. 1979. *The Tiwi of North Australia.* Fieldwork ed. New York: Holt, Rinehart and Winston.

Hattaway H., and A. Jones. 1991. *How the North Won.* Urbana: University of Illinois Press.

Hayden, B. 1981. "Subsistence and Ecological Adaptation of Modern Hunter/Gatherers." In *Omnivorous Primates,* ed. R. Harding and G. Telecki, pp. 344–421. New York: Columbia University Press.

———. 1993. *Archaeology: The Science of Once and Future Things.* New York: Freeman.

Heider, K. 1970. *The Dugum Dani.* Chicago: Aldine.

———. 1979. *Grand Valley Dani: Peaceful Warriors.* New York: Holt, Rinehart and Winston.

Hemming, J. 1978. *Red Gold.* Cambridge, Mass.: Harvard University Press.

Henry, D. 1985. "Preagricultural Sedentism." In *Prehistoric Hunter-Gatherers,* ed. T. Price and J. Brown, pp. 365–84. Orlando, Fla.: Academic Press.

Herdt, G. 1987. *The Sambia: Ritual and Gender in New Guinea.* New York: Holt, Rinehart and Winston.

Hickerson, H. 1962. "The Southwestern Chippewa: An Ethnohistorical Study." *American Anthropologist* 64: Memoir 92.

———. 1970. *The Chippewa and Their Neighbors: A Study in Ethnohistory.* Rev. ed. Prospect Heights, Ill.: Waveland Press.

Hockmann, O. 1990. "Frühneolithische Einhegungen in Europa." *Jahresschrift für Mitteldeutsche Vorgeschichte* 73: 57–86.

Hoebel, E. 1978. *The Cheyennes: Indians of the Great Plains.* 2d ed. New York: Holt, Rinehart and Winston.

Hogbin, I. 1964. *A Guadalcanal Society: The Koaka Speakers.* New York: Holt, Rinehart and Winston.

Hohol, A. S. 1982. "Blood in the Dust." M.A. thesis, University of Illinois at Chicago.

Huber, P. 1973. "Defending the Cosmos: Violence and Social Order Among the Anggor of New Guinea." In *War, Its Causes and Correlates,* ed. M. Nettleship, R. Givens, and A. Nettleship, pp. 619–61. The Hague: Mouton.

Hudson, C. 1976. *The Southeastern Indians.* Knoxville: University of Tennessee Press.

Huntingford, G. 1953. *The Nandi of Kenya.* London: Routledge and Kegan Paul.

Isaac, B. 1983. "Aztec Warfare: Goals and Comportment." *Ethnology* 22:121–31.

Jelinek, J. 1957. "Anthrofagie a pohrebni ritus doby bronzove na podkalde nalezu z moravy a z okolnich uzemi." *Acta Musei Moraviae* 42: 1–33 (cited in T. White, 1992).

————. 1991. "Découvertes d'ossements de la population gravettienne de Moravie." *L'Anthropologie* 95: 137–54.

Jorgensen, J. 1980. *Western Indians*. San Francisco: Freeman.

Jurmain, R. 1988. "Paleoepidemiology of Trauma in a Prehistoric Central California Population." In *Human Paleopathology, Current Synthesis and Future Options*, ed. D. Ortner and A. Aufderheide, pp. 241–48. Washington, D.C.: Smithsonian Institution.

Karsten, R. 1967. "Blood Revenge and War Among the Jibaro Indians of Eastern Ecuador." In *Law and Warfare*, ed. P. Bohannan, pp. 303–25. Garden City, N.Y.: Natural History Press.

Keegan, J. 1976. *The Face of Battle*. New York: Viking.

————. 1987. *The Mask of Command*. New York: Viking.

————. 1989. *Second World War*. London: Hutchinson.

————. 1993. *A History of Warfare*. New York: Knopf.

Keeley, L. 1988. "Hunter-Gatherer Economic Complexity and 'Population Pressure': A Cross-Cultural Analysis." *Journal of Anthropological Archaeology* 7:373–411.

————. 1992. "The Introduction of Agriculture to the Western North European Plain." In *Transitions to Agriculture in Prehistory*, ed. A. Gebrauer and T. Price, pp. 81–95. Madison, Wis.: Prehistory Press.

————. 1993. "Frontier Warfare in the Early Neolithic." Paper given at the American Anthropological Association Annual Meeting, Washington, D.C.

Keeley, L., and D. Cahen, 1989. "Early Neolithic Forts and Villages in Northeastern Belgium: A Preliminary Report." *Journal of Field Archaeology* 16: 157–76.

————. 1990. "Village Specialization in the Early Neolithic of N.W. Europe." Paper read at the Society for American Archaeology Annual Meeting, Las Vegas, Nev.

Kelly, R. 1985. *The Nuer Conquest*. Ann Arbor: University of Michigan Press.

Kennedy, P. 1987. *The Rise and Fall of the Great Powers*. New York: Random House.

Kent, S. 1980. "Pacifism—A Myth of the Plateau." *Northwest Anthropological Research Notes* 14: 125–34.

Kirch, P. 1984. *The Evolution of Polynesian Chiefdoms*. Cambridge: Cambridge University Press.

Klein, R. 1989. *The Human Career*. Chicago: University of Chicago Press.

Knauft, B. 1985. *Good Company and Violence*. Berkeley: University of California Press.

————. 1987. "Reconsidering Violence in Simple Societies." *Current Anthropology* 28: 457–500.

Koch, K.-F. 1974. *War and Peace in Jalemo*. Cambridge, Mass.: Harvard University Press.

————. 1983. "Epilogue." In *The Pacification of Melanesia*, ed. M. Rodman and M. Cooper, pp. 199–207. Lanham, Md.: University Press of America.

Krause, A. 1956. *The Tlingit Indians*. Seattle: University of Washington.

Kroeber, A. 1925. *Handbook of the Indians of California*. Bulletin of the Bureau of American Ethnology, no. 78. Reprint. New York: Dover, 1976.

————. 1965. "A Kato War." In *The California Indians: A Source Book*, ed. R. Heizer and M. Whipple, pp. 397–403. Berkeley: University of California Press.

Lambert, P., and P. Walker. 1991. "Physical Anthropological Evidence for the Evolution of Social Complexity in Coastal Southern California." *Antiquity* 65: 963–73.

Langer, W. 1972. *An Encyclopedia of World History.* 5th ed. Boston: Houghton Mifflin.

Laqueur, W. 1984. *Guerrilla: A Historical and Critical Study.* Boulder, Colo.: Westview Press.

Lee, R. 1979. *The !Kung San.* New York: Cambridge University Press.

Lindeman, G. 1987. *Embattled Courage.* New York: Free Press.

Livingstone, F. 1968. "The Effect of Warfare on the Biology of the Human Species." In *War,* ed. M. Fried, M. Harris, and R. Murphy, pp. 3–16. Garden City, N.Y.: Natural History Press.

MacDonald, G. 1989. *Kiwanga Fort Report.* Hull, Que.: Canadian Museum of Civilization.

MacDonald, G., and J. Cove. 1987. *Tsimshian Narratives 2: Trade and Warfare.* Ottawa: Canadian Museum of Civilization.

McGovern, T. 1985. "The Arctic Frontier of Norse Greenland." In *The Archaeology of Frontiers and Boundaries,* ed. S. Green and S. Perlman, pp. 275–323. Orlando, Fla.: Academic Press.

McInnis, E. 1969. *Canada: A Political and Social History.* 3d ed. Toronto: Holt, Rinehart and Winston.

Maclear, M. 1981. *The Ten Thousand Day War: Vietnam, 1945–1975.* New York: Avon.

McNeill, W. 1982. *The Pursuit of Power.* Chicago: University of Chicago Press.

McPherson, J. 1988. *The Battle Cry of Freedom.* New York: Oxford University Press.

Malinowski, B. 1941. "An Anthropological Analysis of War." *American Journal of Sociology* 46: 521–50.

Malone, P. 1991. *This Skulking Way of War.* Baltimore: Johns Hopkins University Press.

Manchester, W. 1980. *Goodbye, Darkness.* New York: Dell.

Marshall, S.L.A. 1987. *World War I.* Boston: Houghton Mifflin.

Matthews, W. 1877. *Ethnography and Philology of the Hidatsa Indians.* U.S. Geological Survey Miscellaneous Publication, no. 7.

Meggitt, M. 1962. *Desert People.* Chicago: University of Chicago Press.

———. 1977. *Blood Is Their Argument.* Palo Alto, Calif.: Mayfield.

Mellaart, J. 1965. *Earliest Civilizations of the Near East.* New York: McGraw-Hill.

Mercer, J. 1980. *The Canary Islanders.* London: Rex Collins.

Mercer, R. 1988. "Hambledon Hill, Dorset, England." In *Enclosures and Defenses in the Neolithic of Western Europe,* ed. C. Burgess, P. Topping, C. Mordant, and M. Maddison, pp. 77–87. BAR I.S. no. 403(i). Oxford: British Archaeological Reports.

Merk, F. 1978. *History of the Westward Movement.* New York: Knopf.

Milner, G., E. Anderson, and V. Smith. 1991. "Warfare in Late Prehistoric West-Central Illinois." *American Antiquity* 56: 581–603.

Moore, J. 1990. "The Reproductive Success of Cheyenne War Chiefs." *Current Anthropology* 31: 322–29.

Moratto, M. 1984. *California Archaeology.* Orlando, Fla.: Academic Press.

Morren, G. 1984. "Warfare on the Highland Fringe of New Guinea: The Case of the

Mountain Ok." In *Warfare, Culture, and Environment,* ed. R. Ferguson, pp. 169–208. Orlando, Fla.: Academic Press.

———. 1986. *The Miyanmin.* UMI Research Press Studies in Cultural Anthropology, no. 9.

Morris, D. 1965. *The Washing of the Spears.* New York: Simon and Schuster.

Morison, S. E. 1971. *The European Discovery of America: The Northern Voyages A.D. 500–1600.* New York: Oxford University Press.

Murdock, G., and C. Provost. 1973. "Measurement of Cultural Complexity." *Ethnology* 9: 302–30.

Murdock, G., and S. Wilson. 1972. "Settlement Patterns and Community Organization: Cross-Cultural Codes." *Ethnology* 11: 254–95.

Oliver, D. 1974. *Ancient Tahitian Society.* Vol. 1, *Ethnography.* Honolulu: University of Hawaii Press.

Oliver, R. 1991. *The African Experience.* New York: HarperCollins.

Olson, R. 1967. *The Quinault Indians.* Seattle: University of Washington Press.

Otte, M., and L. Keeley. 1990. "The Impact of Regionalism on Palaeolithic Studies." *Current Anthropology* 31: 577–82.

Otterbein, K. 1967. "The Evolution of Zulu Warfare." In *Law and Warfare,* ed. P. Bohannon, pp. 351–57. Garden City, N.Y.: Natural History Press.

———. 1989. *The Evolution of War: A Cross-Cultural Study.* 3d ed. New Haven, Conn.: HRAF Press.

Owsley, D., H. Berryman, and W. Bass. 1977. "Demographic and Osteological Evidence for Warfare at the Larson Site, South Dakota." *Plains Anthropologist Memoir* 13: 119–31.

Pakenham, T. 1991. *The Scramble for Africa.* New York: Random House.

Parker, G. 1988. *The Military Revolution.* New York: Cambridge University Press.

Perret, G. 1989. *A Country Made by War.* New York: Random House.

Pflanz-Cook, S., and E. Cook. 1983. "Manga Pacification." In *The Pacification of Melanesia,* ed. M. Rodman and M. Cooper, pp. 179–98. Lanham, Md.: University Press of America.

Phillipson, D. 1985. *African Archaeology.* New York: Cambridge University Press.

Pilling, A. 1968. "Discussion: Predation and Warfare." In *Man the Hunter,* ed. R. Lee and I. Devore, p. 158. Chicago: Aldine Atherton.

Ploeg, A. 1983. "The Establishment of the Pax Neerlandica in the Bokondini Area." In *The Pacification of Melanesia,* ed. M. Rodman and M. Cooper, pp. 161–78. Lanham, Md.: University Press of America.

Porch, D. 1986. *The Conquest of the Sahara.* Oxford: Oxford University Press.

Pospisil, L. 1958. *The Kapauku Papuans and Their Law.* Yale Publications in Anthropology, no. 54.

———. 1963. *The Kapauku Papuans.* New York: Holt, Rinehart and Winston.

Price, T. D. 1985. "Affluent Foragers of Mesolithic Southern Scandinavia." In *Prehistoric Hunter-Gatherers,* ed. T. Price and J. Brown, pp. 361–64. Orlando, Fla.: Academic Press.

Price, T. D., and J. Brown, eds. 1985. *Prehistoric Hunter-Gatherers.* Orlando, Fla.: Academic Press.

Pryor, F. 1976. "A Neolithic Multiple Burial from Fengate, Peterborough." *Antiquity* 50: 232–33.

Quilter, J. 1991. "Late Preceramic Peru." *Journal of World Prehistory* 5: 387–438.

Rand-McNally. 1988. *Concise World Atlas.* New York: Rand-McNally.

Ray, V. 1963. *Primitive Pragmatists: The Modoc Indians of Northern California.* Seattle: University of Washington Press.

Rhodes, R. 1986. *The Making of the Atomic Bomb.* New York: Simon and Schuster.

Robbins, S. 1982. *Auyana: Those Who Held onto Home.* Seattle: University of Washington Press.

Rochberg-Halton, E. 1991. Letter to the Editor. *Chronicle of Higher Education* 38: B6–B7.

Rodman, M., and M. Cooper. (eds.). 1983. *The Pacification of Melanesia.* Lanham, Md.: University Press of America.

Roesdahl, E. 1991. *The Vikings.* London: Penguin Books.

Rogers, E. 1970. *Indians of the North Pacific Coast.* Pamphlet. Toronto: Royal Ontario Museum.

Rohn, A. 1975. "A Stockaded Basketmaker III Village at Yellow Jacket, Colorado." *Kiva* 40: 113–19.

Romer, J. 1982. *People of the Nile.* London: Michael Joseph.

Roper, M. 1969. "A Survey of the Evidence for Intrahuman Killing in the Pleistocene." *Current Anthropology* 10: 427–59.

Ross, J. 1984. "Effects of Contact on Revenge Hostilities Among the Achuara Jivaro." In *Warfare, Culture, and Environment,* ed. R. Ferguson, pp. 83–110. Orlando, Fla.: Academic Press.

Ross, M. 1983. "Political Decision Making and Conflict: Additional Cross-Cultural Codes and Scales." *Ethnology* 22: 169–92.

———. 1985. "Internal and External Conflict and Violence: Cross-Cultural Evidence and a New Analysis." *Journal of Conflict Resolution* 29: 547–79.

Roudil, J.-L. 1990. "Cardial et Neolithique Ancien Ligure dans le Sud-est de la France." In *Rubane & Cardial,* ed. D. Cahen and M. Otte, pp. 383–91. Liège: ERAUL.

Rouse, I. 1986. *Migrations in Prehistory.* New Haven, Conn.: Yale University Press.

Ryan, L. 1981. *The Aboriginal Tasmanians.* London: University of Queensland Press.

Saunders, C. 1981. "Political Processes in the Southern African Frontier Zone." In *The Frontier in History,* ed. H. Lamar and L. Thompson, pp. 149–71. New Haven, Conn.: Yale University Press.

Schiefenhövel, W. 1993. "Pragmatismus und Utopie als Reaktionen auf kulturellen Wandel-Beispiele aus Melanesien." In *Kulturvergleichende Psychologie,* ed. A. Thomas, pp. 323–37. Göttingen: Hogrefe.

Schwimmer, E. 1966. *The World of the Maori.* Wellington, N.Z.: Reed.

Scott, D., R. Fox, M. Connor, and D. Harmon. 1989. *Archaeological Perspectives on the Battle of the Little Bighorn.* Norman: University of Oklahoma Press.

Secoy, F. 1953. *Changing Military Patterns on the Great Plains.* Monographs of the American Ethnological Society, no. 21. Locust Valley, N.Y.: Augustin.

Sharer, R., and W. Ashmore. 1987. *Archaeology: Discovering Our Past.* Palo Alto, Calif.: Mayfield.

Sherman, W. T. 1886. *Memoirs of General W. T. Sherman.* Rev. ed. Reprint. New York: Library of America, 1990.

Silberbauer, G. 1972. "The G/wi Bushmen." In *Hunters and Gatherers Today,* ed. M. Bicchieri, pp. 271–325. Prospect Heights Ill.: Waveland Press.

Sledge, E. 1981. *With the Old Breed.* New York: Oxford University Press.

Sliva, R., and L. Keeley. 1994. "Frits and Specialized Hide Preparation in the Belgian Early Neolithic." *Journal of Archaeological Science* 21: 91–100.

Slobodin, R. 1960. "Eastern Kutchin Warfare." *Anthropologia* 2: 76–94.

Snarkis, M. 1987. "The Archeological Evidence for Chiefdoms in Eastern and Central Costa Rica." In *Chiefdoms in the Americas,* ed. R. Drennan and C. Uribe, pp. 105–18. Lanham, Md.: University Press of America.

Spears, T. 1981. *Kenya's Past.* London: Longman.

Spencer, R., and J. Jennings. 1977. *The Native Americans.* New York: Harper & Row.

Spier, L. 1930. "Klamath Ethnography." *UCPAAE* 30.

Steward, J. 1938. *Basin-Plateau Sociopolitical Groups.* Bureau of American Ethnology Bulletin no. 120. Reprint. Salt Lake City: University of Utah, 1970.

———. 1941. "Culture Element Distributions: XIII Nevada Shoshone." *UCAR* 4, no. 2.

Steward, J., and L. Faron. 1959. *The Native Peoples of South America.* New York: McGraw-Hill.

Stewart, K. 1965. "Mohave Warfare." In *The California Indians,* ed. R. Heizer and M. Whipple, pp. 369–82. Berkeley: University of California Press.

Stewart, O. 1941. "Culture Element Distributions: XIV Northern Paiute." *UCAR* 4, no. 3.

———. 1942. "Culture Element Distributions: XVIII Ute–Southern Paiute." *UCAR* 6, no. 4.

Sumner, W. 1911. *War and Other Essays.* New Haven, Conn.: Yale University Press.

Svoboda, J., and E. Vlcek. 1991. "La nouvelle sepulture de Dolni Vestonice (DV XVI), Tchécoslovaquie." *L'Anthropologie* 95: 323–28.

Swanton, J. 1979. *The Indians of the Southeastern United States.* Reprint. Washington, D.C.: Smithsonian Institution.

Taylor, J. G. 1974. *Labrador Eskimo Settlements of the Early Contact Period.* National Museum of Man (Canada) Publications in Ethnology, no. 9.

Tefft, S. 1973. "Warfare Regulation: A Cross-Cultural Test of Hypotheses." In *War, Its Causes and Correlates,* ed. M. Nettleship, R. Givens, and A. Nettleship, pp. 693–712. The Hague: Mouton.

Thieme, F. 1968. "The Biological Consequences of War." In *War,* ed. M. Fried, M. Harris, and R. Murphy, pp. 16–21. Garden City, N.Y.: Natural History Press.

Thomas, D. H. 1988. *Archaeology.* 2d ed. New York: Holt, Rinehart and Winston.

Thomas, H. 1993. *Conquest.* New York: Simon and Schuster.

Thompson, L. 1990. *A History of South Africa.* New Haven, Conn.: Yale University Press.

Thompson, L., and H. Lamar. 1981. "Comparative Frontier History." In *The Frontier in History,* ed. H. Lamar and L. Thompson, pp. 149–71. New Haven, Conn.: Yale University Press.

Tonkinson, R. 1978. *The Mardudjara Aborigines.* New York: Holt, Rinehart and Winston.

Turnbull, C. 1962. *The Forest People.* New York: Simon and Schuster.

Turnbull, C. 1965. "The Mbuti Pygmies of the Congo." In *Peoples of Africa,* ed. J. Gibbs, pp. 279–318. New York: Holt, Rinehart and Winston.

Turner, C. 1989. "Teec Nos Pos: More Possible Cannibalism in Northeastern Arizona." *Kiva* 54: 147–52.

Turner, C., and J. Turner. 1990. "Perimortem Damage to Human Skeletal Remains from Wapatki National Monument, Northern Arizona." *Kiva* 55: 187–212.

———. 1992. "On Peter Y. Bullock's 'A Reappraisal of Anasazi Cannibalism.'" *Kiva* 58: 189–205.

Turney-High, H. 1949. *Primitive War: Its Practice and Concepts.* Reissue with new preface and afterword. Columbia: University of South Carolina Press, 1971.

Turney-High, H. 1981. *The Military: The Theory of Land Warfare as Behavioral Science.* West Hanover, Mass.: Cristopher.

Turton, D. 1979. "War, Peace, and Mursi Identity." In *Warfare Among East African Herders,* ed. K. Fukui and D. Turton, pp. 179–219. Osaka, Japan: National Museum of Ethnology.

Underhill, A. 1989. "Warfare During the Chinese Neolithic Period: A Review of the Evidence." In *Cultures in Conflict,* ed. D. Tkaczuk and B. Vivian, pp. 219—37. Calgary: University of Calgary.

Utley, R. 1984. *The Indian Frontier of the American West, 1846–1890.* Albuquerque: University of New Mexico Press.

Utley, R., and W. Washburn. 1977. *Indian Wars.* Boston: Houghton Mifflin.

Van Creveld, M. 1989. *Technology and War.* New York: Free Press.

Vayda, A. 1960. *Maori Warfare.* Auckland, N.Z.: Polynesian Society.

———. 1976. *War in Ecological Perspective.* New York: Plenum.

Vencl, S. 1984. "War and Warfare in Archaeology." *Journal of Anthropological Archaeology* 3: 116–32.

———. 1991. "Interprétation des Blessures Causée par les Armes au Mésolithique." *L'Anthropologie* 95: 219–28.

Villa, P., C. Bouville, J. Courtin, D. Helmer, E. Mahieu, P. Shipman, G. Belluomini, and M. Branca. 1986. "Cannibalism in the Neolithic." *Science* 233: 431–36.

Villa, P., J. Courtin, and D. Helmer. 1988. "Cannibalism in Old World Prehistory." *Rivista di Antropologia* 66 (Supplement): 47–64.

Voegelin, E. 1942. "Culture Element Distributions: XX Northeast California." *UCAR* 7, no. 2.

Wahl, J., and H. König. 1987. "Anthropologisch-Traumologische untersuchung der

Menschlichen Skelettreste aus dem Bandkeramischen Massengrab bei Talheim, Kreis Heilbronn." *Fundberichte aus Baden-Wurtemberg* 12: 65–193.

Walker, P., and P. Lambert. 1989. "Skeletal Evidence for Stress During a Period of Cultural Change in Prehistoric California." In *Advances in Paleopathology, Journal of Paleopathology: Monographic Publ. no. 1*, ed. L. Cappasso, pp. 207–12. Chieti, Italy: Marino Solfanelli.

Warner, W. 1931. "Murngin Warfare." *Oceania* 1: 457–94.

———. 1937. *A Black Civilization*. New York: Harper and Brothers.

Watkins, T. 1989. "The Beginnings of Warfare." In *Warfare in the Ancient World*, ed. Sir J. Hackett, pp. 15–35. New York: Facts on File.

Webb, W. 1974. *Indian Knoll*. Knoxville: University of Tennessee.

Weber, D. 1992. *The Spanish Frontier in North America*. New Haven, Conn.: Yale University Press.

Weigley, R. 1991. *The Age of Battles*. Bloomington: Indiana University Press.

Weinberg, G. 1994. *A World at Arms*. New York: Cambridge University Press.

Wendorf, F. 1968. "Site 117: A Nubian Final Palaeolithic Graveyard near Jebel Sahaba, Sudan." In *The Prehistory of Nubia*, vol. 2, ed. F. Wendorf, pp. 954–95. Dallas: Southern Methodist University Press.

Wendorf, F., and R. Schild. 1986. *The Wadi Kubbaniya Skeleton: A Late Paleolithic Burial from Southern Egypt*. Dallas: Southern Methodist University Press.

Wenke, R. 1988. *Patterns in Prehistory*. 3d ed. New York: Oxford University Press.

White, G. 1983. "War, Peace, and Piety in Santa Isabel, Solomon Islands." In *The Pacification of Melanesia*, ed. M. Rodman and M. Cooper, pp. 109–40. Lanham, Md.: University Press of America.

White, T. 1992. *Prehistoric Cannibalism at Mancos 5MTUMR-2346*. Princeton, N.J.: Princeton University Press.

Whitehead, N. 1990. "The Snake Warriors—Sons of the Tiger's Teeth: A Descriptive Analysis of Carib Warfare ca. 1500–1820." In *The Anthropology of War*, ed. J. Haas, pp. 146–70. New York: Cambridge University Press.

Whittle, A. 1985. *Neolithic Europe*. Cambridge: Cambridge University Press.

Wilcox, D. 1989. "Hohokam Warfare." In *Cultures in Conflict*, ed. D. Tkaczuk and B. Vivian, pp. 163–72. Calgary: University of Calgary.

Wilcox, D., and J. Haas. 1991. "The Scream of the Butterfly: Competition and Conflict in the Prehistoric Southwest." Paper presented at School of American Research, Santa Fe, N.Mex.

Will, G., and H. Spinden. 1906. "The Mandans." *Papers of the Peabody Museum* 3: 81–219.

Willey, P. 1990. *Prehistoric Warfare on the Great Plains*. New York: Garland.

Williams, E. 1970. *From Columbus to Castro*. New York: Vintage Books.

Willmott, H. 1989. *The Great Crusade*. New York: Free Press.

Wilson, M., and L. Thompson. 1983. *A History of South Africa to 1870*. Boulder, Colo.: Westview Press.

Wright, Q. 1942. *A Study of War*. Vol. 1 (abridged ed. published 1964). Chicago: University of Chicago Press.

Zegwaard, G. 1968. "Headhunting Practices of the Asmat of Netherlands New Guinea." In *Peoples and Cultures of the Pacific*, ed. A. Vayda, pp. 421–50. Garden City, N.Y.: Natural History Press.

Zelenietz, M. 1983. "The End of Headhunting in New Georgia." In *The Pacification of Melanesia*, ed. M. Rodman and M. Cooper, pp. 91–108. Lanham, Md.: University Press of America.

Zimmerman, L., and R. Whitten. 1980. "Prehistoric Bones Tell a Grim Tale of Indian v. Indian." *Smithsonian* 11: 100–107.

INDEX